How Effective Sermons Begin

How Effective Sermons Begin

Ben Awbrey

MENTOR

Ben E. Awbrey teaches expository preaching at Midwestern Seminary, Kansas City, Missouri. He received a Doctor of Theology in leadership from New Orleans Baptist Theological Seminary and earned an M.Div. from Southwestern Baptist Theological Seminary. He did graduate work at Talbot Theological Seminary and earned a B.S. from Central State University.

Prior to coming to Midwestern Awbrey served as both pastor and adjunct professor of preaching at The Master's Seminary in California. He has also pastored in Oklahoma and Louisiana.

Copyright © Ben Awbrey 2008

ISBN 978-1-84550-374-1

Published in 2008
in the
Mentor imprint
by
Christian Focus Publications,
Geanies House, Fearn, Ross-shire,
IV20 1TW, Scotland, UK

www.christianfocus.com

Cover design by Daniel van Straaten

Printed and bound by CPD, Wales

All rights reserved. No part of this publication may be re-produced, stored in a retrieval system, or transmitted, in any form, by any means, electronic, mechanical, photocopying, recording or otherwise without the prior permission of the publisher or a license permitting restricted copying. In the U.K. such licenses are issued by the Copyright Licensing Agency, Saffron House, 6-10 Kirby Street, London, EC1 8TS www.cla.co.uk.

Contents

Foreword *by John MacArthur* 7

Foreword *by Richard L. Mayhue* 11

Introduction 15

1. 'Must Hear' Preaching: The Desire of a Preacher and the Delight of a Hearer 21

2. Introducing the Sermon: A Necessity or Nuisance 37

3. Getting Attention: Good But Not Good Enough 75

4. Securing Interest: The Major Work of an Introduction 103

5. Securing Interest: How Interest is Secured in an Introduction 133

6. Stating the Purpose: An Indication of a Passionate Preacher 181

7. Stating the Purpose: An Indication of a Significant Sermon 221

8. Setting the Context: The Earliest Indication of an Expository Sermon 267

9. The Sermon Proposition: The Cornerstone of a Sermon 317

Conclusion 345

References 347

Bibliography 367

Subject Index 377

Scripture Index 383

Foreword
by
John F. MacArthur

The apostle Paul foretold a time when even people in the church 'will not endure sound doctrine; but wanting to have their ears tickled, they will accumulate for themselves teachers in accordance to their own desires, and will turn away their ears from the truth and will turn aside to myths' (2 Tim. 4:3). In light of such indifference about the preaching of God's Word, what should church leaders do? What is the best way to reach a culture that has no taste for biblical preaching?

Scores of books for pastors and church leaders have been written to propose answers to that question over the past few decades. Most of them seem to presuppose that if biblical preaching doesn't capture the hearts and attention of church-goers, church leaders need to come up with alternative methodologies: messages based on something other than Scripture, storytelling, drama, comedy, music – whatever entertains; whatever meets people's 'felt needs'; whatever scratches itching ears. As a result, the evangelical mainstream nowadays is moving steadily away from biblical preaching. Perhaps the preaching of God's Word has never been more out of season.

But notice: the strategy Paul commends to his young protégé Timothy has nothing to do with seeking *other* inventive or entertaining means of trying to reach a new generation. In fact, Paul's answer was a straightforward and unequivocal reaffirmation of the primacy and centrality of biblical preaching – regardless of how trends seem to be blowing at any given time: 'Preach the word; be ready in season and out of season; reprove, rebuke, exhort, with great patience and instruction' (v. 2).

It is significant that those familiar words come in the verse immediately *preceding* the prophetic warning about seasons of apathy and indifference. Before he even mentioned that such a time was on the horizon, Paul had told Timothy plainly what to do about it: *keep preaching the Word.*

Elsewhere, Paul acknowledged that from a worldly perspective, preaching seems a foolish strategy for reaching a world that is hostile to God's truth. Preaching the Bible to people who have no taste for God's Word is practically the polar opposite of 'seeker sensitivity' – and that was no less true in Paul's era than it is in ours: 'For indeed Jews ask for signs and Greeks search for wisdom; but we preach Christ crucified, to Jews a stumbling block and to Gentiles foolishness' (1 Cor. 1:22-23). But Paul says God's strategy for reaching this world is wiser than men in all their so-called wisdom: 'God was well-pleased through the foolishness of the message preached to save those who believe' (v. 21).

Those are especially important words for our generation, because we live in a time of almost unprecedented apathy and indifference. And there is no shortage of strategists and innovators in the evangelical community who think they have better ways for reaching the culture than by preaching God's Word.

Ben Awbrey knows better than that. He understands that the answer to apathy is *better* preaching, not shorter, lighter, or fewer sermons, and certainly not entertainment instead of instruction and exhortation from Scripture. He understands that 'the *gospel*... is the power of God for salvation' (Rom. 1:16). Human cleverness and slick PR tactics are no substitute for that, no matter how such things may garner accolades from the secular culture or from church people eager to have their ears tickled.

Moreover, the Word of God itself *is* more exciting, relevant, timely, and applicable to every heart and life than any substitute message of self-esteem, self-help, or human motivation could ever be. What the faithful preacher needs to do first of all is develop his own passion for studying, understanding, and proclaiming the truth of God's Word – and then share that passion through his preaching. That is the best way to arouse an appetite for the truth of God's Word in our people, and that, in turn, is the only thing that will make a real, positive, life-changing difference in the individual lives of believers as well as the corporate life of the church. This book is a gold mine of practical ways to help preachers do so.

Dr. Awbrey is a careful student of the faithful preacher's task. He approaches the subject not from a merely academic point of view, but as someone totally committed to the absolute authority of Scripture and wholly convinced of the pivotal necessity of preaching in God's plan of redemption (1 Cor. 1:21). I have long appreciated his enthusiasm for preaching and his desire to help other preachers make the most of their gifts and calling. His insights on preaching have proved invaluable to hundreds of pastors and young preachers. I'm glad to see this material in book form, because I know it will multiply the number of preachers who will benefit from Dr. Awbrey's skillful analyses of the biblical task. I hope many will study these pages carefully and put the principles into practice. The church will certainly be strengthened and blessed through the labors of those who do.

Foreword
by
Richard L. Mayhue

The three 'undervalued' components of expository sermon preparation include introductions, illustrations, and conclusions. Due to the complexities of pastoral ministry in general and message preparation in particular, pastors tend to let these three slide. The congregation, in contrast, eagerly looks forward to how its pastor will handle these elements of the message.

You can usually tell how a pastor's week went by his introduction, illustrations, and conclusion; hectic times tend to crowd out or minimize his time spent on them. Whether they are deemed unimportant to the communication process, excessively time consuming in proportion to their perceived value, or unappealing hard work, slighting them can measurably lessen the potential impact of a message.

The general relationship of seasonings and sauces to gourmet cooking parallels the role of introductions, illustrations, and conclusions in preaching. The main meal, or the message, should never be eclipsed by secondary features; nonetheless, these garnishings can dramatically enhance the flavor/interest level of a meal/message well prepared in all other respects.

Realize that none of these three elements can replace the Holy Spirit's work of impacting people with the power of God's

Word. However, to ignore or minimize these proven features of good communication makes a preacher negligent in exercising his human responsibility to be as effective as possible.

By definition, 'to introduce' means to acquaint or to bring into play for the first time. The introduction is to a sermon as an opening kickoff is to a football game, as the initial volleys of gunfire are to a battle, or as a departure from a harbor is to an ocean voyage. It is a time for everyone to acclimate to what follows the initial situation and to gain a sense of direction.

In the most precise sense, introductions to a sermon can be compared to *hors d'oeurves* served before a special meal. The term *hors d'oeurve* in French literally means 'outside the work'. The 'work' itself originally referred to art, literature, or music. It later came to mean food served as an appetizer or 'starter' before the main meal. They caught one's attention, excited one's smell, provoked one's taste, and heightened one's anticipation of the entrée to follow. As *hors d'oeurves* are to a banquet, so introductions should be to a biblical message. They should never compete with what follows but rather tantalizingly lead the audience to the 'work', i.e. the preached Word of God.

The element of *ethos,* i.e., the preacher's perceived credibility in the mind of his audience, can be markedly influenced by the kind and quality of his introduction. This is especially true in cases where listeners have no previous acquaintance with their preacher. As the old adage goes, 'First impressions are lasting impressions.' The initial impact of the introduction may even shape the final effect of a message.

Only a preacher's imagination and creativity limit the kinds of effective introductions. The introduction employed, however, should be tailored to fit a speaker's relationship to his audience, the occasion for the message, and the intended outcome of the sermon. Every introduction should have a clear purpose—both to the preacher and the congregation. It should never be hastily prepared or indiscriminately tacked on to a message.

John Stott reminds us that 'It is an enormous privilege to be called to preach in the contemporary world, and to be a biblical expositor! For one then stands in the pulpit with God's Word in his hands, God's Spirit in his heart, God's people before his eyes, waiting expectantly for God's voice to be heard and obeyed.'[1]

With this great privilege comes an equally important responsibility. We all need to carry out our sacred duty to exposition at the highest level of excellence, an excellence that extends even to our introductions.

In all of my considerable reading over a lifetime on biblical exposition, this excellent volume on 'introductions' by Dr. Ben Awbrey proves to be the most thorough and complete that I have ever encountered. To the expositional preacher who zealously desires to proclaim every element of the message with excellence, I commend this work on sermon introductions.

Introduction

Effective and pleasing sermon introductions are like pleasing landscapes. They do not happen automatically or accidentally. They are the result of the implementation of time-honored principles. If the principles for introducing a sermon are disregarded, they are disregarded at the expense of the preacher and the hearers of the message. Effective sermon introductions, like pleasing landscapes, are the result of one who has a deep concern and passion for a desired commodity. Just as a landscaper is personally convinced that the diligent and strenuous effort of his work will make a difference, so must the preacher[1] be assured even more so of the efficacy of his sermonic work, in general, and his work in introducing a sermon specifically.

It is definitely the case that the work of introducing a sermon is undervalued.[2] And it is potentially the case that a preacher may, upon occasion, lose sight of the eternal significance of the whole enterprise of preaching. Therefore, it is good counsel in general 'to think on all that can happen to one mortal in one service. God's greatest miracle happens often under preaching. Let a man think on the eternal consequences of one half hour.'[3] As wise as it is to be reminded about the significance of preaching, I believe it to be an excellent idea to consider what is to be done in the beginning portion of our preaching effort – the introduction of our sermons.

In order for one to take seriously the task and put forth the effort to make improvement in the quest for introducing sermons more effectively he must be consumed with the passion to do only the very best he can do in his preaching. This consuming passion for excellence is what my homiletics professor, Howard Yim, a Korean-American, called 'the oriental art of perfecting a masterpiece and mastering a craft'. In order for one to preach as well as he is able, one must possess a diligent spirit and be marked by a passion for excellence. Such a man will stint no cost in the endeavor to preach well. This speaks of the kind of person he is, as well as the character he possesses, in reference to his preaching. If one is truly desirous of preaching excellently, then one must take seriously the objective of improvement in the area of the sermon introduction.

However, for a preacher to do a consistently effective job in his sermon introductions, he must bear the burden of a desire to be heard by the audience. He cannot abide the thought of being greeted with half-hearted interest regarding the things of God. Yet this is a man who is the exception rather than the rule. Just as certainly as there will be people who receive truth from every preacher in a half-hearted fashion there will be preachers who handle truth from every passage in a haphazard fashion – in their sermons and especially in their sermon introductions. I couldn't agree more heartily with the indictment advanced by Spurgeon regarding men who bear no such burden of desire for the work of their sermon introductions. His comments are as follows:

> There are preachers who care very little whether they are attended to or not; so long as they can hold on through the allotted time it is of very small importance to them whether their people hear for eternity, or hear in vain: the sooner such

ministers sleep in the churchyard and preach by the verse on their gravestones the better.[4]

As appropriate as these remarks were in Spurgeon's day, I would suggest that they are even more so today.

A sermon introduction that signals a congregation that the sermon about to be delivered is a 'must hear' matter is predicated upon some basic yet significant convictions held by the preacher regarding his sermon introductions. The convictions a preacher holds regarding the role and importance of the sermon introduction determine much of the presence of the preacher who will preach to them. It is at the crucial juncture of the sermon introduction that the preacher not only informs the hearers about the message they will hear but also about the messenger who will preach that message to them. The introduction a preacher makes about himself during the act of introducing his sermon is both inevitable and influential. Haddon Robinson surmised the following:

> During the introduction an audience gains impressions of a speaker that often determine whether or not they will accept what he says. If he appears nervous, hostile, or unprepared, they are inclined to reject him. If he seems alert, friendly, and interesting, they decide he is an able person with a positive attitude toward himself and his listeners.[5]

Regardless of whatever changes might occur in the arena of preaching, the sermon introduction will remain a significant factor.

The introduction is an opportunity for the preacher to make a favorable impression on the congregation that will help him to do the very thing he is there to do – serve the people through the agency of God's Word. Through a solid understanding of and a good procedure in introducing his sermons, a sermon introduction can be a servant to the servant of God in his preaching. It is to the accomplishment of this end that this book is written. My prayer is that men of God can serve the people of God well through the enhancement of their preaching from the Word of God. I trust you will discover that an effective sermon introduction makes an immediate impact upon the people to whom you preach and that you will experience the joy of introducing God's truths in a manner that will be considered as 'must hear' material by those who hear you preach.

Though this book will offer instruction for introducing a sermon, it must be understood that effective introductions, like effective preaching in general, may be aided by homiletical insights but effectiveness in preaching is far more a byproduct of one's personal walk with the living God rather than compliance with homiletical procedure. The adage, 'The sum is greater than its parts' is never truer than when it is applied to preaching a sermon. Therefore, the insights of this book, or any other book on preaching, will be useful only for those who truly are spiritually fit for the high calling of preaching the Word of God. Additionally, homiletical instruction cannot take the place of the gift of preaching. Nevertheless, the setting aside of practical insights helpful in the act of communicating biblical truth is unwarranted and unwise. It is my purpose to offer the instruction of this book to make the most of one's giftedness in preaching as well as one's opportunities to preach.

Words to Live and Preach by

The Profitability of the Spoken Word

Proverbs 12:8 – A man will be praised according to his insight, but one of perverse mind will be despised.

Proverbs 12:25 – Anxiety in the heart of a man weighs it down, but a good word makes it glad.

Proverbs 15:4 – A soothing tongue is a tree of life, but perversion in it crushes the spirit.

Proverbs 15:23 – A man has joy in an apt answer, and how delightful is a timely word!

Proverbs 16:13 – Righteous lips are the delight of kings, and he who speaks right is loved.

Proverbs 18:4 – The words of a man's mouth are deep waters; the fountain of wisdom is a bubbling brook.

Proverbs 19:8 – He who gets wisdom loves his own soul; He who keeps understanding will find good.

Proverbs 22:11 – He who loves purity of heart and whose speech is gracious, the king is his friend.

Proverbs 30:5-6 – Every word of God is tested; He is a shield to those who take refuge in Him. Do not add to His words or He will reprove you, and you will be proved a liar.

Chapter One

'Must Hear' Preaching: The Desire of a Preacher and the Delight of a Hearer

'This is a sermon that I must hear!' Few are the people who would make such a response to a forthcoming sermon by the time a preacher has *completed* his sermon introduction. In fact, this would be an uncommon response for most listeners having heard the typical introduction of most preachers on any given Sunday. Even the best of preachers often fail to prepare listeners for 'must hear'[1] preaching. The truth is, despite considerable giftedness in preaching, thorough seminary training, and years spent laboring strenuously at the task of preaching, most preachers do less than praiseworthy work in their sermon introductions. As one preaching professor noted, 'The lack of proper sermon preparation usually appears more emphatically in the introduction than in any other portion of the discourse; and it may almost be said that a bad introduction is worse than any other bad feature in formal discourse.'[2] But this is only how it is, not how it should be and can be!

Preachers can and should do excellent work in preaching, including the introductions to their sermons. There are, however, six convictions regarding sermon introductions a preacher must possess if he is to do excellent work in introducing his sermons. One who holds these convictions regarding the work of introducing a sermon will demonstrate the desired presence of a preacher who is likely to be heard by an audience. All six are beneficial for a preacher to achieve a 'must hear' verdict from his hearers.

Conviction Number One
'Must hear' preaching is not simply the net effect of the opening words of an introduction, but rather it is the cumulative effect of the completed introduction to a sermon. It is not the responsibility of, nor is it a possibility for, a preacher to effect the rapt attention of his hearers in the opening words of a sermon introduction. Rapt attention is a cumulative effect. Regardless of the nature of one's opening remarks, no matter how shocking, startling, amusing, humorous, insightful, etc., they may be interesting but they cannot bring rapt attention. A profoundly secured interest of the audience is the responsibility of a preacher, and it must be accomplished in the sermon introduction, but it cannot be accomplished by a few sentences of opening remarks.

Without demeaning the significance that one's opening remarks may have, one's opening statements are just a portion of the introduction and the opening statements can be an element of an effective introduction but they cannot constitute, by themselves, an effective introduction. Such well-intended instruction as the following confuses the role of the opening words with the objective of the entire sermon introduction. 'The minister's opening words have to mean, "Wait a minute! Don't touch that dial; this is something you want to hear!"'[3] This reveals either an all-too-common-view that places unmerited value upon the opening statements and/or an all-too-common-view that devalues the significance that an entire sermon introduction has in preaching. There is the effect that the opening statements can have, and then, there is the far more substantial effect that the completed sermon introduction must have. The two are related but they definitely are different.

It is the introduction that makes the needed impression on the hearer regarding the *sermon* to be preached. It is the opening words that make an impression on the hearer regarding the *introduction* to be delivered. Both the opening words and the introduction make an impression. The opening words make an initial impression that will aid in hearing the introduction, and the introduction makes a completed impression that will aid in hearing the sermon. With a careful distinction made between the opening statements and the sermon introduction, it is exceedingly wise to apply the following counsel to both the introduction and to the opening statements of the introduction. 'Do not let the introduction become an end in itself, but keep it a means to an end. Make it attractive and winsome. Work it out with the greatest care. Do not forget that, as elsewhere so in public discourse, the first impression is often the decisive one.'[4]

The initial portion of the introduction is strategic. The initial battle of the opening comments must be won so that the larger battle of the introduction may be successful. As one writer expressed the matter succinctly, 'The first few minutes should lay down a magnetic line between the pulpit and the pew which shall vibrate with electric response all the way through.'[5] Spurgeon codified his intent for his sermon introductions by the following:

> I prefer to make the introduction of my sermon very like that of the town-crier, who rings his bell and cries, 'Oh, yes! Oh yes! This is to give notice,' merely to let people know that he has news for them, and wants them to listen. To do that, the introduction should have something striking in it. It is well to fire a startling shot as the signal gun to clear the decks for action.[6]

The opening remarks specifically and the entire introduction generally should be designed to be effective. But the greater necessity for effectiveness must be apportioned for the entire introduction not just the opening statements of the introduction.

Conviction Number Two
The preacher must believe that the message to be preached is one of great value. This will be the case only if the study of the passage has been of great value to the preacher. If a preacher has been excited about the discovery of the truth of the passage, he will be excited about the declaration of the truth of that passage. If the study of the Scriptures, from which the sermon will come, has been personally significant to the preacher, then the audience will sense that the message is significant to him. If the audience senses that the sermon is significant to the preacher then it may well become significant to the hearers. C. H. Spurgeon called this personal significance of the truth to be preached a fire burning in his soul.[7] It is the fire that burns in the preacher's soul that makes him earnest and allows him to generate heat to the hearers so that they may be warmed. He wrote,

> You may clothe a man in blankets until he is fairly warm, because there is life in him; but you cannot heat a stone in that fashion. Life always begets a measure of warmth, and the possibility of more; and as you have life, there is within you the capacity for heat. Some preachers are of such a cold nature that no known means could warm them.
>
> The attempt to find heat in some men's sermons reminds me of Aesop's fable of the apes and the glowworm. The apes found a glowworm shining on the bank, and straightway gathered round it to warm themselves. They placed sticks over it, and tried to make a fire; but it did not burn. It was a very pretty thing, and looked like flame; but they could not warm their cold hands with its cold light. So have I known ministers, whose light was destitute of heat; and, consequently, the poor sticks around them have never kindled into a flame, nor have frozen hearts been melted by their influence.

> It is dreadful work to listen to a sermon, and feel all the while as if you were sitting out in a snowstorm, or dwelling in a house of ice, clear but cold, orderly but killing. You have said to yourself, 'That was a well-divided and well-planned sermon, but I cannot make out what was the matter with it;' the secret being that there was the wood, but no fire to kindle it.[8]

For a preacher not to burn with a fire for the truth of the message he will preach is more than just a lamentable situation. It is an indictment upon the preacher. To the contrary, however, his excitement about the truth he has discovered will be obvious to all who hear him preach and it will be obvious, as it must be, in the introduction of the message.

The most basic, central, non-negotiable, requirement of a sermon introduction is to create an impression on the audience from the outset that you have something to say worth hearing, and are so much in earnest that you mean for them to listen to it.[9] The introduction will forecast the great value of the message to come and reveal the passion and conviction the preacher has for the truths to be proclaimed in the exposition of the text.

Perhaps the most obvious failure of the common sermon introduction is the missing commodity of earnestness in the preacher. J. W. Alexander cited a lack of earnestness as 'the great reason why we have so little good preaching'.[10] Specifically he wrote, 'To be eloquent one must be in earnest; he must not only act as if he were in earnest, or try to be in earnest, but be in earnest, or he cannot be effective. We have loud and vehement, we have smooth and graceful, we have splendid and elaborate preaching, but very little that is earnest.'[11] If a sermon is worth hearing it should be apparent to the hearers by the demonstration of a true earnestness on behalf of the preacher. And that true earnestness of the preacher should be apparent in the introduction of his sermon.

In hearing a sermon introduction, the hearers must observe the fact of the preacher's earnestness, the hearers should discern the matter about which the preacher is indeed earnest, and the hearers should get a sense for why the preacher is so earnest about this matter. If this is not the case then the preacher must understand that his introduction is ineffective in the sense that it fails to communicate to his hearers what they need to know and perceive. The insight of Alfred Garvie is true not only for the sermon but is particularly valuable for the sermon introduction. He wrote:

> It is not merely an intellectual, but also an emotional and a volitional communication which constitutes real preaching. The preacher not only thinks, but also feels and wills. He not only seeks to know the truth of the Gospel, but also to feel its worth with his whole heart, and to exert his will fully that others may claim this good.
>
> The power of preaching depends on passion, the intensity of the emotion which the truth itself inspires in the preacher. There must not only be light, but heat also. A sermon delivered in an unimpassioned way, as though the preacher cared not at all either for his message or for the reception his hearers might give to it, cannot be an effective sermon. Emotion is communicative, nay, intense emotion is contagious; the mood in which the preacher speaks generates the mood in which the congregation hears. But this emotion must not be undirected and uncontrolled excitement, because then there will be heat only, without light, and without work. Volition must check and guide emotion. The preacher must will to do something, and he must concentrate the energy of his will on that purpose. Preaching is a deed, and not a word only. A resolute purpose and a strenuous energy in the preacher have a commanding influence over his hearers. To feel deeply and will strongly is as necessary to the preacher as to think clearly.[12]

If a preacher is not convinced of the great value of the particular passage to be preached then, quite frankly, he is in no condition to preach, to say nothing of introducing his sermon effectively. In such a state there can be no earnestness of spirit and no depth of conviction regarding the truth he is to proclaim. Not only the introduction but the sermon itself is destined for a less than optimal treatment.

William Taylor offered advice that must be applied in the preaching of the sermon and the introduction specifically. 'If, therefore, you have no positive convictions, keep out of the pulpit until you get them; and when you get them, they will make for themselves a manly and earnest utterance.'[13] Again, Taylor insists upon earnestness in preaching as he wrote: 'It is the irrepressible in a man that makes him earnest. If he can keep anything in, then let him keep it, for such a thing, generally speaking, is not worth letting out, and his utterance of it will have no force.'[14]

If a preacher is not convinced of the great value of the particular passage to be preached then he simply will not be able to communicate to the congregation that the message is of vital importance. In fact, the very opposite will inevitably be the case. Regardless of what is said or how much is said the net effect of his sermon introduction will be to convey his own estimation of the sermon to come – a 'ho-hum', 'take it or leave it' issue. Such a careless attitude for the substance of the sermon and the reception of his hearers is a violation of all good counsel regarding the proclamation of biblical truth. Therefore, it is crucial that a preacher preach as if he intended to be listened to and he should go into the pulpit with that intention in his mind. This will evidence the significance of his words and will put him into immediate contact with the minds of those whom he will address. If this is not the case then a rather sad cause and effect scenario will be set in motion, namely that: 'Some people preach as though they wished not to be listened to; and the people instinctively take notice of this apparent desire, and act accordingly.'[15] No preacher who takes his calling seriously could settle for this.

Conviction Number Three
The preacher must believe that the sermon introduction is far more than just a trite, perfunctory, rite-of-passage into the sermon itself.

This perception of a sermon introduction will undermine the remotest possibility of an effective introduction. A low view of the work of introducing sermons is impossible to conceal because it is conveyed clearly through everything said and done by the preacher in his introduction of the sermon. 'A preacher's manner, his tones, his attitude even, serve to introduce him to his hearers and enlist their interest in him. He may repel or attract his auditors before he has been speaking five minutes.'[16] There is nothing compelling about hearing a man introduce a sermon if the preacher has a view that the sermon introduction is just a trivial pursuit.

The needs of the hearers are not addressed in the sermon introductions of the preacher who views this portion of his sermonic work as an insignificant thing. Such a preacher belies the very purpose he must achieve on behalf of his hearers. From the outset of the sermon a preacher must not fail to be about the true function of preaching – to bring the valuable truths from Scripture into immediate contact with the understanding, the feelings, and the will of those who are present. Therefore, an elevation of thought, feeling, and utterance certainly is appropriate for such a purpose. If the biblical text comes from God and the exposition of that text concerns the eternal interests of those who receive it, need one say more to lift the subject into a position of unique importance, and to claim for it the highest treatment?[17]

It is the idea that the introduction is an insignificant portion of a sermon and that an introduction accomplishes a nominal role in the overall scheme of the sermon that effects a convictionless, passionless, irrelevant tone in the preacher's voice. Such a tone is deadly in preaching. It betrays the best of material and content. It weakens the receptivity of all that will hear the message of that day.

The preacher's expression of the content of the gospel is a decisive element in preaching effectively. Charles Bridges commented that a passionless presentation of truth 'awakens but little interest, and produces no effect. Our people feel little obligation to receive what, from the spiritless mode of presentment, seems to be of minor importance – at least not worthy of inconvenient consideration, or expensive sacrifices.'[18] The perceived power of scriptural truth often is weakened by an indecisive mode of statement. When the truth of Scripture is set forth in a feeble and hesitating tone, it evokes either a careless investigation into the Scriptures, a doubtful opinion of the truthfulness of what the preacher is saying about the Scriptures, or an indistinct apprehension of the value and efficacy of what the preacher has to say about the Scriptures.

If the preacher's tone can be debilitating for the reception of truth in the body of the message then it must be understood that it can be even more ruinous in the introduction of a sermon. Such a tone in preaching must be avoided because it defeats everything that the preacher tries to do for the congregation in any sermon introduction on any occasion, which may be summarized as a motivation of personal interest in the subject, created in the congregation 'by the preacher'.[19]

How can a preacher who obviously is unexcited about the truths he will be preaching, as reflected by his tone, create excitement in the hearts of his hearers for truths that have left him passionless? It will be an exceedingly difficult task, if not an utterly impossible task, for a passionless preacher to create anticipation for the message by those who hear him. For a preacher to preach Scriptural truth in a spiritless, irrelevant tone is tragic. As one man aptly wrote, 'A tame and spiritless discourse, coldly uttered, as if the Word of Life were as dull as last year's almanack, as formal as the publication of banns, may even do positive harm.'[20]

But, as bad as that sounds and as tragic as that seems to be, that is not totally tragic. It can be worse. When a preacher starts with a passionless tone and stays with this tone throughout the message, he has accomplished a tragedy in the pulpit. A passionless message, prefaced by a passionless introduction, is the ultimate bad sermon!

Conviction Number Four

The preacher must understand that the sermon introduction is not just a collage of abbreviated opening remarks that must be dispensed with in short order. A sermon introduction is not the homiletical equivalent of the tonsils or the appendix to the human anatomy and physiology. For the overall sake of one's preaching, and specifically one's sermon introductions, a preacher must view this homiletical component as equivalent to the pituitary gland of the human body or one of the other *vital* organs of the body.

The sermon must, one would suppose beforehand, be solemn and affecting, loving and urgent, full of persuasion, warning, and rebuke. Every sentence is purposed to do its share of persuasion. Each hearer should bear witness to the presence of a speaker earnestly desiring to save some soul from death, or to sow in some heart truth and peace.[21] If this is true of the preacher as he preaches the body of the message then it will be indicated by the introduction to that message. The valuable role of the sermon introduction is clarified by the following insight:

> People may eye you, smile while you are speaking, and even compliment your sermon when they leave the building, but unless you speak to that inner ear, the ear of the heart, the soul of the individual, you have not spoken. The introduction will get the ear open for the sermon.[22]

The sad reality is that it is common for sermons to fail to speak to the inner ear of the heart because the opening of the heart's inner ear is accomplished through the agency of an effective introduction. But many introductions fail to do what an introduction to a sermon must do – open the ears of the hearers for an effective reception of the sermon.

A sermon introduction is a servant to the preacher. It must work for him. It has tasks it must accomplish for the preacher on behalf of his hearers. Being much more than a collection of words and ideas that are stated before a congregation, a sermon introduction must transfer the weight and significance of the substance it contains.

When there is a failure of a preacher to transfer the significance of the material he is treating, in the introduction or the body of a sermon, there will be a rather daunting barrier to effective communication that will be interjected by the preacher. What has been reported to be true of the preaching in England would be true of the sermon introduction of many American preachers – 'There is a wall of crystal between him and his hearers; some light passes through it, but hardly any heat.'[23] The spectacle of such heat-deprived light, whether in the introduction or in the body of the sermon, is not a friendly foe.

The congregation must observe, in the introduction especially, that the preacher has an earnest desire to minister to them through the vehicle of the sermon. As of the sermon introduction, the audience must sense that the preacher has a valuable and specific purpose in preaching his message.

All analogies aside, the truth is that a sermon introduction is important because preaching is important! Everything pertaining to preaching is important, including the introduction to the sermon. No preacher would be wise to discount anything that might help him to preach more effectively. One element vital to the cause of more effective preaching is preaching the sermon introduction more effectively. Even though the sermon introduction is a relatively small consideration in the overall enterprise of preaching it is none-the-less uniquely strategic in order to preach more effectively.

Conviction Number Five

The preacher must believe that the sermon introduction, like every other part of a sermon, deserves and requires his most diligent effort. Enhancement in the preaching of one's sermon introduction certainly is attainable. However, enhancement may not be attained without considerable additional effort.

A preacher must make a commitment that he will not slight the preparation of sermon introductions. Instead, he must resolve himself to the fact that he will work hard in this aspect of his sermon preparation. Such a resolve is necessary because diligent work in sermon preparation, even the body of the sermon, is not automatic.

Every preacher knows from personal experience the stinging guilt of the conscience from putting forth less than his best effort in a sermon. Yet few would probably feel much remorse for a less than one's best effort in preparing a sermon introduction. Why? Well, first of all, it is easier to slight an introduction since it is just a portion of a sermon and probably, in the theory of most preachers, just a very small portion at that. Furthermore, the introduction is not involved directly in the exposition of a scriptural text. Therefore, if less than diligent effort is expended for the sermon introduction then it is not really a big deal. It is just a minor offense, if it is any offense at all.

James S. Stewart reminds us of the perpetual opportunity to shortchange our preparation for preaching but we must resist such opportunities and supply the strenuous labor that is demanded upon us by our calling to preach the Word. Reflect long over Stewart's words as he writes:

> There will be subtle temptations to scamp the work of preparation. You will be tempted to rationalize your other crowding duties into a justification for relaxing the inexorable discipline of your study-desk.[24]

Stewart is quite insightful as he continues:

> And can we honestly pray over a bit of scamped work, or any sermon into which we have not cared to put our best? Dr. Sloan Coffin once declared that 'the recipe for compounding many a current sermon might be written: "Take a teaspoonful of weak thought, add water, and serve." The fact that it is frequently served hot, may enable the concoction to warm the hearers; but it cannot be called nourishing.'[25]

And finally,

> Yours is a task, I repeat, which demands and deserves sheer hard work, sweat of brain and discipline of soul.[26]

As to the possibility of scamped work in preparing to preach, the greatest area of culpability for many preachers would be in the preparation of the sermon introduction.

The hard work, sweat of brain and discipline of soul is required in every area of preparation not just portions of it. A preacher who works hard and does well in preaching is one who does a good job in introducing his messages just as he works hard and does well in other parts of sermon preparation and delivery. If this is not the case, he is not a preacher who is as effective as he should be.

Conviction Number Six
A preacher must understand that effective introductions are not produced easily. Inadequate introductions come easily. But an introduction that accomplishes all its objectives and does so in a manner that is clear, concrete, and concise will not be easy. It never has been nor will it ever be easy to produce effective introductions. As one man, well over one hundred years ago, wisely wrote: 'The exordium has been called a preacher's cross. It is the most facile subject of criticism, but the most difficult of execution.'[27]

In like manner, Alexander Vinet warned his readers of the unique nature of a sermon introduction as he wrote, 'let it be remembered that no part is either more difficult or in more danger of mismanagement.'[28] Additionally, he commented on the stra-tegic nature of a sermon introduction and the requirements placed upon one who would preach effectively in this most crucial area of the sermon. Vinet places appropriate significance to a sermon introduction in the following statements.

> Finally, I require in the exordium clearness, justness, correctness, purity of language and style; in a word, I may say perfection. In respect to ideas and style, the exordium in truth, cannot be too faultless. The orator's position is critical now, for the hearer, not being as yet warmly interested, can give his whole attention to details, and the orator, as yet, has been able to do nothing to obtain indulgence even to his slightest faults. No part of the discourse needs as much exactness, or as much address, as the exordium, none being heard with more coolness and none more severely judged. He may be well assured that the attentive hearer will not forgive those faults in the exordium which he will pardon in the body of the discourse, after we have communicated to him our own warmth. All incorrectness, redundance, exaggeration, want of precision, obscurity, he will remark, and nothing will he forgive. Now, this first impression is often decisive and always important. The success of a discourse often depends on the beginning; from first impressions, whether good or bad, we do not easily recover. It is more important that we be free from faults than adorned with beauty.[29]

Obviously, because of its significant role in the sermon, a preacher cannot afford to give casual effort to an introduction and he must provide a significant effort because of the overall degree of difficulty in introducing a sermon well.

The fact that the sermon introduction is an area of the sermonic process marked by difficulty is established by the many ways in which the most basic intentions of an introduction can be foiled rather easily.

Since a sermon introduction is a common area of underachievement and an effective introduction is not produced easily, how then does one prepare a sermon introduction that will result in 'must hear' preaching? It takes a combination of six elements which compose the substance of a sermon introduction that will be the kind of introduction that accomplishes what an introduction should accomplish for any sermon, *but especially an expository sermon.*

In a sermon introduction the preacher must get attention, secure interest, state the purpose of the sermon, set the biblical context from which the sermon is derived, state the proposition of the sermon, and end the sermon introduction with a repeated statement of the sermon proposition. These six elements are necessary components of a sermon introduction that constitutes must hear preaching. These six elements are content-based necessities for a truly effective sermon introduction. But these content-based necessities will not surface in the introduction, or will not be present in sufficient quality, if the preacher does not possess the previously mentioned convictions for the work of preparing a sermon introduction.

It is certain that a preacher controls the content that is present in the introduction of a sermon. It is equally certain that a preacher's convictions regarding a sermon introduction are determinative in controlling the preacher as he makes careful and critical choices about the content of the introduction he prepares. The choices he makes concerning the quality and the quantity of material he includes in the introduction will be determined by the convictions that guide him. The first step in doing a better job in the area of preparing effective sermon introductions is to attain a greater respect for and hold stronger convictions regarding the work of introducing a sermon.

I strongly urge you to discern the strength of your commitment to these convictions regarding the sermon introduction. If conviction is lacking in any of these areas, my plea is for you to pray that God will change your heart regarding the work of introducing your expositions of God's Word. It is His Word you preach and you preach it to His people. He and they deserve the very best you can do in your preaching. To do your best in preaching will necessitate your clearest thinking and strongest commitment to excellence in every aspect of the sermons you preach, and that includes the sermon introduction!

Words to Live and Preach by

Giving Correction

Proverbs 9:7-9 – He who corrects a scoffer gets dishonor for himself, and he who reproves a wicked man gets insults for himself. Do not reprove a scoffer, or he will hate you, reprove a wise man and he will love you. Give instruction to a wise man, and he will be still wiser, teach a righteous man, and he will increase his learning.

Proverbs 15:12 – A scoffer does not love one who reproves him, he will not go to the wise.

Proverbs 22:10 – Drive out the scoffer, and contention will go out, even strife and dishonor will cease.

Proverbs 23:9 – Do not speak in the hearing of a fool, for he will despise the wisdom of your words.

Proverbs 25:12 –Like apples of gold and an ornament of fine gold is a wise reprover to a listening ear.

Proverbs 26:4-5 – Do not answer a fool according to his folly, Lest you also be like him. Answer a fool as his folly deserves, lest he be wise in his own eyes.

Proverbs 28:23 – He who rebukes a man will afterward find more favor than he who flatters with the tongue.

Proverbs 29:9 – When a wise man has a controversy with a foolish man, the foolish man either rages or laughs, and there is no rest.

Chapter Two

Introducing the Sermon: A Necessity or Nuisance

A sermon introduction is to preaching what the showing of a house is to the sale of real estate, or what a test drive is to the purchase of a vehicle. How foolish it is to think that a house would be procured without an inspection by the potential owner or that a vehicle would be bought without examination by the potential buyer. If the test-drive or the inspection does not go well then there will be no subsequent financial transaction.

In a general way, the same is applicable in preaching. Certainly there are prospective buyers of automobiles and houses who desire to procure that which is unkempt, unattractive, and displeasing – a 'fixer-upper'. It is in the best interest of a skilled craftsman or mechanic to secure inexpensive houses or cars because they can be turned into quality possessions that are cost-effective. However, there is not much of a market for 'fixer-upper' sermons! Yet, many preachers showcase their homiletical commodities with introductions that clearly forecast that the sermon to be heard is nothing other than a sermonic fixer-upper!

Many preachers construct sermon introductions that fail to secure the significant interest of their hearers rather than to reveal to them the value that the sermons will have for their lives. When this is the case, the introduction serves as an advertisement that a sermonic 'fixer-upper' is coming their way. An introduction that serves the purpose to advertise that a less-than-significant message will be presented is an advertisement that no preacher can afford to make.

One, then, might begin to wonder if it is wise to have an introduction at all if it is prone to be a potential liability to the sermon. One leading homiletician wrote in his massive text on preaching that 'no introduction is better than a bad one'.[1] And in addition, John A. Broadus wrote in his classic text, *A Treatise On the Preparation And Delivery Of Sermons*: '"Well begun is half done." And ill begun is apt to be wholly ruined.'[2]

Anyone who has had the privilege to preach occasionally would have sufficient grounds by which they could agree with Broadus' statement. But this statement was never intended as an argument for opting out of a sermon introduction simply from the inherent risk that it could be done poorly. In fact, he argued that a sermon without an introduction would be incomplete. This is quite obvious as he wrote:

> It can scarcely be necessary to argue at length to the effect that sermons ought generally to have an introduction. Men have a natural aversion to abruptness, and delight in a somewhat gradual approach. A building is rarely pleasing in appearance, without a porch, or something corresponding to a porch. The shining light of dawn, which shineth more and more till the perfect day, teaches us a lesson. And so any composition or address which has no introduction, is apt to look incomplete.[3]

However, the thrust of his instruction regarding a sermon introduction cannot be overlooked as he penned the words, 'In all preaching, let there be a good introduction, or none at all.'[4]

Even though there is a risk that an introduction might be done poorly, it is wise to have one. Furthermore, there is much good to be achieved by an effective introduction. However, there is no wise counsel for the accommodation of a poor introduction. That simply is not an option. Therefore, two basic assertions regarding sermon introductions need to be made. A sermon must have an introduction. And a sermon introduction must be effective.

Woodrow Kroll summarized the matter succinctly with his words, 'The introduction is a component of extreme importance. It is the introduction which captures the minds of the audience. If the introduction fails, the entire sermon is a failure.'[5] Obviously, the introduction is of great significance and it must be done well or the sermon will not be as effective as it could have been and should have been.

The Necessity of a Sermon Introduction

Must a sermon have an introduction? One certainly has the right to inquire about the necessary inclusion of an introduction for a sermon. However, I believe the answer to the question is a three-fold yes. A sermon needs an introduction because the people, the preacher, and the passage to be preached need it. Or as Arthur Hoyt wrote, 'Some introduction, however short, is generally demanded by the preacher, by the truth, and by the audience.'[6]

The People

The people to whom a preacher preaches constitutes the greatest need for a sermon introduction. The sermon as well as the sermon introduction is for their benefit. An introduction to a sermon will help them to derive more from a message than a message that does not have an introduction. This is so because a sermon introduction accomplishes five closely associated needs hearers have as they begin to hear anyone preach. These include heightened focus, an overcoming of inertia, natural elevation, a communication bridge, and alleviation of abruptness.

Heightened Focus

Everyone who hears a sermon possesses the need for the preacher to help him or her to focus upon what is being communicated. Regardless of the preacher or the congregation, those who hear sermons are not prepared to hear a message at the most productive level when the preacher begins to preach. Certainly some are more prepared to listen than others at the beginning of a sermon but all can and should be taken from whatever level of learning readiness they begin with to a higher level.

Just as the preacher needs to prepare the sermon he is to preach to the people, he also needs to prepare the people to hear the message to be preached to them. The intent to have the people understand the truth to be brought to them in the sermon can be negated by a preacher who supposes that his hearers are already prepared to hear the sermon profitably without the intervention of a sermon introduction. He has violated the chief supposition of a preacher for the endeavor of a preaching an introduction to a sermon – 'suppose them not prepared, composed.'[7] A preacher may suppose that the hearers are prepared to hear the sermon profitably at the end of his introduction but he must not suppose this when he enters the pulpit to begin the preaching process.

Overcoming Inertia

If, at the beginning of a sermon, a preacher is going to suppose anything regarding the people to whom he will preach, he must suppose that there will be an 'initial inertia' of indifference or apathy. To overcome this initial inertia, it is essential that there shall be an introduction that will awaken the lethargic, stir the apathetic and, at the same time, gain the sympathetic ear of all who are present. 'An introduction that does not arouse the attention of the hearers will leave the preacher without an audience, when he comes to the discussion of his theme.'[8]

To suppose that each individual of the congregation bears a degree of indifference toward the forthcoming message is a wise supposition and will provide the preacher with an enhanced purpose for everything that is said in the introduction. During the introduction the preacher needs to serve his hearers by turning their initial inertia into established enthusiasm for the sermon to be preached. However, even when the futile supposition that the hearers are already prepared and composed is not made, and the appropriate supposition that the hearers need to be nurtured into an enthusiastic state is made, optimum reception of the truth is not automatic at this juncture.

Natural Elevation
A preacher can fail to achieve preparing and composing his hearers in the introduction if his content and style does not unfold and elevate in a natural manner. A natural progression of content and an elevation of style are essential within the introduction. In order to achieve a hearing, the preacher must start as close as possible to where his hearers are in terms of excitement regarding the sermon they are about to hear. This will require the preacher to restrain his excitement of the truth he is about to proclaim by a subdued pitch, pace, and projection of voice. Increasing each of these as he progresses into his introduction, a preacher can carry his hearers along with him as they increasingly become excited about the truth that has become such a passion to the preacher. Even though he begins the introduction in acceptable fashion and naturally ascends to an elevated level of pitch, pace, and projection of voice it may not be easy to do so. But do so he must, if he is to keep from losing his audience in route to the text.

In like manner, a judicious speaker will commence with elementary views, and proceed by natural gradations to those more closely associated to the text. As to the natural progression of content and style, a preacher is like a train which does not start off at full speed, but rather by a slow beginning and measured motion at the introduction of its course gradually attains its full velocity. The preacher should so arrange his matter that he may advance to higher and higher results; otherwise, striking on too high a key he will be doomed to descend, and perhaps fall flat before reaching his conclusion.[9] This brings us to the next need of the hearers – a communication bridge.

Communication Bridge
The preacher has to build a bridge of communication from the introduction to the sermon. This bridge is not an option since there is quite naturally a communication gap between the preacher and his congregation as he begins to speak. This communication gap is in reality an information gap and an appreciation gap that exists between the preacher and the people in reference to the passage to be preached.

The information gap that exists is a disparity of knowledge between the preacher's understanding of the text and the hearer's understanding of the text. In the study of the text, days before he preaches the sermon, the preacher has saturated his heart and mind in the truth of the passage. However, this has not been the case with those to whom he will preach. They come to the preaching event in a comparatively emaciated state. He has discovered the truth and prepared himself to disclose his discoveries to the people. Now he has to prepare the hearts and minds of his hearers to receive the truth he will bring to them in his sermon. A preacher prepares the message in his study days before he preaches the sermon. However, a preacher prepares the people to hear the message in the worship setting just moments before the sermon, the body of the message, is preached. Both preparations must be made and both are important.

Because the preacher has studied diligently the text of Scripture that he will expound, he can bring his hearers to an initial appreciation and understanding of the importance of the text in the introduction and, therefore, begin to close the information gap between the preacher and the audience. The initial information about the passage will be provided in the introduction in the form of content depicting how important the subject-matter of the passage is to the lives of all whom will hear the exposition of the passage. Therefore, bridging the appreciation gap of the hearers primarily bridges the information gap. I like what Robert L. Dabney said concerning this necessity.

> If the speaker has done his duty to himself and his subject, he has mastered it by previous study, and comes to the pulpit with his soul inspired and warmed with it. He cannot assume that his hearers are in this animated state. It may even be true that they are ignorant what his subject is to be. Now, this contrast between their state of feeling and his is unfavorable, at the beginning, to the instruction of an active sympathy. When he is all fire and they as yet are ice, a sudden contact between his mind and theirs will produce rather a shock and revulsion than sympathetic harmony. His emotion is, to their quietude, extravagance. He must raise them first a part of the way toward his own level.[10]

Alleviation of Abruptness

The final need of the congregation to be met by the preacher in his introduction has to do with the curtailment of abruptness in the preaching process. The abruptness that must be avoided is not that of a shocking or surprising statement or question raised by the preacher. This form of abruptness can be quite useful. The abruptness that the preacher must not place upon his hearers is to thrust them into the discussion of the passage to be preached before they are prepared to contemplate it.

Alexander Vinet raised the questions, 'Is the exordium necessary, natural? Or is it but a factitious and conventional ornament?'[11] In summary, his response was that it was necessarily natural to have an introduction so as to provide the beauty of conversation that was devoid of abruptness. He argued that 'even in accidental conversation, no one begins *ex abrupto*, if he is free to do otherwise.'[12]

He suggested three reasons for not starting a sermon in an abrupt fashion. In the first place, there is a certain degree of weight in the mere fact of beginning a discourse with an exordium. We appear to have more regard for our subject, when we do not approach it immediately, abruptly. Secondly, it is useful to compose the hearer for a moment, lest he enter into the depth of the subject with a wandering mind. Thirdly, a preacher should seek to put his hearer in a state of mind in relation to his subject, similar to his own. 'It is with the orator and the hearer as with instruments which are tuned before a concert.'[13]

To begin immediately with the message would be a mistake because they would be denied the preacher's preparation for them to hear his message. The preacher desires to have his hearers in a state of earnest desire and anticipation to hear the sermon. Without his preparation of the people, he will not preach for their optimum enhancement. He will launch into the valuable things of Scripture before they have a keen desire to receive it. In essence, the preacher will begin his sermonic journey before the hearers are ready to travel. The preacher must engage the hearers. But the preacher must engage the hearers for the substance of the sermon but not, at least initially, by the substance of the sermon. The introduction is the appropriate and necessary vehicle for the preacher to interest his hearers for the substance of the sermon he will preach to them.

The hearers are engaged for the sermon by the introduction. Quintillian wrote, 'The reason for an exordium can be no other than to dispose the auditory to be favorable to us, in the other parts of the discourse.... By it (the exordium, or the introduction) we so far gain an ascendant over the mind of the judge, as to be able to proceed farther.'[14]

Anyone who has been trained to share the gospel will see the importance of the principle of an introduction that precedes a body of content. Before one begins to disclose the substantial truths comprising the gospel, the teller of the Good News is instructed[15] to engage the recipient in conversation of preliminary matters such as family, interests, religious background, and exploratory questions. What matters is the gospel, not so much the preliminary issues. But the preliminary issues are important because they allow one to be engaged profitably in conversation that leads to disclosure of the gospel.

To begin a conversation with the gospel without any preliminary discussion would seem terribly abrupt and one would not expect to gain much of a hearing by usage of a mode of conversation that would be so startling to the hearer. Without any previous preparation of the recipient of the gospel for the truths of the gospel the hearer will be inclined naturally to indifference or disinterest. So it is in preaching to the saints for their ongoing edification. Before the preacher brings them to the substance of his sermon he must prepare them for the content to come and not take them by surprise with it.

The Preacher
The preacher too is in need of the sermon introduction. The needs of the preacher are primarily the flipside of the needs of the hearers. The introduction provides the preacher an opportunity to minister to his hearers in preparation to receive the Word while at the same time he ministers to his own needs associated with his task to proclaim the Word. The five needs of the hearers merge together to establish a three-fold need of a preacher. Every preacher has the need for a *favorable reception* by the congregation, a need to establish *communicative momentum* or to be in sync with the congregation, and a need to sense that the congregation is an *interested congregation* – they have a strong desire to hear the message to be preached.

Favorable Reception
A favorable reception is indispensable to a preacher. Every time a preacher preaches he wants to sense that his hearers are favorably disposed to him to the extent that they greet him

with a basic willingness to hear him at least during the outset of this preaching occasion. If this is not the case then he is preaching to a hostile audience who possesses a prejudice against him, or perhaps he is preaching to an indifferent congregation who has been so consistently disappointed that they no longer hold out any hope of hearing a worthwhile message from him.

A preacher begins to perceive a favorable reception through the common courtesy of the congregation to give attention to one who is a messenger of God who is there to serve them as he ministers to them through God's Word. Additionally, a favorable reception is sensed even more adeptly as the congregation demonstrates the ability and willingness to follow the train of thought of the preacher's initial material of his sermon introduction.

Communicative Momentum

The needs of the preacher go beyond a favorable reception. Having sensed the courteousness of the people toward him and the initial material of the introduction, the preacher must build upon these so that they do not become initial yet fleeting realities that disappear from the preaching occasion. In other words, a favorable reception must become sustained once it is sensed. If it is not sustained then the preacher will notice that he no longer possesses what he was able to accrue. This obviously is an unproductive and an unwelcomed chain of events. The preacher needs to be received and then make progress throughout the introduction. A regression militates against the momentum which a preacher needs to make in order to bring the people to the sermon, the exposition of the biblical text, in a heightened state of interest. This need of the preacher is one of communicative *momentum*, or certitude.

The preacher possesses this need of communicative momentum, or certitude, every time he preaches. No matter how well he has preached before, that reality does not exempt him from the necessity to do in this sermon what was required for him to preach effectively in times past. No preacher preaches well automatically. Hugh Kerr says, 'Great preaching is not self-sustaining. Even in the life of an individual preacher there are heights and depressions. Preaching, like the landscape, seems to be made up of hills and valleys, heights and depths and long level spaces.'[16] Even in the preaching ministry of a great preacher it is true that not all of his sermons possess the same excellence. However, a great preacher desires to preach well every time he preaches. And though many years of excellent preaching can provide the confidence of a proven track-record, this still does not subtract from his need/desire to preach well the next time he preaches.

Past success in preaching cannot assure success for the next sermon any more than a great athlete cannot be assured of a great performance in his next competition. Since past success cannot assure next-time success, the preacher desires to establish a productive flow of communication in the sermon introduction that suggests to him that he is beginning to do again what he has done before, preach productively. When this is sensed, he has established communicative momentum for the rest of the sermon. Until this occurs or if it fails to occur, the preacher feels as though he is out of sync, that he is not on track, and that is very disconcerting.

Specifically, a preacher has a need to sense that his introduction is making progress so that the initial attention of his hearers is being strengthened. This momentum, or communicative certitude, in the introduction provides the preacher the needed feedback that all is going well and he feels in sync with his congregation and his material. To achieve communicative certitude is an important battle to be won in an attempt to win the war of an excellent introduction. Failure to win the battle of momentum does not spell certain defeat for the preacher but it definitely makes the sought after victory much harder to achieve. A preacher needs to win the battle for communicative certitude!

Since communicative certitude needs to take place in the sermon introduction, the preacher must prepare introductory material that will produce this for him. If he cannot do this in his preparation to preach there is an uneasy feeling that he must take with him in the pulpit. The reason for this is simple – he does not feel he can introduce the sermon effectively since he is not that interested in the sermon he will preach. He is not that interested in the material he will preach because he is yet to discover the true genius of the passage. If he has not been able to discover the riches of the text then he is not ready to preach. To use the words of Richard C. Borden, 'If you know not how to start nor how to finish you know not yet as you ought to know.'[17] Not knowing what you ought to know is not a platform for effective preaching, in general, or for an effective introduction, specifically.

An Interested Congregation
Having worked so hard on interpreting the passage and preparing a sermon from that passage, the preacher needs to know that those who will hear the message will be interested in what he has to say. In other words, it is significant to the preacher to know that, by the time the introduction is finished, the message he will preach is perceived to be a vital one by those who will hear it. If this is not the case then the preacher gets a sense that the preaching effort on this particular occasion is going to be a difficult, uphill task. In fact, if the preacher fails to secure the vital interest of the congregation, then although having won the first two battles he needed to win (to secure a favorable reception and to secure communicative momentum), he *has* lost the war in regards to the sermon introduction. This must be the only appropriate assessment since he failed in achieving the main objective of the sermon introduction – to engender rapt interest of the congregation to the message, the passage of Scripture, to be preached. The preacher cannot afford to fail in reaching this objective.

Establishing the vital interest of the hearers regarding the message to be preached is the magnum opus of the introduction. To fail here, is to ultimately fail in the introduction. The preacher has a need to succeed in the sermon introduction to the extent that he has much more than just receptivity and momentum going for him within the introduction itself. He needs to succeed so well in the introduction that he has won a major victory and has established momentum for the sermon at hand. Nothing is more encouraging to a preacher than for him to sense, by the end of the introduction, that those to whom he will preach have a vital interest in the text/sermon he is to expound.

By the time the preacher completes his introduction he has either gained significant homiletical momentum for the task of proclaiming his message or he has failed to do so. The former is a great advantage for the preacher. The latter is a significant detriment for him.

The Passage

A sermon introduction is warranted not only because the people who will hear the message need it and the one preaching the message needs it but also the passage from which the sermon is derived has need of the sermon introduction. The passage to be preached has three needs that are met by an effective introduction.

First of all, there is a need for the passage to be understood regarding its placement in the biblical book at the particular juncture where it is found. In other words, an effective introduction will answer the compound-question, 'Why is this passage *here at all* in this book and why is it precisely *right here* within this book?' Secondly, there is a need for a passage of Scripture to be appreciated for its unique contribution to the progressive revelation of the scriptural canon because one grasps a general understanding for its existence within the canon of Scripture. Thirdly, there is the need of the passage to help shape a cohesive codification of the foregoing exposition that has taken place as the contents of a biblical book are being expounded verse-by-verse, *or in other words, to provide a connection with the surrounding verses, especially the verses preceding the preaching passage.* The introduction provides an opportunity for the progress the expositor has made in expounding a biblical book to be quickly and concisely reviewed before any analysis is done in the text composing the sermon to be delivered.

In a word, what an effective introduction supplies for a passage is context. Just as context is a crucial consideration in hermeneutics, so it is important in homiletics, especially expository preaching. Unfortunately though, consideration of the passage's context in the introduction is an undervalued component in most homiletical pedagogy and practice. I believe this is indicative of the common aversion to expository preaching.

A text has a context and a text that is to be understood and expounded must be understood and expounded in view of its context. A preacher who can introduce his sermon without time and effort to explain the context of the passage either does not understand the context of the passage himself, or he understands it but assumes that the time and effort spent dealing with the context is not justifiable in the preaching of this sermon. When this is done, regardless of the reason, this typically serves as a foreshadowing that a negligible or nonexistent expositional effort is on the horizon.

Establishing the context is uniquely important in expository preaching. Because the expositor is typically working sequentially through a book of the Bible he desires his hearers to understand the overall flow of the book that has been established to this point in his preaching. And, perhaps even more importantly, he wants them to understand the wider and the immediately preceding contexts. Even if the preacher is involved with a topic that is being expounded, it is helpful to survey the progress that has been made, that is, the instruction that has been provided already on that subject-matter in the previous weeks.

The Effectiveness of a Sermon Introduction

Among other significant functions, one should understand that an introduction acts as a commercial for the message to follow. Through the introduction the hearers are given a 'preview of coming attractions'. That is, they are given an idea of what the sermon will hold for them in terms of the potential power of the forthcoming message and the passion of the messenger before them. Haddon Robinson adeptly captured the importance of the introduction regarding the preacher. He wrote, 'There are three types of preachers: those to whom you cannot listen; those to whom you can listen; and those to whom you must listen. During the introduction the congregation usually decides the kind of speaker addressing them that morning.'[18] This is a profoundly daunting reality! If one agrees with Robinson's assessment, as I do, then one must feel the weighty responsibility of assembling an introduction that will not furnish the congregation grounds by which they may dismiss the preacher and whatever message he would care to deliver to them upon this occasion.

It is inevitable that the introduction reveals to a congregation the type of preacher who will be preaching to them that day. But it is imperative that the introduction serves to accomplish more than simply getting the favorable attention of the hearers toward the preacher and the prospective message he intends to deliver.

The purpose of an introduction is commonly defined in such terminology as getting the attention of the hearers or introducing the text of the sermon or introducing the subject of the sermon. There is no doubt that these things must be done. However, these things, even having been done, are not vital enough to accomplish the ultimate purpose of a sermon introduction. There is still much work to be done in the introduction before proceeding to the exposition of the text/ preaching of the sermon. In fact, the lion-share of the work to be accomplished in a sermon introduction lies beyond getting the hearers' attention and introducing the text and subject of the sermon. It is counter-productive for preachers to think that they have labored sufficiently in the introduction if they have only achieved these most rudimentary objectives. As long as preachers think that the introduction is only about the more basic objectives of getting the hearer's attention, introducing the text of the sermon, and introducing the subject-matter of the sermon, there will be underachievement in the work of introducing sermons.

The Length of a Sermon Introduction

The escalation of the purpose for sermon introductions almost guarantees that the time spent introducing the sermon will increase. This is a critical consideration. Who would dare doubt that time is a very important issue in preaching? And in like manner, who would doubt the wisdom of trying to curtail the time spent introducing the sermon so that one might have more time for the preaching of the message? These questions notwithstanding, it is beneficial to raise an often-asked question and reinstate an old answer that will seem new. The often-asked question is – 'How long should an introduction be?' The reinstated answer to the question is – *'As long as it takes to do what must be done in a sermon introduction!'*

For consistent improvement in sermon introductions to be achieved, preachers must bury the idea that a certain amount of minutes or a given percentage of one's preaching time is to be afforded for the work of introducing the message. Such a burial will be a difficult thing for most preachers to pull off because they probably have seen modeled, been taught, and read frequently the various numerical and percentage quotas for sermon introductions. To labor under a numerical or percentage quota is to minimize the worth of a sermon introduction.

If a preacher accepts a time-based limit for a sermon introduction he is prioritizing 'the time spent in' versus 'the affect of' introducing the message. In other words, he reveals that the more important goal of a sermon introduction is to be finished with it rather than accomplishing what must be done in it. In holding such a view, the work of introducing a sermon will only be a trivial and perfunctory matter and the resulting introductions may be brief but less than effective.

Having stated the main assertion in answering the often-asked question of how long should an introduction be, a second assertion must be supplied with equal force. *'Though a sermon introduction must be as long as necessary to do what must be done, it must not be one second longer than necessary to do what must be done!'*

If a preacher can do what must be done in a given introduction in seven minutes and five seconds then do so in seven minutes and five seconds but not one second more. Genuine concern that no time be wasted in a sermon introduction is a necessity, not an option. 'It is bad policy to waste the moments when the congregation is all attention with unimportant or trivial remarks'[19] remains wise counsel and is unheeded at one's own peril.

A sermon introduction is not more effective just because it is longer. In a word, brevity *is* an essential consideration for a sermon introduction as long as one understands that brevity means to be as brief as one can be in doing all that needs to be done in the introduction. Brevity is a counterproductive consideration if by it one means that the introduction is a product consisting of a few sentences to be spoken before one begins to preach a sermon.

A clear and emphatic proposition must be understood at this point – I am not making a case for *unnecessarily* long sermon introductions! There is no premium on long introductions simply because they are long any more than there is a premium on short introductions simply because they are short. The measure of a sermon introduction is not the time spent by the preacher in presenting it but what happens to the hearers during the introduction, regardless of the time spent introducing the sermon. The crucial consideration regarding brevity in sermon introductions is not the time spent presenting the material contained in the introduction but the very careful and purposeful inclusion of all the material that is to be included in the introduction of a sermon. The *meaningful incorporation of content*, not the *time spent presenting the content*, is the more important issue for sermon introductions.

If the content of the introduction is qualitative then the quantitative reality of the introduction, regardless of how lengthy it may be, will *seem* brief. Brevity and length in a sermon are subjective realities. A sermon or an introduction can seem long regardless of the amount of time actually committed to the effort. 'It is possible for one man to be even more dreary in ten minutes than another would be in an hour and a half.'[20] What Lyman Beecher lecturer Charles Reynolds Brown said in his lectures pertaining to a sermon is just as true of the sermon introduction. Brown's comments regarding the relevance of time spent in delivering a sermon are even more instructive in our extremely time-sensitive society.

> Let me hasten to say that the clock has nothing to do with the length of a sermon. Nothing whatever! Clocks know nothing about the matter: clocks are in no wise competent to pass upon the proportions of a sermon. A long sermon is a sermon that seems long. It may have lasted an hour or it may have lasted but fifteen minutes. If it seems long, it is long – it is too long. And the short sermon is one that ends while people are still wishing for more. It may have lasted only twenty minutes or it may have lasted for an hour and a half. If it leaves the people wishing for more, they do not know nor care what the clock said about the length of it.[21]

What a great and valuable insight! As another man wrote, 'There is no excuse for a long sermon.'[22] That too is true and helpful as long as the rationale for the statement is understood – if the sermon is good then it will not *seem* long and if it is not good then it ought not to *be* long!

The same reasoning must be applied to the introduction of the sermon. A sermon introduction is brief enough if people want to hear the sermon that the introduction introduced. In other words, if the people want to hear the sermon more, having heard the introduction, than they did before they heard the introduction then that introduction was brief enough. On the other hand, if the people want to hear the sermon less, having heard the introduction, than they did before the introduction then the introduction was much too long regardless of the few minutes it may have taken to present it.

The amount of time given to the introduction is still an important concern. Homileticians have documented the need for brevity in sermon introductions for many years. William G. T. Shedd's assessment of brevity in the sermon introduction, though written in the middle of the nineteenth century, is timeless.

> Still, brevity should be a distinguishing characteristic of the exordium; and where one sermon is faulty from being too abruptly introduced, one hundred are faulty from a too long and tiresome preface. It is easier to expand the common thoughts of the introduction, than to fill out full, and thoroughly elaborate, the argumentative parts of the discourse; and hence we too often listen to sermons which remind us of the Galatian church which began in the spirit, but ended in the flesh. The sermon opens with a promising introduction, which attracts attention, conciliates the audience, and paves the way to a noble and fertile theme. But, instead of bringing the exordium to a close, and commencing with the development of a subject, or the proof of a proposition, the sermonizer repeats, or unduly expands, his introductory matter, as if he dreaded to take hold of his theme. The consequence is that the theme itself is not handled with any strength of firmness of grasp, and the long and labored introduction only serves as a foil, to set off the brevity and inferiority of the body of the discourse.[23]

As true as this might have been in the nineteenth century it is even more so today.

Our culture absolutely demands brevity. Certainly, no preacher today can afford to expand his introductory matter unduly. 'We face a congregation, a situation, and the clock. We will waste no time. We must gain the immediate attention of those who are present.'[24] It is unwise and impossible to preach without feeling the relentless pressure of time that is passing quickly.

Another plea for brevity in the introduction is contained in the words 'it is necessary that the development of the idea of the exordium should be brief. By detaining the people on the threshold of a house into which we have promised them entrance, we give them good reason to be impatient.'[25] Many preachers, however, will need to spend more time introducing their sermons simply because they consistently fail to do what needs to be done in an introduction. In other words, they cannot do what must be done in an introduction in the time they generally allot for a sermon introduction.

It is common for a preacher to have finished his introduction even though some elements of an introduction have not been incorporated or have been incorporated in a less-than-significant manner. It will require additional time to strengthen what is weak or absent because more material is needed. Therefore, the necessary priority and perspective is one of enhancement of the sermon introduction rather than expansion of the sermon introduction. Expansion is simply an unavoidable consequence entailed in the strengthening of weak, ineffective introductions due to a paucity of significant material. Expansion, also, is a welcomed corrective for introductions that cannot do what an introduction is required to do.

A common attribute of weak introductions is that they do not possess enough substantial material for them to be strong. But it may be a common weakness of a substantial introduction that too much time was expended needlessly in presenting the material that composes the introduction of the sermon. David Breed addressed the delicate balance needed in a sermon introduction to transport a substantial load of material in a brisk clip of time.

> A plain worshiper, who had been much upon the sea in the days of the old sailing vessels, remarked with regard to the sermons of a certain minister that they were 'clipper-built.' Those who recall the special design of such vessels will understand his reference. The peculiar quality of the old clippers was in the formation of their prows, rather than in the general form of the vessel. The 'cut-water' was sharp, clean, and projected backward upon lines which offered the least possible resistance to the waves. Therefore they were fast sailers, while at the same time capable of carrying considerable freight. And the introduction to the sermon is the 'cut-water'; it, too, should offer the least possible resistance. It should be no burden upon the attention of the congregation, but rather the reverse. A scow may carry more freight than a clipper, but its sailing qualities are so imperfect that it is capable of making but a single passage while the other vessel is making half a dozen. The clipper is the more effective, and there are some sermons weighted with an immense amount of learning, thought, and argument, which are not effective, only because they are not 'clipper-built.'[26]

Time is a very critical factor but content is ultimately critical. A preacher must incorporate what he feels necessary for the introduction to be a vital one, but he must communicate it as succinctly as he can.

In an effort to try to establish a guideline to help a preacher determine the length of a sermon introduction, common sense rather than some rigid rule should be used. The following argument is thoroughly sound and to the point regarding content versus time. 'He who is saying nothing, cannot have done too soon. He who is saying something, will always say that best in the fewest words. When the nail is driven home, all after-hammering is superfluous; but if we stop before we have driven it home, we might as well never have begun to drive it.'[27]

Broadus provides two very general but helpful insights regarding the length of the sermon introduction, the second of which is commonly ignored by those who teach and write upon the subject. He warned that 'the introduction must not be too long' and, more importantly, that 'the attempt of some writers to tell how many sentences an introduction should contain is exceedingly unwise.'[28] Haddon Robinson writes, 'Unfortunately no percentages help us here.'[29] Rather than offering some form of a quota Robinson, instead, offers a principle that is not only wise but helpful. His counsel is that a sermon introduction must do what it is intended to do – 'Until that is done, the introduction is incomplete; after that the introduction is too long.'[30] Amen, and amen!

Yet many have offered, and some continue to offer, quantitative quotas for the amount of minutes or the percentage of preaching time that should be given to the introduction. A selection of the various quotas are represented as follows: 'not more than 5 to 15 percent';[31] 'never, at longest, occupy more than an eighth of a sermon';[32] 'five minutes, or less, should be ample for a forty minute address';[33] 'the first three minutes of the sermon';[34] 'Five minutes out of the thirty granted to the sermon should be ample';[35] 'as a general guideline, introductions may run between seven and twelve sentences in length.'[36] The lack of wisdom in ascribing numerical or percentage quotas to an introduction is hinted at by the fact that the quotas offered are so wide in range that they must be arbitrary designations.

Again, the argumentation of Charles Reynolds Brown for the length of a sermon must be applied to sermon introductions rather than some arbitrary quota.

> The sermon always is nothing more nor less than a tool! What size should a tool be? How long should a scythe be? How heavy should an axe be? This cannot be determined by certain fixed presuppositions or by any a priori principles about the formation of tools. It is to be determined altogether by the demands of

the task to which this particular tool is to be applied. A man will mow more grass with a scythe of reasonable length than he would with a scythe twenty feet long. He will cut more wood with a five pound axe than he could with one weighing twenty pounds. The sermon also is a tool and its length is to be determined entirely by those considerations which indicate its fitness or its unfitness to accomplish a desired spiritual result.... The question of length is a practical question altogether and it is to be answered by the application of the pragmatic test. What length of sermon works best? What length of sermon accomplishes most in creating, nurturing and directing Christian impulse? If that can be determined, we shall have the proper length of discourse indicated. Whatever brand of philosophy you may prefer touching other vital interests, in determining the length of your sermon, you would better all be pragmatists. The length of sermon that works best in producing spiritual results is the right length.[37]

No one should pontificate upon the quantifiable length of the sermon introduction. In like manner, no preacher should submit to some arbitrarily devised quota for introducing his sermons.

A wise preacher will seek to introduce his message in a manner that will be brief enough so that it does not seem long. Someone reported that a 'Reverend' Jones became known as 'the *Neverend*' Jones.[38] This must not be the case in our preaching, in general, and in our sermon introductions, specifically. It was reported that an old woman said of the preaching of the Welsh preacher, John Owen, that he was so long spreading the table she lost her appetite for the meal.[39] An eminent preacher, much inclined to the fault of long introductions, was accosted by a plain old man with the following words: 'Well, you kept us so long in the porch this morning that we hardly got into the house at all.'[40] It is important that such anecdotes are not affixed to us because of our preaching introductions that are too long. It is important to understand what Ilion T. Jones wrote,

'Nothing will kill interest more certainly than a laborious beginning.'[41]

In the long run, if a preacher takes great care in regards to the content of the introduction, he will effectively take the appropriate care for the length of the introduction. In other words, the quality of the content takes care of the time concern for the introduction! Inversely, the perceived length of the introduction is a commentary upon the quality of the content of the introduction!

Jerry Vines writes, 'Long introductions are a waste of time.'[42] But, this is not necessarily true. If an introduction is effective, even if it requires more than a few minutes to deliver, it is not at all a waste of time. If an introduction is effective, then whatever amount of time is required to deliver it is time well spent. 'Long introductions are a waste of time' is as true as the statement 'short introductions are not a waste of time.' But this, too, is not necessarily true. A short, ineffective introduction is also a waste of time!

The point of distinction, though, between a short, ineffective sermon introduction and a long, ineffective sermon introduction is that the short version wastes less time. So the secondary point is clear. If you are going to preach an ineffective sermon introduction, by all means make it a brief one! But ineffectiveness is not the issue anyway. To preach an effective introduction is the issue and effectiveness is the priority. Invest whatever time is necessary to provide an introduction that indicates a 'must hear' exposition is in store for your congregation and that amount of time will be time invested wisely.

More Eye Contact and Less Paper in a Sermon Introduction

Unfortunately, introductions that contain a substantial amount of material may create a great barrier to effective communication that is not related to time. This barrier is found in the form of sermon notes that a preacher may feel he needs to rely upon if he were to marshal more than just the scant amount of material that a brief introduction would require. Sermon notes must be managed well, but this is especially so during the crucial time in which the introduction of the message is delivered.

A substantial introduction must not generate an unwieldy mass of paper that a preacher must manage in the pulpit. In the introduction portion of a sermon it is vital that a preacher make eye contact with those who will hear him preach. He must engage them not only conceptually with the material he will cover in the introduction but he must engage them personally by sustained, individual eye contact. Through eye contact the preacher makes the communication of truth a personal issue so that the congregation can sense that he is proclaiming the truth *to* them and *for* them, not simply *before* them. Alex Montoya states:

> Most preachers think the primary use of the eyes is to read their notes or manuscripts. That is secondary. The primary use of the eyes is to make contact with the listener. Through your eyes, you allow the listeners to look into your soul, even as you look into theirs. The eyes also most fully reveal the state of your emotions. Anger, sadness, joy, gladness, and love – all these come most clearly through your eyes.[43]

A preacher cannot afford to treat eye contact with the congregation as a luxury item or a peripheral issue.

Since over-attention to sermon notes may curtail the crucial eye contact necessary to preach effectively, a preacher must implement whatever measures necessary to assure a relatively note-free sermon introduction. Every preacher will have to determine what amount of sermon notes works best for him in preaching. Regardless of how much or little paper he takes with him in the pulpit he must strive to be as note-free as he can be in the sermon introduction. It is certain that to whatever extent a preacher is dependent upon sermon notes he is sure to lose eye contact to the same degree, and he may wane in passion as well.

Additionally, Charles Koller offers two incentives for note-free preaching that deserve consideration. 'First, it is recognized that most congregations prefer note free preaching.' Second, 'there are, and always have been, ministers who preach effectively from manuscript or copious notes in the pulpit, as well as some who read their sermons in full; but the same preachers would be even more effective if they could stand note free in the pulpit.'[44] John Baird, who condemned notes as 'distracting to the speaker and the audience', argues that almost everyone admires the freedom of the speaker who can talk without notes. He is free to gesture since his hands are not filled with papers or busy shuffling those obtrusive little cards which many speakers use. He is free to move about since he is not dependent upon the pulpit or stand which holds his notes. He is free to maintain eye contact with his audience since it is not necessary for him to look down at his notes.[45]

From the vantage-point of the listeners, notes are a distraction. They must be limited. Beyond preventing distractions, speaking without notes provides certain benefits to a speaker. Again, Baird is convincing as he says, 'If you want to look guilty, bashful, or weak, just neglect to look at your audience. On the other hand, if you want to appear confident, powerful, dynamic, and straightforward, look them in the eye. Concentrate every effort on looking at the audience and keeping their attention on you.'[46] The benefits described above are related to the ethos, or the character, of the preacher.

In preaching, a preacher dare not sacrifice his character or even tolerate anything that may be part of his delivery in preaching that may perceptually impeach his character. And just as emphatically, a preacher does not want to indicate that he is less than passionate and not full of conviction regarding the truth he preaches. But, a preacher's pathos or passion, emotion, and conviction he has for the message he preaches is perceived in part by his eye contact, or lack of eye contact. Simply put, 'It is the face that makes the audience believe that you believe what you say.'[47] Even more specifically, 'It is the eyes that convey sincerity and conviction.'[48] Eye contact plays an important role in the audience's perception of the man preaching to them as well as his concern for the message he is preaching.

Having established the benefits of better eye contact through the use of little or no notes, it must be acknowledged that many preachers would contest the validity of preaching without any notes at all. And I would be among them. But certainly a preacher can and should divest himself of the distractions accompanying sermon notes and incorporate the benefits of note free preaching in the *sermon introduction*!

In establishing a case for the significance of the message to be preached, the overall purpose of a sermon introduction, eye contact and passion must not be diminished. Stephen Olford's comments regarding the matter of deciding what form of notes are to be used in delivering a sermon are equally justified in curtailing notes used for delivering a sermon introduction. He reminds us that truth, clarity, and passion are desired in the delivery of the message. One has to assess how the use of a manuscript impacts each one of these three important aspects of the delivery of a specific message. For example, if a preacher feels that he is freer in delivery without any notes, but he loses some clarity in the exposition, this needs to be viewed very carefully.[49] In the introduction, where the preacher typically will not be expounding the text, he simply seeks to convey how crucial the exposition of the passage will be for their lives. This can be done, typically, with the use of very little or no notes at all.

A careful understanding between information and communication must be understood and applied to the sermon introduction. 'Information is giving out; communication is getting through.'[50] Sermon notes are more necessary for the exposition of the text in the body of the sermon. But the introduction is the time and place to communicate far more than to inform! Fewer notes and more eye contact are critical in the introduction. The introduction must make it clear to all whom hear that you are not preaching this message *because you have to say something* but rather you are preaching this message *because you have something to say*.[51] At best, reference to notes indicates that you are trying to say something (but you cannot say it without quite a bit of help) while note-free preaching indicates that you have something to say and are saying it. Notes indicate information. Eye contact indicates communication.

Communication is thwarted in a two-fold way when a preacher sacrifices eye contact by over attention to sermon notes. 'First, the sermon will become less intelligible and more uncertain in its results. Second, an impersonal attitude will creep into your delivery. The element of personal interest and concern will evaporate.'[52]

Extemporaneous Preaching in a Sermon Introduction

Before considering further the subject-matter of more eye contact and fewer notes, I believe it may be profitable, and perhaps necessary, to deal with a question and an assertion that some may still be harboring. The question being, 'What about a preacher like Jonathan Edwards?' The assertion being, 'He was used greatly by God in his day and he did not make eye contact with his hearers because he read from a manuscript and read from the manuscript in a monotone!' The assertions about Edwards are true. The following is recorded about the preaching of Edwards.

> In the delivery of his sermons he was unsensational. His voice, neither loud nor strong, had little inflectional variety. He did not use gestures, and a heavy dependence on his manuscript prevented any direct rapport with his congregation. Edward's

practice was to hold the manuscript volume in his left hand, the elbow resting on the cushion on the Bible, his right hand rarely raised but to turn the leaves, and his person almost motionless.[53]

But the example of Jonathan Edwards should not deter anyone from doing what must be done *today* in order to preach as effectively as one may preach. Without any attempt on my part to be sarcastic or unnecessarily blunt, the following must be kept in mind. In the providence of a sovereign God, He chose to use Jonathan Edwards as a choice instrument to bring about the Great Awakening. God used him mightily despite his delivery idiosyncrasies. Do you believe God is bound and determined to use you the way He used Edwards? Although Edwards was used mightily in his day with his delivery, these days are not those days, the days of Jonathan Edwards. Should you ever become Jonathan Edwards and should you ever preach to the people to whom Edwards preached, you should feel free to preach like Edwards! Jonathan Edwards' delivery worked well for Jonathan Edwards, when *he* was preaching in *his day*.

What means may be deemed as necessary for one to preach a substantial amount of material in a sermon introduction and still be relatively note-free? The necessity called for is extemporaneous *preaching*. Most crucial for a correct understanding of extemporaneous preaching is that it is a method in which a preacher studies a subject thoroughly and then prepares to preach it with the help of a few notes as possible.[54] Thoroughness and freedom from notes are the hallmarks of extemporaneous preaching.

There must be no confusion about the rigors of preparation for this method of sermon delivery. This is not a method for an indolent man. Time and effort are not economized by extemporaneous preaching. Time and effort expended in the act of writing may be curtailed but the same amount of time and effort, perhaps more, will be spent understanding, internalizing, and familiarizing oneself with the material to be delivered. However, the crux of the matter regarding extemporaneous preaching is not the shift in one's approach in preparation but the result of one's preparation in the act of preaching. Extemporaneous preaching allows listeners to retain thirty-six percent more of the content as well as causing them to be more sympathetic and attentive to the speaker.[55]

I believe four things may be helpful for one to preach extemporaneously. Actually, the last three things to be considered are mandatory for preaching extemporaneously, though the first consideration is only an option. Some, however, would view this consideration to be equally as imperative, perhaps more so, than the other three. The optional consideration for extemporaneous preaching is a highly polished manuscript. The imperative considerations for extemporaneous preaching are thorough internalization of the content of the sermon introduction, a brief and sketchy outline of the sermon introduction content taken to the pulpit, and the preparation of the sermon introduction must finalize the sermon preparation process.

A Highly Polished Manuscript
First, a highly polished manuscript of the sermon introduction, which will allow precision of thought and clarity on paper, probably will not be so beneficial for the pulpit. There was a time when many were the advocates of writing sermons, especially homileticians of the late nineteenth and early part of the twentieth century. At present, there is a strong sentiment for sermonic material to be prepared for the ear, not the eye. In other words, the preparation is geared for a sermon intended to be heard as opposed to being read. Therefore, not written language but oral language, orality, in a word, is the demand of the day.

Extemporaneous speech is the preferred vehicle by which a preacher may convey a substantial amount of material to a congregation and do it in such a way that they receive the content easily, since it is spoken for oral consumption. Furthermore, through extemporaneous speech the preacher can deliver content freely since he has little written material to manage. Jay Adams clarifies the merits of extemporaneous preaching. Adams is of the conviction that the case for extemporaneous preaching first may be based upon the fact that in the Scriptures preaching is always extemporaneous. As to the nature of extemporaneous preaching, he makes it clear that extemporaneous does not mean unprepared, but rather speaking in which the preacher, after careful preparation, chooses much of his language at the time of delivery. Furthermore, extemporaneous preaching does not preclude the use of an outline to which the preacher may make occasional reference. Many of his words may be words that were chosen previously because of their accuracy, precision or crucial importance in making a particular point.[56]

I will have to admit that my practice and penchant in the past and still to the present is not for a written sermon, nor a manuscript of the introduction. However, in the very few occasions where I have wordsmithed a sermon, or a portion of a sermon, it has been confined primarily to the sermon introduction. Even though I have written sparingly, I can vouch for the merits of writing that many have so strenuously demanded.

In the 1875 Yale Lectures on preaching, John Hall insisted upon sermonic writing with the utmost care as he addressed the divinity students with these words:

> Write every word, or an equivalent for every word, and set down every idea you ought to give to the people, and in its relative place. Write, if necessary, more than once, first a brief, then a precis of greater length, then a full and complete presentation of the whole matter as you are to give it to the people. I say this to you with the utmost explicitness, and with the strongest emphasis. Forego every bottle but the ink-bottle. Write regularly, conscientiously, and at your best. Whether you take your manuscript to the pulpit, or burn it when you have done your

best upon it, or leave it to be burned by ungrateful posterity, is of secondary, that you write is of the first, importance. If you inquire why this is urged so vehemently, let me reply succinctly. It is the way to prune off redundancies. It is the way to exactness of phraseology. It is the best method of taking one's own measure.[57]

However, many will feel more comfortable with writing an expanded outline rather than a manuscript, concluding that the precision and polish of a well-honed manuscript, even of the sermon introduction, to be too great an expenditure for too little of a return.

So the question is this – what is the final form of all that you have prepared? Should this be written out in full, or should it not? I believe Martyn Lloyd-Jones provides an acceptable argument that gives to each man the freedom to do as he deems best for himself. Consider what Lloyd-Jones says and let this be an encouragement to you in your approach to sermon preparation as you prepare the body, the conclusion, and the introduction of the sermon.

> Once more it seems to me that the only sane thing to say is that you must not lay down an absolute law about this matter; because you will find that your laws will not stand up to the test of the history of preaching. Charles Haddon Spurgeon, that great preacher, did not write out his sermons in full; he just prepared and used a skeleton. He did not approve of the writing of sermons, in general.... On the other hand, Dr. Thomas Chalmers, the great leader of the Free Church of Scotland, and a great preacher, found that he had to write out his sermons fully. He tried many times to become an extemporary preacher but felt each time it was a complete failure; he just could not do it. So he had to write his sermons out in full. The result was that a completely written manuscript of the sermon became and has continued to be a tradition in Scotland until today.[58]

However, if one chooses for the final product of one's preparation to be few notes or no notes at all, what is crucial is for the preacher to preach and not to try to recite what has been committed to memory. A recitation of memorized material is not preaching and such an attempt to do so gets in the way of preaching. The following are what Francois Fenelon, the great court preacher of Louis the XIV, considered to be advantageous to not memorizing a speech: the speaker is self-possessed, he speaks naturally; his utterances are lively and full of movement; the warmth that possesses him converts itself into terms and figures that he will not be able to prepare in his study.[59]

Thorough Internalization
Second, having produced a manuscript or an expanded outline, it must be internalized, *and done so in a very thorough manner.* This will require the repetitious reading and thinking through the material so that one may gain a mastery of the content by very thorough familiarity. This means that the preacher is to engross himself in the message so that he strengthens his own interest and conviction in the message.

Jerry Vines suggests the following for mastering one's sermon material. Thoroughly understand what you will be saying. Have a strong organization for your material. Understand the logical relationships of the ideas of the material, knowing how the various ideas fit together. Rehearse the thought sequences in your mind, mastering the pictures of the sermon material. Study the material on Saturday night and Sunday morning. Overlearn your material so that you are so familiar with what you are going to say that it is a part of you.[60]

A Sketchy Pulpit Outline
Third, perhaps to help insure that the written manuscript or expanded outline cannot become a barrier, a brief, sketchy outline of the contents of the sermon introduction can be taken into the pulpit. A brief sketchy outline will serve as a set of prompters to remind him of the material that has

been wordsmithed and internalized. Visually rich keys such as indention, capitalization, font size, underlining, and color coding are helpful in recalling the sequence and substance of material to be delivered as suggested by the brief outline.

The Final Step of Sermon Preparation
Fourth, the introduction, regardless of whatever form it will ultimately take, must be produced only after the sermon body and conclusion have been prepared. Thomas Potter presented the case very cogently as to why the introduction should be produced last. He says, 'If we write our exordium at the very commencement, and before we have thoroughly digested our materials and arranged our plan, how can it possibly shadow forth the main features of our discourse? In such cases we write, not introductions to suit our sermons, but sermons to suit our introductions.'[61]

Obviously then, the introduction is something that is not easily produced nor is it something that is produced satisfactorily simply because one has been preaching for years. Alexander Vinet's comments are insightful in this regard.

> Among experienced preachers we find few examples of exordiums altogether defective; we find few good ones among preachers at their beginning. We hence naturally infer, that there is in this part of the discourse something of special delicacy, but nothing which demands peculiar faculties. It is with exordiums as with nice and exact mechanical operations, in which the workman finally succeeds, but not without having broken more than one of the instruments which he uses.[62]

Preaching sermon introductions that are more effective is an achievable goal. It will require from a preacher more time and effort. It, typically, will necessitate more material than a preacher is used to providing as well as testing more stringently his stewardship regarding the time he allots for this portion of the sermon. He will need to be so familiar with the content of the introduction and have this material so internalized that his obvious passion for the truth is revealed by sustained, individual eye contact with the hearers through extemporaneous speech. Is it worth the additional difficulties? Absolutely!

Ineffective introductions, with all that they fail to achieve, for the preacher and especially for the listeners, are the ultimate 'too high of a price' to be paid in the preaching enterprise. It is time for preachers to stop payments on the homiletical boondoggles of ineffective sermon introductions. A preacher's inability to establish in the heart of the hearers a desire to hear his sermon is an indictment on his own interest in that which he will preach. If this is not the case then it surely is indicative of the fact that he does not understand what to do in an introduction, or how to go about introducing a sermon effectively. The thrust of this book will be devoted to the elements that should be part of an effective introduction and how to structure the truth of the texts that will be expounded in the sermons that have been effectively introduced.

Consider the following Questions

1. Do you assume that your hearers are already interested in the sermon you will preach? If you do or do not make this assumption, what is the rationale for your assumption?

2. Are you concerned enough about your hearers that you are willing to overcome the initial inertia of the indifferent or apathetic hearers in the congregation?

3. Does the introduction reflect the fact that you are excited about the truth you will proclaim? Is there a natural elevation in excitement as the sermon introduction progresses?

4. Do you incorporate material in the introduction that is designed to get your hearers in tune with your own

understanding and appreciation for the sermon to be preacher to them?

5. When you are about to preach, which of the following is more indicative of your prevailing focus and driving force for preaching: a desire to preach well in this sermon, or an appreciation for an effective preaching ministry in past days?

6. Do you accept the idea that the sermon introduction is a personal challenge for you to hook the hearers' interest or do you shrink back from such a high challenge?

7. Do you consider establishing the context of the sermonic text unnecessary or an ineffective use of time in a sermon introduction?

8. Do you really believe that a sermon introduction actually depicts the kind of preacher you are on this particular occasion?

9. Are you willing to fight the battle of achieving the necessary effect of a sermon introduction yet doing so in the least amount of time possible? In other words, are you committed to preparing 'clipper-built' introductions that can transport a significant amount of material in a brief amount of time?

10. Do you agree that any percentage of preaching time or specific time-allotments are unwise for sermon introductions?

11. In your preaching, does the sermon introduction demonstrate the greatest amount of sustained eye contact you provide for your hearers?

12. Do your introductions indicate that you preach because you have something to say or that you preach because you are required to say something?

13. Do your sermon introductions depict thorough preparation and personal internalization or do they suggest inadequate preparation and insufficient mastery of content?

Words to Live and Preach by

Accepting Correction

Proverbs 3:11-2 – My son, do not reject the discipline of the Lord or loathe His reproof, for whom the Lord loves He reproves, even as a father corrects the son in whom he delights.

Proverbs 8:32-6 – Now therefore, O sons, listen to me, for blessed are they who keep my ways. Heed instruction and be wise, and do not neglect it. Blessed is the man who listens to me, watching daily at my gates, waiting at my doorposts. For he who finds me finds life and obtains favor from the Lord. But he who sins against me injures himself; all those who hate me love death.

Proverbs 10:8 – The wise of heart will receive commands, but a babbling fool will be ruined.

Proverbs 10:17 – He is on the path of life who heeds instruction, but he who ignores reproof goes astray.

Proverbs 12:1 – Whoever loves discipline loves knowledge, but he who hates reproof is stupid.

Proverbs 12:15 – The way of the fool is right in his own eyes, but a wise man is he who listens to counsel.

Proverbs 13:18 – Poverty and shame will come to him who neglects instruction, but he who regards reproof will be honored.

Proverbs 15:5 – A fool rejects his father's discipline, but he who regards reproof is sensible.

Proverbs 19:20 – Listen to counsel and accept discipline, that you may be wise the rest of your days.

Chapter Three

Getting Attention: Good But Not Good Enough

Attuning the Minds of the Hearers

One of the most basic functions of a sermon introduction is to cause the hearers to become attentive to the preacher for the sake of the sermon content he is about to deliver as he expounds a biblical text. It is necessary to attune the hearers to the message they will hear lest they encounter the sermon with wandering minds, or with minds that have not been initially prepared to engage the sermon meaningfully.

Therefore, the earliest portion of the introduction must effectively attune the mind of the hearers to the preacher so that he may communicate more significantly later in the sermon introduction and in the sermon itself. Like a professional athlete who must warm up and stretch out before the competition begins, so must a hearer be prepared by warming up to the message they will hear. Alexander Vinet depicts this function of the sermon introduction as analogous to the need an orchestra has to tune their instruments before a concert.[1]

Such an attuning of the hearers' minds is accomplished by incorporating attention-getting material at the very beginning of the introduction. It is only as the hearers become attentive to the preacher that he can proceed farther with them in the sermon introduction. The attention-getting material must bear some relationship to the subject-matter of the sermon. The attention-getting material of the sermon introduction is designed to prepare the hearers to understand well what will be spoken throughout the remainder of the introduction. The completed introduction is designed to prepare the hearers to understand the sermon to be preached to them. To use another analogy, as a good farmer must stir up the soil before sowing seed, so must a good preacher stir the mind of the hearer to receive the seed of the Word.

Attention-Getting Material – A Sermon Introduction's Introduction

A crucial understanding of the attention-getting material is this: the attention-getting material directly attunes the hearers to receive the remainder of the introduction, and thereby, indirectly attunes them to receive the sermon. The relationship of the completed introduction to the sermon must be obvious or it is not a good introduction. A good introduction is marked by its indispensable relationship to the sermon which is characterized by a relationship that 'is united as intimately as the flower is united to the stem'.[2] But this intimate relationship between the sermon and the introduction must be relegated to the completed introduction. The attention-getting material typically will not bear such intimacy. The attention-getting material will surface the subject-matter of the sermon, but it will be the interest-securing material that will bring the introduction and sermon into the desired intimate relationship.

The initial portion of a sermon introduction will have a less direct bearing upon the sermon than the heart of the introduction will have to the sermon, and an even lesser bearing to the terminal end of introduction. Just as one drives south from Mandeville, Louisiana to New Orleans on the 24-mile causeway bridge over Lake Pontchartrain, one is connected rather indirectly to the city of New Orleans as one leaves the North Shore having gained entrance upon the causeway. Thirteen miles out on the causeway, one is more closely connected to New Orleans than when the bridge was first engaged on the North Shore, but one enters the city of New Orleans only when the causeway bridge has been traversed and one is no longer over water. On the trip from the North Shore to the South Shore of Lake Pontchartrain, one is involved in a course of a sustained, progressive connection throughout one's drive across the lake. So it is with a sermon introduction. The attention-getting material of a sermon introduction possesses an important, although indirect, connection to the sermon just as the northern most portion of the causeway bridge bears an indirect connection to New Orleans.

The initial discussion of a sermon introduction, designed to get the attention of the hearers, will not bring them immediately to the desired connection with the text. It does, however, have an indirect role to play in the ultimate arrival to the text to be expounded. But do matters that have no direct relationship with the text have a place in a sermon introduction? Yes, they do. As Gardiner Spring wrote in his chapter, *The Truth of Which the Pulpit is the Vehicle,*

> that the God of heaven is the God of Truth so truth is infinitely dear to his pure and holy mind. There is truth which, while it has its own appropriate sphere of influence, is an important auxiliary to the truth proclaimed from the pulpit. Therefore, there is no conflict between the truth of God's Word and any other truth in the universe; rather there is a delightful harmony between this and all other truth. They form one beautifully compacted system, and all unite in proclaiming the perfection and glory of their great Author. But even though they may confirm, illustrate, and adorn each other, they do not have the same place, nor are they revealed for the same purposes.[3]

Spring was obviously writing about the important role that universal truth – matters of general revelation and personal observation – possesses to relate to higher truth, the special revelation of God's Word. His point is valuable – lesser truth's greatest value is found in its ability to relate to higher truth. Though Spring was not making reference to the introduction of a sermon to the body of the sermon, or even the relationship of material included in a sermon introduction, his point is valid – lesser truth has a place if it serves a purpose to establish more significant truth.

And so it is with the attention-getting material of a sermon introduction. Attention-getting material, though not as significant as the interest-securing material and other elements of the introduction, still has a role to play in the sermon introduction.

The Valuable Role of Getting Attention in a Sermon Introduction

Paul provides a great illustration of how each seemingly insignificant part gains significance by its connection with more prominent and important members. He argues in I Corinthians12:14-25 that an individual part of a body is not insignificant just because it does not accomplish the purpose of another body part. So it is with the individual elements of a sermon introduction. Each element has its place in the introduction because it accomplishes something for the overall good of the introduction. Just as one can assert the right of, and appreciation for, the existence of a nose to a face, even though it is not an eye, so can one validate the existence of attention-getting material in a sermon introduction. Just as a nose is not an eye, attention-getting material is different from interest-securing material. And just as it is desirable for one to both see and smell, so it desirable to both get attention and secure interest in a sermon introduction. So it is in the attention-getting material of a sermon introduction – it also has a rightful place. Such auxiliary discussion of material has its place in an introduction as long as it facilitates the purpose to surface the text's subject-matter that the sermon will expound.

The thing that must be understood is this – if a preacher loses the battle to get the attention of his hearers, then the war to secure their interest is already lost. A preacher must not lose the battle to get the attention of his hearers. For a preacher, getting the hearer's attention is simply not an option! This means he will have to supply attention-getting material that will attune the minds of his hearers to the subsequent and more significant substance of the sermon introduction. At the conclusion of this chapter, in Appendix One, I have incorporated examples of attention-getting material from five introductions preached by five different men. This should help to understand the role of attention-getting material in a sermon introduction.

Three Reasons why Getting Attention is Difficult but Necessary

The culture around us

A product of our present culture is people who are not particularly well-suited to hear a good exposition of a text of Scripture. Preachers have to reckon with a TV-conditioned congregation. We have a colossal task on our hands if we hope to counteract the baneful tendencies of much modern television. We can no longer assume that people greatly desire to listen to sermons. Nor is it wise to assume that they indeed are able to listen to a sermon in a truly productive manner. When they are accustomed to the swiftly moving images of the screen, how can we expect them to give their attention to a person talking to them about people and events millennia removed from their lives? Is this not beyond their normal level of need for sustained effort to concentrate? For many of our hearers it is well beyond what they are accustomed to do. As a consequence, before the introduction is over and the sermon has begun, some may well switch off. Without getting the attention of the hearers early in the introduction you can almost hear the click of the hearers shutting down their minds. And though this is certainly no reason to give up on preaching, for there is something unique and irreplaceable about preaching since God has committed Himself to use preaching for man's spiritual advancement, it certainly is a reason that we shall have to fight for people's attention.

Whatever is dull, drab, or monotonous cannot compete in the television age. Television challenges preachers to make our presentation of the truth attractive by demonstrating that it is the God-given supply for that which is needed and missing in the lives of his hearers. John Stott has rightly stated it when he writes, 'Although nothing can supplant preaching, it definitely needs to be supplemented.'[4] Certainly, one supplement which preaching needs is a sermon introduction that can quickly connect to a culture that is vastly disconnected with biblical truth.

The hearers before us
It is certain that there are some individuals in a congregation, and even some entire congregations whose attention you do not readily gain. In every congregation there are some people whose attention is far more difficult to gain than others. They must be encouraged and compelled to listen. Our hearers cannot be shamed into listening, nor made to listen for that would be 'like throwing a bush at a bird to catch it' as Spurgeon so graphically put it. The fact is, if anyone is to be blamed for a congregation not being attentive to the sermon, in most cases the preacher has only to look to himself as the ultimate problem. Although it may be the duty of the hearers to attend to the sermon, it is far more the preacher's duty to compel them to be attentive to the truth of God's Word. What applies to the art of fishing applies to the art of preaching – a skilled fisherman is able to catch fish. Non-compliant fish are not a problem to a good fisherman. He simply provides bait that they are interested in. The bottom-line in fishing is this – a fisherman must attract the fish to

his hook, and if the fish are not attracted to his baited hook the fisherman is to blame, not the fish. So it is in preaching. A preacher must compel his hearers to hear what the Lord desires to say to them. The preacher who recommended to an old lady to take snuff in order to keep from dozing was very properly rebuked by her reply that, 'If he would put more snuff into the sermon she would be awake enough.'[5] We must bear the responsibility to put significant truth in our sermon introductions in order to compel hearers to listen, to cause them to want to hear our sermons.

But even though it is always the responsibility of the preacher to gain the attention of his hearers, the truth is that it is a more difficult task for some as opposed to others. Though the difficulty to gain the attention of hearers may be more difficult in this culture and in these days, it has always been a necessity for preachers at any time and in any culture. Observe G. Campbell Morgan's determination not to falter in the battle to interest the indifferent person in the sermon introduction. Morgan writes:

> I don't think we can characterize any audience by a single word, but we do have those in our audience who are patently indifferent. I don't know how it is with other men, but I preach *to* congregations, never *before* them. I see the people. I cannot help it. I am conscious of anybody who is indifferent. I do not look at the person, but half the work of the introduction is to get that person.[6]

Morgan realized that attentiveness is a relative reality within a congregation. Some hearers were not as attentive as other hearers. So it is for every preacher in the preaching of any sermon before any congregation.

The task before us
In preaching, more than just the presentation of material is needed. The hearers must think. This requires active

attention. When less than active attention is being given, the mind being only partially aroused, gains only faint and fragmentary conceptions which will be as inaccurate and as useless as they are fleeting. As bad as disinterest is, we must understand that lack of interest pales in comparison to lack of accurate understanding of what is heard. Inaccurate understanding of what is heard must be recognized as the ultimate negative consequence of inattentiveness! A preacher may be parceling out incredibly insightful information but a hearer will get from this rich supply only as much as his level of attentiveness can shape in his own mind.[7]

Getting Attention Means Providing Something to Attend to

In order to get attention, the first golden rule is, always say something worth hearing. Most people instinctively possess a desire to hear a good thing. All people have an even more dominant instinct that prevents their seeing the good of attentively listening to mere words. It is not too severe of a criticism to say that there are preachers whose words stand in an inordinately large proportion to their thoughts. This causes them to be exceedingly rich in words and extremely poor in thought. In fact, their words serve only to hide their thoughts. They pour out heaps of chaff but only a handful of wheat. Such preaching will not be heard attentively, effectively, or regularly. A sermon introduction is especially prone to be nothing more than a handful of chaff! The exhortation given by Spurgeon is needed not only for the body of the sermon but is even more applicable to the sermon introduction. Consider Spurgeon's words with the sermon introduction in mind:

> Give your hearers something which they can treasure up and remember; something likely to be useful to them, something striking, something that a man might get up in the middle of the night to hear, and which is worth his walking fifty miles to

listen to. You are quite capable of doing that. Do it, brethren. Do it continually, and you will have all the attention you can desire.[8]

This, however, requires that the preacher has discovered for himself that which is truly useful in his study of the passage and can successfully present it as useful in a striking way in his introduction.

Four Requirements of Attention-Getting Material

So important was an introduction in the theory of Roman oratory that the great Roman orator Quintillian quipped that 'a flawed introduction is like a scarred face'. His point being that one who was approached by a man with a scarred face or an orator with a flawed introduction would give only a glance to the bearer of either.[9] Many preachers fail to understand that point. As a consequence, these preachers pave the way for their sermon to be heard ineffectively.

To prevent producing an introduction that merits only a glance from the hearers, a preacher must understand what the introduction is to accomplish. Warren Wiersbe, who himself was an incredibly effective preacher, suggests three main goals for the sermon introduction: getting our listeners' attention, telling them what the sermon is to be about, and convincing them that if they listen, it will do them good.[10]

But the question must be asked, what is necessary to do an effective job of getting our hearers attention? Or, to frame the question a bit more insightfully, what constitutes effectiveness in getting attention? The material used in the initial portion of the introduction which is designed to get the hearers' attention, if effective, will satisfy four requirements – attention must be commanded immediately, attention must be achieved briefly, attention must be directed toward a subject-matter, and attention must be turned into interest.

1. Attention Must Be Commanded Immediately

Effective homiletical instruction and practice have all but insisted upon the immediate command of attention by one's hearers. C. H. Spurgeon stated the need for a sermon to command attention as he made the observation that, 'Over the head of military announcements our English officers always place the word "ATTENTION!" in large capitals, and we need some such word over all our sermons.'[11] Haddon Robinson is even more specific as he uses the terminology that a sermon introduction 'should command attention'.[12] Richard Mayhue writes, 'If a preacher fails to gain his audience's attention with a captivating introduction, he has probably lost them for the rest of the message.'[13] Again, Robinson writes with greater urgency as he warns and counsels regarding a sermon introduction. According to Robinson, 'If a preacher does not capture attention in the first thirty seconds, he may never gain it at all.... However he begins, the preacher should make the most of his first twenty-five words to seize attention. An ear-grabbing opening suggests that what follows may be well worth everyone's time.'[14] The case for an immediate command of the hearer's attention is validated well.

In order to be able to effect such a high standard for one's immediate success in the introduction, it may be wise to challenge yourself strenuously about the significance of your earliest statements in the sermon introduction. In other words, assume that the audience is bored or is thinking about other matters, and that your first task is to command attention. It has been said that in preaching a preacher is to 'Light your match on the first strike'. This means that a preacher must never waste time or words before getting into the subject-matter of the sermon. The consequence for failing to do so is that not only that precious time is being wasted, but members of the congregation are being turned off from the sermon before they were ever really turned on to the introduction. In reference to the sermon introduction, Jay Adams suggests that 'The first sentence should usually be gripping, if not striking'.¹⁵ Likewise, Spurgeon wrote, to get people's attention 'we must astonish them with something they were not looking for'.¹⁶ This too is certainly good counsel and this is obviously a worthwhile goal to pursue for one's opening statements. Yet the question is, How does one accomplish this? Another question seems to be worthy of consideration: to what extent is it possible to accomplish this consistently in one's sermon introductions?

Statements like those mentioned above put a great deal of stress on the opening statements of a sermon introduction. It seems to be a very tall order to make such progress with one's opening statements. It is tougher still when one considers the prospects of doing this successfully from sermon to sermon, through the years, while preaching to the same people. Haddon Robinson is helpful in listing the following ways to get the attention of the hearers in one's opening statements: paradox, the use of a familiar expression in an unfamiliar context, rhetorical questions, startling facts or statistics, humor, provocative comments regarding the subject-matter of the text, stories, and a bottom-line assertion regarding the claims of the text.¹⁷

2. Attention Must Be Achieved Briefly

Warren Wiersbe writes that rule number one for the introduction is to *Plan to hit the pulpit running*. By this he means that a preacher must not only design the first sentence so it will grab the attention of the congregation but that he will be able to accomplish what needs to be done in an introduction with economy of time. In other words, the day of the casual introduction is over. He writes, 'Years of experience in radio ministry have taught me the importance of those first few sentences in getting people to listen. They can turn us off very quickly, even if they're sitting in the pews looking at us.'¹⁸

It is hard to imagine that a preacher of Wiersbe's stature would have a working knowledge of being turned off quickly by anyone. But such is the nature of preaching, as well as the nature of those to whom we preach. And that just helps to understand an important point – we cannot take a long time to get the hearer's attention.

Once we have their attention we must move on because there is even more important work to be accomplished before the introduction is completed. We get attention so that we may do other things, things of greater significance than attentiveness. The opening statements of a preacher's introduction are like a sprinter's initial response once the gun is fired to start a sprint. It is crucial for a sprinter to bust out of the blocks cleanly and quickly. But a sprinter gets out of the blocks as quickly as possible in order to do what is necessary – to run the race and run it well. The race to be run in preaching only starts by getting attention, and having gotten the attention of the hearers we have to preach and preach well. But as with a sprinter, if a preacher does not start clearly and quickly, his race, which is the preaching of a sermon, may be lost already.

3. Attention Must Be Directed toward a Subject-matter

As indicated above, a preacher must gain the attention of the congregation at once or he may not gain it at all. For this reason the beginning of the sermon is of supreme importance; it is even more important than the ending of the sermon. Typically, the sermon conclusion is considered to be more important than the sermon introduction. However, consider the following – First of all, if people have not been made to listen at the beginning, it is unlikely that they will be doing so twenty minutes or half-an-hour later. Therefore, it is advisable that a preacher should plunge straight into his subject. His business is so urgent that he has no time to waste. He must make headway with his hearers in the introduction for the sake of the sermon body and the conclusion of the sermon. Secondly, how important is a conclusion to a sermon that has not been followed with interest and accurate understanding?

A ponderous beginning may be suitable when one is dealing with a specialized audience of people trained to listen and assembled with the sole and deliberate purpose of hearing a weighty utterance on a subject in which they are interested and on which they are already informed. Yet, nobody would contend that a typical congregation is such an audience. It is made up of a mixed company of people – mixed in every way. They have come in different states of mind. Some are tired, some are distracted, some are intending to devote the sermon time to other important concerns. But many of these people are the same in that they are not going to pay close attention to the preacher unless they can be made to feel that what the preacher is going to say to them in his sermon is likely to be at least as interesting as their own thoughts.[19]

The preacher must hold the attention of the congregation, but he can only do this as the hearers are interested in his sermon. People attend to a thing voluntarily only while they are so interested that they cannot take their minds off it. Otherwise, they have to make themselves listen, and most people are not prepared to exercise their wills very much in this matter unless they can see a good reason for the effort. And when it comes to listening to sermons, most people cannot see the reason. Nothing seems to hang on it. They won't have to pass an examination on the subject-matter. And let us be fair – for the great majority sustained attention over a long period is difficult.[20] Even though it is not easy, the preacher must be able to direct attention of the hearers to the subject-matter of the sermon.

When we consider attention, what exactly are we talking about? How is attention to be understood? What does it mean to get attention? Attention means the direction of the mind upon some object. This direction of the mind is the act of bringing something into the focus of consciousness. Consciousness is possessed in a quality of focus and a quality of margin. The focus is occupied by our awareness of the thing that is being attended to. The margin is occupied by thoughts, sensations, and feelings that are in the range of consciousness, but are vague, indistinct, and not dominant. Attention is not a constant or invariable condition. Attention can change so that something which, moments ago, was focused upon is now being marginalized and that which, moments ago, was marginal has become a focus.[21]

The act of consciousness change from focus to margin is a flitting attention or passive attention. It is passive because it involves no effort of the will. A marginal thought surfaces or a new stimulus from the environment simply intervenes surreptitiously to become focal. But the essential characteristic of the human mind is that it can control, rather than be controlled by, marginal thinking and surrounding forces. This distinctively human type of attention is called active attention because it requires a force of the will to focus upon a matter in spite of competing mental and environmental allurements to do otherwise.[22]

The important point of understanding for a preacher is that active attention is not always economical. For the most part active attention is costly. It typically requires much from the mental reserves of the hearer. When hearers are absorbed in our preaching, active attention is more economical because they are caught up with our subject-matter. As we preach, our hearers are being encroached upon by marginal and environmental matters. Therefore, the state of being absorbed in our subject-matter inevitably will change. We will have to make sure that the substance of our preaching consists of material that is so personally significant that is re-absorbs them in our sermon.[23]

4. Attention Must Be Turned into Interest
In the initial portion of an introduction, it is well sometimes to indicate one's conviction of the supreme importance of the particular theme, sometimes to declare its gravity, sometimes to suggest its comfort, sometimes to admit its difficulty. All these things help to bring the audience into attention.[24]

However, one may wonder if this is truly a concern of men who are devoted to preaching the Bible. Those who are genuinely concerned about, and devoted to, the proclamation of the Bible should be especially interested that they do all they can to command the attention of their hearers. The great Puritan preacher, Richard Baxter, employed every lawful aid of native wit and acquired art; anecdote and allegory; metaphor and simile, to gain the attention and to win the hearts of his hearers for his Master.[25] Could the same diligence to command attention be true of the typical preacher today? I think not, and this is detrimental because far more than gaining attention is crucial for preaching.

Introductions should catch attention, arouse interest in and create a desire to learn more about the subject-matter. In short, a sermon introduction should evoke:

A – Attention
I – Interest
D – Desire[26]

As crucial as it is to get the attention of the hearers, it is more important to secure their interest. When the hearers are truly interested in the preacher's introduction they will desire to understand the text he intends to expound to them.

Needed concern has been given to the necessity to get the hearers' attention immediately and briefly. However important the opening words of an introduction may be and no matter how effective the opening words may be, a preacher must not confuse getting the attention of the congregation with securing the interest of the congregation. A very 'interesting' opening in the introduction certainly gets attention of the hearers and may *start* the process of securing interest. But, a best-case scenario is that this attention-getting beginning has only started to secure the interest of the hearers.

Getting the attention of the hearers will not accomplish the greatest work of an introduction, which is to secure the interest of the hearers. The task of securing interest is far more than the opening words can achieve. Securing interest, or 'hooking' the congregation, will be the topic of the next chapter, but for now I want to distinguish getting attention and securing interest as two separate tasks of a sermon introduction.

Many are the instances in literature on preaching when getting attention and securing interest are used interchangeably. For example, the following advice is given – 'use that first sentence to place a "hook" in the introduction and arouse the interest of your hearers.'[27] I agree with the advice as offered but I also want to clarify that a 'hook' – an interesting first sentence – in the introduction may 'arouse' interest in the hearers but it will not 'secure the interest' of the congregation because much more than an interesting opening sentence is needed for secured interest to be accomplished.

Perhaps an analogy will be helpful at this point. If one is fishing, one can bait one's hook and cast it in the water. But having done this one has not caught or hooked a fish. Now, obviously, if one never put a hook in the water one will not catch a fish. But the bane of fishing is having a baited hook cast into the water while waiting to hook a fish – the very reason why the hook was committed to the water in the first place.

A wise Russian proverb goes like this: 'It is the same with men as with donkeys: whoever would hold them fast must get a very good grip on their ears!'[28] Though initial attention is valuable, the initial attentiveness will wane and it cannot be sustained by whatever may be used to a good effect in the opening of the introduction. And quite frankly, it is wrong to even think that a preacher would want them to hang onto the opening remarks. The opening statements have a job to do but having done their job they need to be forgotten, to die a sacrificial death, for the sake that progress can be made so that the initial attention of the hearers can be turned into secured interest for the sermon to be preached. The last thing a preacher wants is for his sermon to not be heard because the hearers are still enamored by, and continue to rehearse in their minds, the attention-getting material used by the preacher in his introduction. So by all means, we want to get a grip on the ears of our hearers but we want to let go of their ears so that we may ultimately grip their hearts while we are still in the introduction, before we ever get to the sermon itself.

A preacher can get a grip on the hearer's ear in a hurry. And this he should do. But the mind and heart of the hearers will require additional time, effort, and substance supplied by the preacher in order to secure their interest. But as every preacher knows, time is of such a premium. Should he seriously consider spending more time beyond the opening statements, and whatever brief amount of material following the opening statements, to try to secure interest? Not only should he consider it, but he should do it! And if he does it, he must spend more time and supply more material than just the opening statements and that which immediately follows can achieve. Why? The answer lies in how the mind works.

The human mind, which, in its healthy state, has a sense of dignity and self-respect, does not like to be hurried, or compelled to move by another's impulse rather than by its own voluntary act; it will not be pushed, but may be drawn. Some preparation of the mind is needed on the part of the hearers for the full influence of the preacher to be felt, or for the permanent influence and adoption of new ideas.[29]

Attention and interest, though distinct, work in reciprocity. A hearer's interest in the subject-matter determines his attentiveness to the material. As the hearer's interest grows, his attentiveness increases and the preacher is able to be a better teacher on his behalf. Yet, it is only as a preacher gets the attention of his hearers that he is able to secure their interest. Attention and interest are not luxuries for expository preaching but are mandatory.[30]

As crucial as the opening statements are in the introduction, designed to get the attention of his hearers, how he continues in the introduction once attention is gained is even more important for a preacher. It is of little significance to get the hearers' attention if he fails to secure their interest.

Before we turn our attention to securing interest and the means by which interest may be secured, let's briefly conclude this chapter with a clarifying comparison regarding the nature and characterizing qualities of securing interest material and getting attention material. In comparing the nature of the material, securing interest material is of primary interest while getting attention material is of secondary interest. This is so because of the characterizing qualities of primary versus secondary interest. Primary interest is afforded to material that is characterized by the qualities of specific, immediate, and personal. Secondary interest, that which is attained through attention-getting material, is characterized by the qualities of general, remote, and impersonal.

The *general* versus *specific* quality has to do with subject-matter under discussion. If it is subject-matter that is leading to, but different from, the subject-matter that the sermon will ultimately address then the material is general. Once the discussion has surfaced the subject-matter that will be the focus of the sermon, the subject-matter has become specific.

The *remote* versus *immediate* quality has to do with the biblical text to be expounded. All discussion that does not make a direct connection with the sermon text is remote. Once the discussion is no longer serving as a preface to the text but rather the text is being referenced directly, the material has become immediate.

The *impersonal* versus *personal* quality has to do with the hearers themselves. Once the preacher begins to address the hearers in regard to the lives they are living in light of the subject-matter of the sermon and the claims of the text to be expounded, the discussion has moved from the impersonal to the personal.

Consider the Following Questions

1. Do you agree that attuning the minds of the hearers in a sermon introduction is as necessary as the need for athletes to warm up before a competition, for orchestras to tune up before a performance, and for soil to be stirred up before the planting of seed? What reasons were given for the necessity to attune the minds of the hearers?

2. What are the implications of a 'TV conditioned congregation' to a preacher in the preparation and delivery of his sermon introductions?

3. How is it possible that a preacher must bear the responsibility for his hearers' disinterest in his preaching?

4. What is the ultimate negative consequence of disinterested hearers?

5. What is the first golden rule of getting attention and why is it so?

6. In examining the five examples of attention-getting material in appendix 1, how many of Haddon Robinson's eight ways to get attention in the opening statements can you find?

7. What is the rationale for the sermon introduction being a matter of extreme importance, even more important than the conclusion of the sermon?

8. What does it mean to get attention in terms of focused and marginal consciousness? What is the inevitable reality of the hearer's consciousness in listening to a sermon and what are the implications of this for a preacher?

9. Can you contrast getting attention and securing interest in terms of what each one grips, the relationship between the two, and the time required for each to occur in the hearers?

10. How does getting attention and securing interest work in reciprocity?

11. Can you compare attention-getting material and interest-securing material by their differing natures and characterizing qualities?

Appendix One
Five Examples of Attention-Getting Material

Example 1 – Excerpt from sermon introduction by Dr. Joel Gregory

I suppose that many of us must feel some identification with Jacob in our own generation – a man on the run. If we didn't feel it any other way we might sense it by reading the titles of some of the best-sellers, because they seem to have to do with our struggle as we run against time. You go look in the bookstore and you read titles like, Getting Control of Your Time And Your Life or Making Time Work For You or How to Put More Time in Your Life. And in that famous series of books led by The One Minute Manager, The One Minute Father, The One Minute Mother. I'm sure that many of you are waiting with bated breath for The One Minute Preacher. That one hasn't been published yet.

You know, Jacob was born on the run. Even as his older twin brother emerged from the womb, Jacob was given his name – heel snatcher, heel grabber because he was overreaching, trying to grab Esau's heel even as the two were born. And that became the story of his life. He was a man on the run. He deceived his father Isaac and cheated his brother Esau out of the birthright and the blessing. That was the ancient equivalent of running away with the only copy of the family will as well as the key to the safety deposit box.

He was on the run from Esau but then he ran into his father-in-law Laban. No people ever deserved one another as much as Jacob and Laban. That was like diamond cutting diamond, as one commentator put it. But finally he had to run away from Laban, too. And in the midst of his life, seated on the East side of the Jordan by its tributary, Jabbok, Jacob ran out of resources and he ran into God. He came to the end of his rope and he sat alone with his only resource being the resource that God gave him. I've tried to put the truth of this in the little synopsis of the message in your worship folder. If you were to concentrate this into a statement that you could take home with you it would be this – that a person without resources can prevail with God in prayer, changing his nature and his situation.

Example 2 – Excerpt from sermon introduction by Dr. Tom Eliff

One of the most frustrating experiences of life is to sense that you are busy, that you are investing your life, your energy, your resources, your time, your abilities and yet you are not certain that the direction of your energy, the focus of your talents, is accomplishing what it ought to be and what it could be accomplishing. I believe there are probably many people here this morning who believe that, in some sense, your life is being wasted on the world. You sense that you are capable of more, you know more, you believe that God wants to use you more effectively than you are being used and yet you are not sure just which way you ought to turn. It's frustrating isn't it, to live a life and not be certain that you are living it out according to the purpose God has planned for you?

Now, if we were to go to the major cities across this nation today and walk into most of the convention centers and the conference halls, we would find that, either in the larger arenas or in some conference hall off to the side, someone would be speaking about how to set goals, how to manage your life, how to be a success. Success and success motivation is the hot topic of the 90s. People want to know that they are using their lives to accomplish all that they could be using it for, that they are getting the most for their money, and for their time, and for their ability. And I want to say to you unequivocally this morning that the only way you will ever get out of your life all that you could get out of your life, the only way you can ever experience all that you can experience and enjoy all that you are capable of enjoying and to have the sense of fulfillment that you ought to have, the only way you can do that is to live your life according to God-given goals.

Now here is what you will discover in most of those seminars. You'll be encouraged to sit down and write out on a piece of paper, either that you brought or one that they provide for you, what you want to get out of life. And so you think about the things that you like, you think about the things you would like to do, the things you would like to possess. You think about your personality, your dreams, your wishes, your desires, your ambitions. And out there at the end you realize this is the way I would like to live, this is the way I would like to retire perhaps, these are the resources I would like to enjoy, this is what I would like to be driving, this is how I would like to be living, and this is how I would like to be positioned. And so you begin to write down on that piece of paper, as soon as you can get it crystallized in your mind, the things you want for your life. Because, after all, who knows you better than yourself?

Well, the answer to that is this. God knows you better than you know yourself. God knows you better than you know yourself. He knows exactly what you are capable of doing. He knows what is the maximum in your life that you could enjoy. And He knows how you can receive it. He knows the life you ought to live in order to get it. And so if you want to enjoy life to its fullest, if you want to live in the Canaan, so to speak – the promised land of the Christian experience, you're going to have to live your life according to God-given goals.

Example 3 – Excerpt from sermon introduction by Dr. Charles Swindoll

If you're a lover of people then you are a lover of history. If you're a lover of history then you're a person after my own heart, because I have found in my study of the Scriptures and in the study of great people that you cannot separate the greatness of the person from the context of his times. As a matter of fact, people who have steel in their character have it forged out between the anvil and hammer of their times.

It's true of every great man or woman that has ever lived. It's true of military men such as Lee or MacArthur or Eisenhower. It's true of poets such as Poe, Browning, Byron. It's true of philosophers – Pascal, Schleiermacher, great men of the histories. It's true also of song writers – Isaac Watts and so many of his ilk, including, of course, Charles Wesley in his days. It is certainly true of Bible characters.

Our tendency is to plunge into the blooming greatness of Elijah's life and to miss the anvil and the hammer of his times. And I don't want us to do that. I want us to see how God forged out of those difficult years a very unique, leathery, gaunt, individual who was able to meet the rigors of his day. And once we see the context of his life, I think we will appreciate all the more the beauty of his person.

This was brought home to me a number of years ago when my family and I were camping in New England in the fall of the year. We were blanketed by the yellow, and the burnt orange, and the red of the Maple trees, surrounded by the Birch, the beauty of Vermont and New Hampshire. And my oldest daughter who was then two, three, four years old ran up to me with a fist full of little wild flowers and she said in her own inimitable way, 'Look, how pretty!' And I remember looking down at her hand with all those flowers in it and I said, 'Honey, show me where you got them.' And so we walked a long way away, very near a ledge, that if you had stepped three more feet you would have fallen perhaps fifty or sixty feet down. There were thorns. There were weeds. There were rocks. And in the middle of all of this, there was a wasp's nest not too far away and hornets buzzing around. I appreciated that fist full of flowers all the more once I saw where they had come from. Here they had grown unappreciated, unseen, unknown, except by the eyes of a little girl who had gotten too far away from camp and was enraptured with these little blossoms that had grown.

Men of God are like that. Elijah is like that. In the ledges and the rocks and the weeds and the thorns of godless times our Lord gives the green light to the birth and the growth of a man far ahead of his time. And then he blooms and blossoms and is usually hated during his day but immortalized years later. I am confident that's the way it was with Elijah.

Example 4 – Excerpt from sermon introduction by Dr. Stephen Olford

Dr. Henry Bieler, the author of *Food Is Your Best Medicine*, tells us that the number one killing power in America today is the heart attack. In fact, one million people die every year in this country through heart disease. And that disease is started and accelerated and consummated by what is known in the medical world as arteriosclerosis. And every time we breathe somebody has a heart attack across this country. So that one of the greatest enemies to physical health in this land of ours today with all our civilization, with all our advances, and all our affluence is heart problems, heart troubles, heart disease.

But you know, this is just as true in the spiritual realm. And as a matter of fact the Holy Spirit uses a Greek term from which we get our modern term 'sclerosis' to indicate what is true of Christian people all across America today and beyond America, not only among the unregenerate but among Christian people. And last night I started by asking, 'How many of you have come here with a burdened heart?' How many of you as you drove up or flew through the air communicated one with the other as those two on the way to Emmaus with sad hearts, dull hearts, and you've come longing that you may go away with burning hearts? I want to ask another question tonight, I wonder how many of you have come to be with us with hardened hearts? You've become sophisticated, professional, calloused. You're affected by sclerosis in the spiritual life. This is a grim reality that we need to face.

Example 5 – Excerpt from sermon introduction by Dr. Haddon Robinson

One of the great cathedrals in Great Britain is St. Paul's in London. It was designed and built by Sir Christopher Wren after the original cathedral built during medieval times was destroyed in the fire of 1666. Sir Christopher Wren died before St. Paul's was finished and there is no monument in the cathedral to his memory. Instead, he is buried in a crypt in the basement. And on that crypt on a plaque inscribed in Latin are the words, 'If you would see his monument, look around you.'

The visitor to St. Paul's can see, on every side, evidence of Sir Christopher Wren's existence and also of his consummate skill. Many times those of us who are Christians say to our skeptical friends, 'If you would see God's monument, look around you. For the heavens declare God's glory and all the earth shows the thumb-print of His hand.' But if you wanted to know Sir Christopher Wren it would not be enough to simply look at Saint Paul's. That cathedral would tell you something about his brilliance and his power. But there is another side to Sir Christopher Wren you could not know. You would not know by looking at Saint Paul's whether he was married. You would not know if he was a good husband, a faithful friend, a devoted father.

And so, if you were to look at creation in order to know God there are some things the creation would tell you. They would tell you that God is a God of power, a God of magnificent imagination. But there is another side to God that you might miss. In fact, looking at the creation you might be led astray. You might come to conclude that whenever God works He does so with all the splendor of a tropic sunrise, with all the magnificence of a mountain range. If you came to that conclusion you would miss the other side of God.

What is more, you might miss God's working in the world and God's working in your life.

Almost seven hundred years before the birth of Jesus Christ, Isaiah the prophet was concerned that the people of Israel might miss the other side of God. In a Mt. Everest passage of the Bible – Isaiah chapter fifty-three – Isaiah addresses himself to that problem.

Words to Live and Preach by

The Mouth of the Righteous Man

Proverbs 10:21 – The lips of the righteous feed many, but fools die for lack of understanding.

Proverbs 10:31-2 – The mouth of the righteous flows with wisdom, but the perverted tongue will be cut out. The lips of the righteous bring forth what is acceptable, but the mouth of the wicked, what is perverted.

Proverbs 12:5 – The thoughts of the righteous are just, but the counsels of the wicked are deceitful.

Proverbs 15:1 – A gentle answer turns away wrath, but a harsh word stirs up anger.

Proverbs 15:7 – The lips of the wise spread knowledge, but the hearts of fools are not so.

Proverbs 15:28 – The heart of the righteous ponders how to answer, but the mouth of the wicked pours out evil things.

Proverbs 16:23-4 – The heart of the wise teaches his mouth, and adds persuasiveness to his lips. Pleasant words are a honeycomb, sweet to the soul and healing to the bones.

Proverbs 18:21 – Death and life are in the power of the tongue, and those who love it will eat its fruit.

Proverbs 20:15 – There is gold, and an abundance of jewels; but the lips of knowledge are a more precious thing.

Proverbs 25:15 – By forbearance a ruler may be persuaded, and a soft tongue breaks the bone.

Chapter Four

Securing Interest: The Major Work of an Introduction

Interest versus Attention

In order to understand interest, which must be secured in the introduction of the sermon, it must be distinguished clearly from attention. Interest and attention are often used interchangeably. However, only one kind of attention may rightly be considered as synonymous with interest. Attention may be of three types: voluntary attention, involuntary attention, and nonvoluntary attention. Voluntary attention is given because of a sense of duty. Involuntary attention is given to some invading hindrance, such as the antics of a disobedient child in the next pew or the intervening mental replay of a recent occurrence or the incessant clamor to focus upon an upcoming event. But there is also nonvoluntary attention. Nonvoluntary attention is given because of intrinsic interest in a subject; and of course this is the only type of attention that a preacher really wants.

It is this nonvoluntary attention that we must recognize as secured interest. More importantly, this is the kind of attention a preacher must have. Why? He simply will not be able to preach effectively without this kind of attention being paid to him by his hearers. As we shall discuss later in fuller detail, secured interest captivates the hearers because the preacher makes valuable insights demonstrating the connection of biblical truth and their lives. It cannot be overemphasized that a sermon, in general, and a sermon introduction specifically, must bear a prominent personal relevance to the hearers. It has been observed that:

> People are most interested in what concerns them personally. Lord Northcliffe, the British newspaper publisher, once said that people are more interested in 'themselves' than in anything else. The average man is more disturbed about a dull razor blade than about a revolt in Indo-China.[1]

The chances of gaining interest will be greatly enhanced if the preacher establishes the relevancy of the sermon in the minds of his listeners. Nonvoluntary attention occurs only as a hearer's interest is secured. Securing the hearer's interest is the major work to be done in an introduction and it must be accomplished.

Again, it is crucial to remember that securing interest material bears the characteristic qualities of being specific, immediate, and personal. Nonvoluntary attention can be attained only by material of this nature since such material is of primary interest to the hearers. Voluntary attention may be obtained and maintained by material that is general, remote, and impersonal but the hearers cannot be 'hooked' by such material since it is of secondary interest.

Interest and Expository Preaching

In expository preaching especially, it is important that we have the right conception of interest in preaching. Don De Welt makes a point that must be recognized and honored by expository preachers particularly. He writes, 'If a sermon is not interesting they are not going to listen – regardless of how well organized or scriptural it might be. If they do not listen – and I mean with the inner ear Jesus spoke about – then why preach? It is not just a good plan to have the attention and interest of your congregation, *it is an imperative*![2]

In expository preaching the expositor, like any other preacher, must be sure to gain a favorable hearing by showing his hearers that his exposition is important for their lives. An expositor's general purpose is to move the listeners to action, to help them make certain decisions on the basis of the sermon he will deliver.[3]

Rightly understood and practiced, the purpose of expository preaching is not only to explain a passage of Scripture, increasing the hearer's knowledge of the Bible, but also 'to afford the hearers guidance and insight for change, growth, and a responsible life of faith'.[4] The best exposition draws attention to the light that is in the Word of God by explaining its meaning, while at the same time calling attention to the human situation and promise of hope because of that light. When this balance is maintained, the exposition will always serve human experience, meeting human needs since the preaching is centering on a biblical passage. Like all good preaching, exposition must be designed and delivered to make hearers understand, feel, and act.[5]

Expository preaching must be a preaching event in which the expositor is at the same time a man compelled by two different but not competing factors – pathos or passion, and compassion. The expositor is all about the Word of God in his preaching. Yet, the expositor is all about the people to whom he preaches. Both must be a vital reality in the heart and mind of the expositor in order for expository preaching to be as effective as it should be. The very portion of Scripture which has been studied and taken as the text to be preached must fill the man with passion – a passion for the truth, a passion to declare it clearly and accurately. A passion for preaching is a great thing but it is not enough. There must also be an equal compassion, or passion for the people, to help them by what is expounded. In other words, compassion for the people of God, a genuine desire to minister to people through the exposition of the truth, is just as mandatory for an expositor as delivering a passionate and faithful declaration of truth. Though both are important, this does not assure that both are a reality in any preaching event.

Compassion for the people can be absent in a very accurate handling of a portion of Scripture. On the other hand, a compassionate message may be delivered to the people of God which is nothing other than a shoddy, shallow representation of the truth of the text, or even worse, an outright misrepresentation of the passage. Both of these must be condemned, and neither of these is to be present in expository preaching. Lloyd-Jones is correct in his insistence that:

> To love to preach is one thing, to love those to whom we preach quite another. The trouble with some of us is that we love preaching, but we are not always careful to make sure that we love the people to whom we are actually preaching. If you lack this element of compassion for the people you will also lack the pathos which is a very vital element in all true preaching. Our Lord looked out upon the multitude and saw them as sheep without a shepherd, and was filled with compassion. And if you know nothing of this you should not be in a pulpit, for this is certain to come out in your preaching.[6]

The ability to secure the interest of the hearers in the sermon introduction is early evidence that a capable expositor is in the pulpit. His passion for the truth to be expounded will be evident by his ability to indicate to his hearers that the passage to be preached will be significant for them just as his compassion for the people will be obvious as they sense his desire to declare this life-changing truth to them.

To be honest, expository preaching is too often lacking in both pathos or passion, and compassion. This is typical in the body of the sermon, but even more pronounced in the sermon introduction. Particularly, though not exclusively, expository preaching needs a thorough rethinking and substantial overhaul for the sermon introduction. When the sermon introduction is sufficiently overhauled, it will reflect compassion and passion in a preacher who is able to secure the interest of his hearers.

The Expositor and His Hearers

Many an expositor presupposes an unwise and, for the most part, a false state of reality – that his hearers are as interested and excited about his sermon as he is. But this is untrue. Because of God's privileged calling upon his life, the expositor has had the responsibility to study the Scriptures. The result of his discovery of Scriptural truth is not only insight into the Word of God but a great deal of joy from the process and the product of his discovery. His hearers, however, have not been given such a privilege to spend the previous week in extended study of the Bible. The inescapable result is that the expositor bears an excitement for the sermon he will preach that his hearers simply do not have.

The typical expositor's sermon introduction seems to indicate a presupposition that the congregation should be just as interested in the sermon he will preach as he is. Certainly his hearers should be equally interested in biblical truth! But to begin a sermon based upon this presupposition will only lead to a weak introduction. On the basis of the introduction, there are times when it seems as though the preacher thinks his hearers live only to attend church for the resolution to some technical, textual issue. They do not. They want to know how to live the Christian life in a fallen world in such a way that will bring glory to God, fulfillment for themselves, and benefit the lives of others. They want to be addressed in terms of their own needs, their own language, and their own interests.[7]

It is not to be taken for granted that the people who listen to a sermon are, by virtue of that fact, interested in it. As expository preachers, we ought not to assume that because a truth is compelling to ourselves, it is necessarily as fascinating for our hearers. It is part of our calling to make the truth we love relevant and interesting to our people.[8]

Congregations are by no means always interested. Some people in the congregation will be interested, others will be interested occasionally, but more than a few will not be sufficiently interested in whatever theme is presented. Yet, every preacher must know that, if he is to impress the minds and hearts of his hearers with the truth of his message, he must, by all means, get them interested in what he is saying. If this interest is not secured at the outset, the probabilities are that it will not be secured at all throughout the sermon. As a Bible expositor, to fail to secure the ears of your hearers is to fail to secure their minds. This means that the Word of God will not receive the hearing which it rightly deserves. It is, therefore, the responsibility of the preacher to present his matter so interestingly that the audience cannot help but listen and be interested.[9]

One of the most sage and valid points of counsel regarding a sermon introduction has been offered by Haddon Robinson: 'It has been suggested that there are three kinds of preachers: those to whom you cannot listen; those to whom you can listen; and those to whom you must listen. During the introduction the congregation usually decides the kind of speaker addressing them that morning.'[10] One preacher takes the following tact in introducing his sermons: 'When I begin my sermons I dare the person not to listen to me. Not that I'm that great – it's just that I've got something to say that's too important to ignore.'[11] This is a wise approach to take in introducing an expository sermon, an approach that is obviously and unfortunately taken infrequently.

For one who aspires to be a Bible expositor, such an approach is not only admirable, it is warranted by the truth he will proclaim. If the hearers of a sermon introduction sense that the message to be preached to them will be significant to them, the preacher has done well in his sermon introduction. Since the Word of God is significant to the lives of the hearers, why shouldn't the sermon be perceived as such by the hearers, from the earliest part of the sermon? Yet, many times this is not the case.

Howard Hendricks states that the number one problem in communicating biblical truth is the failure to motivate the hearers into action. The problem of the hearers lies not in the area of their IQ, or their intelligence quotient, but in their MQ, or their motivation quotient.[12] For preaching to be most effective, the hearers will need to become properly motivated. Humanly speaking, the preacher will have to be used by God in such a way that as he begins preaching to his hearers they will undergo a motivational upgrade. The sooner this takes place, the better it will be for the preacher, his hearers, and the sermon he is preaching. A motivational upgrade will not take place through a sermon they are not interested in because they have not perceived the importance of the sermon to their lives. A significant sermon must be introduced as such.

Expository preaching has for its end instruction in righteousness. The expository preacher recognizes the tremendous importance of Bible knowledge and the way in which the personal understanding of Scripture determines one's conduct and character. An expository preacher, therefore, gives himself faithfully to line-upon-line, precept-upon-precept teaching. At all times, in expository preaching, what he stresses is the Bible itself, believing that if people know the Scriptures they will be led to live by them. However, sometimes what he stresses is theology, unfolding a system of thought based upon the Scriptures, and taking various passages and fitting them into what may be a most ingenious pattern. At other times what he stresses is the acceptance of the Christian walk, some specific submission to the Lordship of Jesus Christ, with its many implications as the way of life. Regardless of the specific character of the exposition, expository preaching accomplishes far more than can ever be known by the preacher. It results in the development of Christian character, the equipping of believers for ministry, and the enabling of a more meaningful, productive life.[13] Though each of these may be stressed variously from week to week, each should accompany every sermon.

Greek scholar A. T. Robertson had a picturesque way of bemoaning the fact that God's people are deprived the meat of the Word from the very ones who are charged by God to feed them. Let his words seep into your soul until you can resolve that the following indictment will never be true of you and your preaching!

> The poor hungry sheep look up to the food rack, and are not fed. All they hear is the wind whistling through.
> Preachers are divinely called to preach, to preach in power and demonstration of the Spirit. Too many sermons are bland, innocuous, soporific. They deal in vague abstractions, pleasing platitudes, psychological theories, and watered-down theology, instead of telling people how to get the righteousness of God in their hearts through Christ.[14]

He is right. The meat of the Word, as it is commonly found in the typical sermon, may be more analogous to a small sliver of dry, stale, shriveled-up beef jerky! It may be meat, but only in a technical sense and in a marginal way!

William Barclay is correct when he asserts, 'There has been far too much topical preaching and far too little expository preaching.'[15] When Scripture is expounded, preaching will supply what is seriously lacking, or put in other words – to a large extent preaching ought to be teaching.[16] And as if preaching without substantive exposition is not bad enough, there is a notion, believed by many, that the Bible is not worthy of serious scrutiny or its content deserving of faith and practice.

Joseph R. Sizoo is right when he observed that as bad as it is for the Bible to be discredited and disavowed, it is worse for it to be disregarded, as when people brush it aside asserting that it is 'unscientific' and 'it had a place in the day of the tallow candle and the horse-and-buggy'.[17] Expository preaching that explains the text, thus providing theological understanding and practical, personal compliance of the Bible's meaning, demonstrates a preacher's appropriate regard for the Scriptures. An expositor's regard for the Scriptures must not only impact the sermon he will preach but it must also affect how he introduces the sermon he will preach!

The Decline of Expository Preaching

Why is it that there are comparatively few men who are faithful expositors of God's Word? D. Martyn Lloyd-Jones provided a threefold answer to the question of why preaching had suffered a decline in his day in Britain. His answers were so adept that they serve to indicate a rationale for the decline of preaching at any time in any culture. Lloyd-Jones suggested that the failure to believe in the authority of the Bible in preaching is 'the first and greatest cause of this decline'. Hence,

> While men believed in the Scriptures as the authoritative Word of God and spoke on the basis of that authority you had great preaching. But once that went, and men began to speculate, and to theorize, and to put up hypotheses and so on, the eloquence and the greatness of the spoken word inevitably declined and began to wane. You cannot really deal with speculations and conjectures in the same way as preaching had formerly dealt with the great themes of the Scriptures. But as belief in the great doctrines of the Bible began to go out, and sermons were replaced by ethical addresses and homilies, and moral uplift and socio-political talk, it is not surprising that preaching declined.[18]

A second detrimental factor was the rise of the great 'pulpiteers' in the second half of the nineteenth century, among whom Henry Ward Beecher was cited as an example. Lloyd-Jones writes,

> He illustrates perfectly the chief characteristics of the pulpiteer. The term itself is very interesting, and I believe it is a very

accurate one. These men were pulpiteers rather than preachers. I mean that they were men who could occupy a pulpit and dominate it, and dominate the people. They were professionals. There was a good deal of the element of showmanship in them, and they were experts at handling congregations and playing on their emotions. In the end they could do almost what they liked with them.... These pulpiteers were to me – with my view of preaching – an abomination; and it is they who are in many ways largely responsible for this present reaction (the decline of preaching).[19]

The third factor cited was 'the wrong conception of what a sermon really is, and therefore of what preaching really is.' This was due to the publication of the sermons, particularly the publication of the sermons of men who were endowed with a real literary gift, who moved away from the truth of the message to literary expression, historical allusion, and quotation. These men 'were essayists rather than preachers; but as they published these essays as sermons, they were accepted as sermons.' 'A good deal of the decline in preaching is attributed to those literary effusions which have passed under the name of sermons and of preaching' so as to confuse the Church as to what a sermon should be and what preaching really is. People began to talk about and expect an address or a lecture rather than a sermon.[20] A true sermon, especially an expository sermon, must distinguish itself from a lecture right from the sermon introduction!

Reversing the Decline of Expository Preaching
The solution to the problem of the decline of preaching for Lloyd-Jones was simple and straightforward: 'the primary task... of the Christian minister is the preaching of the Word of God.'[21] How very appropriate are Lloyd-Jones' three reasons for the decline of preaching for our time and our culture! How sorely needed is his single solution to this decline! Take counsel from the salient elements of his solution as they interface with the three problems for the decline of preaching. A *Christian*

minister is a man who is not a showman, not a performer, but a Christian who is truly a minister, serving God's people with the Word of God rather than performing before them and playing on their emotions. What the Christian minister is committed to is *preaching*, declaring the Word of God, not lecturing, not addressing, not essaying the congregation. What the Christian minister preaches is *the Word of God*, not anything else, because the Word of God alone is the sole authority for all those who profess to know Him and owe to Him alone their utmost obedience.

Lloyd-Jones' solution for the reversing the decline of expository preaching is needed today. Our present culture is more averse than ever to expository preaching because, in many cases, what is sought is the antithesis of expository preaching – showmen who seek to amuse their hearers with material that only hints of biblical texts. However, reversing the decline in expository preaching will not be made by a man who is committed to things that will cause him to be less of an expositor. This will only continue the decline of expository preaching. Reversing the decline of expository preaching will only be accomplished through excellence in expository preaching. Those who desire to understand the Bible will not be disappointed by good expository preaching. Those who do not desire to understand Scripture will be pleased with much contemporary preaching. The truth is, expository preaching is not for everybody. But expository preaching that is truly excellent may be found compelling to those who are not seeking it!

Expository preacher John MacArthur on his *Grace To You* radio broadcast was asked a question regarding the non-negotiables for determining the criteria for joining or leaving a church. His response was as follows:

> There is one, basic, dominating thing – how do they handle the Word of God? How do they handle the Word of God? The Church is to be the pillar and ground of the truth. The

distinguishing element of the Church is that it rises up in society in its foundation, in all of its structure, to give proclamation and testimony to divine truth. It's very simple – the truth of God is the most important thing in the world, because you can't know God, Christ, the Holy Spirit, man, sin, the future, the past, anything, without the revelation of God. So, I tell people this all the time. You choose a Church on the basis of the centrality of the proclamation of the Word of God. That's the key. And when that happens, all things generally come into balance. God will be honored and worshipped because, of course, He is the One who is, Himself, revealed in Scripture. Christ will be lifted up and glorified because He is the theme in Scripture. The doctrine of salvation, with all of its range from justification through sanctification to glorification, will be expressed in accurate terms. So, I only ask one question – what is the role of the Word of God in the Church?

Phil Johnson, the one interviewing MacArthur, states,

That's such a simple principle but, if you think about modern evangelicalism, that truth seems utterly lost and obscured because of what they are doing today.

MacArthur continues,

Well, they are pushing the Word of God out. They have a better way to do it. They have a better way to do it.[22]

This *Grace To You* excerpt is as accurate as it is appalling! We live in a day when the Word of God receives a vote of 'no confidence' from many of those who should be proclaiming its timeless truths as the only basis for one's faith and conduct. Surely no man who speaks to his fellow men has a more taxing, or more thrilling, task than a preacher.[23] Before him are gathered people who have a great variety of spiritual experience, understanding, need, and interest. And it is his task to teach, interest, and persuade them all from the same passage. But in an effort to make the task of preaching less taxing or to make it more interesting, some seek to do away with biblical exposition altogether. The rationale is predicated upon the sentiment that explaining the Bible is hard work and people aren't interested in what the Bible says as much as they are interested in how they can live lives of greater comfort, success, and pleasure. Why not give them what they want? Besides, if I don't give it to them they will find someone who will. Quickly and easily it is concluded that expository preaching doesn't stand a chance of being effective in this day and in this culture, and if attempted it will not work.

The ability and willingness to quickly dismiss expository preaching because of societal factors is not new. Men have been proclaiming the death of expository preaching and trying to eulogize its demise for many decades! In reality, all they are doing is to display their refusal to acknowledge that God has chosen to work through His Word and through the Holy Spirit of God to bring regeneration to the lost and sanctification to the redeemed, regardless of the conditions of the society in which they live! Take for example this death sentence to expository preaching declared in 1930, based upon the conditions of American society at that time.

> No one will deny that the conditions of life in our age are a challenge to those who would interpret the things of the spirit. A large part of the public lacks the mental concentration, if not the capacity, to follow sustained thought; and that state of fact creates a changed atmosphere for preaching. For one thing, it makes expository preaching, so fruitful in other days, well-nigh impossible, at least in America. Such preaching must of necessity assume some knowledge of the Bible, in respect to which most of our hearers are ignorant.[24]

This sordid view of expository preaching has only increased in the intervening decades to the point that preaching is not recognized as preaching unless it is a communication event to promote self-affirmation and self-aggrandizement to each hearer. This, of course, is perversion! What people need is knowledge of God's Word, that is, to understand how the Word of God supplies needed truth which is not found in the world because the world cannot understand divine revelation. All of the sermon, including the sermon introduction, should indicate the sufficiency of the Word of God as God's resource to meet man's needs.

The Need for Interest in a Sermon Introduction
It is the indication that the sermon will examine valuable and needed truth that causes the introduction to be perceived by the hearers as a good one. However, there seems to be a strange fear in homiletical literature of doing too good a job of developing a sermon introduction. In other words, the fear is that the sermon introduction will be far better than the sermon. Is this not an unnecessary fear? This fear is depicted as building a substantial foundation (an excellent sermon introduction) which is appropriate for an impressive building (an excellent sermon), only to build upon the substantial foundation a 'chicken coop' (a poor sermon). Well, as I see it, the problem here is not the excellent introduction which shows up the poor sermon! The problem is that the sermon was poor! Sure, there is incongruity between a good introduction and a bad sermon. But can the problem honestly be the fault of a good introduction? Is there really any virtue in having a bad introduction and a bad sermon? I have heard some bad sermons. The overwhelming majority of them were accompanied by bad introductions. Once in a while, a good introduction will accompany a bad sermon. My response has always been this, 'Well, at least the introduction was worth hearing!' Certainly it is a shame if the sermon is not a good one. But a bad sermon will not be made better by an equally bad introduction! A bad sermon is not bad because the introduction that accompanied it was a good introduction! To be sure, a good introduction cannot make a bad sermon a good one. Bad sermons are a problem beyond the purview of this book. This book is concerned with the more typical

problem of good sermons accompanied by bad introductions. Jay Adams, who has a good understanding of the relationship between a sermon introduction and the sermon, put it this way: 'A good introduction must be followed by a good sermon, or the rest becomes a let-down. But why shouldn't it be followed by a good sermon?'[25]

Good preaching is not an option. Less-than-good preaching inevitably will be an occasional reality, but when it occurs it is always an unacceptable and unfortunate thing. A preacher must endeavor to prepare an excellent sermon and an excellent introduction for the sermon. If a sermon introduction may be feared as being 'too good' for a sermon body, then the preacher must go back and attend to his most basic responsibility – the sermon body. To know that the sermon is less-than-good is self-defeating and a preacher will not be well-advised to craft an equally inept introduction. Congruity between a bad introduction and a bad sermon is unthinkable. Incongruity between a good introduction and a bad sermon is unfortunate. Congruity between a good introduction and a good sermon is irreproachable! Don't be afraid to construct a sermon introduction that is 'too good' but certainly be concerned about developing a sermon body that is less than excellent! Take the counsel of John MacArthur regarding 'the ultimate key to effective preaching' which is: 'Very simply, stay in your study until you know that the Lord will gladly accept what you have prepared to preach because it rightly represents His Word.'[26]

A hearer must attend with interest to the material to be learned.[27] The cardinal rule, then, is that the preacher must be interesting. The sad fact is that often he is not. Sir Leslie Stephen said that eighteenth-century sermons fell into three categories – dull, duller, and dullest.[28]

A congregation will not be interested unless the preacher himself is interested in what he is saying. It is said that an old Duke of Devonshire so bored himself by his speech in the House of Lords that he yawned in the middle of it. I have never seen a preacher do that, but I have heard some sermons that were so lacking in interest that, if it were to happen, I would think it to be an accurate depiction of, and an appropriate response, to the sermon. 'How many sleep under us,' said Richard Baxter, 'because our hearts and tongues are sleepy, and we bring not with us so much skill and zeal as to awake them.'[29] A bored preacher will preach a boring sermon which is introduced by a boring introduction that fails to secure interest.

Monotony, in all its forms, militates against securing interest. As a listener, one cannot concentrate long on anything that does not change or is expected to change. There is a variety of monotony that can be implemented by a preacher. There is monotony of voice pattern with the same inflections recurring in every sentence – his voice rising and falling interminably to the same notes. There is monotony of voice pitch, pace, projection, and punch from sentence to sentence throughout the sermon. This not only indicates that the preacher is not interested in what he is saying, but it also makes it an inevitable certainty that the hearers will not be interested in the sermon either.

Dullness in the pulpit is a sin because it is avoidable! But this requires the preacher to understand the passage from which he is to preach well enough so that he himself can be gripped by the vital reality of the truth he desires his hearers to be gripped by. When a preacher isn't clear in the subject-matter of the sermon because he hasn't understood the passage clearly himself, his confusion breeds confusion in his hearers. Just as it is with confusion, so it is in the matter of interest – interest breeds interest and disinterest breeds disinterest.

Sermons catch fire when flint strikes steel. When the flint of a person's problems strikes the steel of the Word of God, a spark ignites that burns in the mind. Directing our preaching at people's needs is not a mere persuasive technique; it is the task of ministry.[30] People will listen to the preacher, not because they should listen, but because they want to listen if they understand that his message will be of significant help in their lives. Haddon Robinson had this to say about the importance of an applicable sermon introduction:

> Early in the sermon, listeners should realize that the pastor is talking to them about them. He raises a question, probes a problem, identifies a need, opens up a vital issue to which the passage speaks. Application starts in the introduction, not in the conclusion. Should a preacher of even limited ability bring to the surface people's questions, problems, hurts, and desires to deal with them from the Bible, he will be acclaimed a genius. More important than that, he will through his preaching bring the grace of God to bear on the agonizing worries and tensions of daily life.[31]

The best introductions will be those which make contact at some point with life as the people know and understand it. Few are prepared at once to be interested in the geography of the Holy Land or the doings of a remote King of Israel of whom they have never heard. Even a story from the Gospels or the Acts of the Apostles will not grip them unless it is approached by some road which started from their own experience or at least from the world in which they are familiar. Sometimes an anecdote will help, but it must be relevant. We have no business to throw out a story, humorous or otherwise, like the opening gambit of an after-dinner speaker, even if it happens to be a good one. In any case, unless the theme quickly and naturally connects with the lives of the hearers, any interest aroused will at once be lost.[32] Whoever brings the implications of the gospel to bear with relevance and power to any aspect of life can be sure of an interested congregation.[33]

One factor that determines the effectiveness of a sermon is the degree to which the sermon, though a public declaration of divine truth proclaimed to a number of people, is an individual and very personally relevant message.[34] It is the function of a good introduction to convince the hearer that the sermon is a personally significant message.

When the expositor conveys this to his hearers he will be inevitably seen as a significant messenger. How else can it be but that one who bears an urgent message would be any other than an urgent messenger? As the message is in the heart of the preacher, so is the preacher before the people. An exposition viewed by the expositor to be insignificant will render that expositor as insignificant before his hearers. The scathing indictment of Howard Hendricks should very infrequently, if ever, be true of a Bible expositor. He writes:

> I don't mean to be cruel, but I'm compelled to be honest: If all those involved in Christian teaching had to become salesmen to make a living, most of them would starve to death. We're teaching the most exciting truth in all the world – eternal truth – and doing it as if it were cold mashed potatoes.
>
> You listen to some guy talking about supposedly the most important thing in all the world, and it sounds like item twenty-one on a priority list of twenty. You're just sure he doesn't feel it in his gut. And you think, *If this is exciting to him, I hate to see him when he's bored.*[35]

But the truth is, we will not be able to conceal our excitement any more than we are able to conceal our lack of excitement regarding the sermon to be preached.

A common criticism of Christians is that they are not as excited about the truth claims they hold as they ought to be. The rebuke of, 'If one-tenth of what you believe is true, you ought to be ten times as excited as you are,' deserves to be shouldered by many who expound the Bible, the only thing really worth being impassioned about.[36]

It has been stated that 'Action springs out of what we fundamentally desire'.[37] Sound advice for any expository preacher who desires to be both interesting and persuasive before his hearers is: first and foremost in the sermon introduction, arouse in your hearers an eager desire for the truth to be expounded. He who can do this has the whole congregation with him. He who cannot preaches an unattended message!

If the expositor truly desires to see God's people living the truth, he must give them the truth. In order to help them receive the truth that he will provide for them, he must show them that it will be beneficial to their lives. Failure in doing this is indicative that the preacher did not study to the extent that he sees for himself the vital connection of the truth to be preached to the lives he and his hearers are living. He simply has not understood the passage sufficiently. If he has understood the text sufficiently, but does not introduce the sermon effectively, it must be that he has an insufficient understanding of what must take place in preaching, especially in the sermon introduction. What he fails to understand specifically is that he must take what he understands, the truth of the passage to be expounded, and quickly make a connection to the interests of his hearers – which will always be in reference to their own lives. To fail to understand the vital connection between the truth of the text to be expounded and the lives of the hearers is ignorance. To understand the connection between the truth of the text to be expounded and the lives of the hearers, and fail to make this connection clear in the sermon introduction, is foolishness. Consider the following plea for preaching that is intended to encourage preachers to strive to make their sermons a matter of personal relevance to the hearers.

> I go fishing up in Maine every summer. Personally I am very fond of strawberries and cream; but I find that for some strange reason fish prefer worms. So when I go fishing, I don't think about what I want. I think about what they want. I don't bait the hook with strawberries and cream. Rather, I dangle a worm or a grasshopper in front of the fish and say: 'Wouldn't you like to have that?' Why not use the same common sense when fishing for men?[38]

Common sense dictates that you need to indicate how the truth of the text, which you are about to expound, is instrumental in meeting their needs, the apex of their true interest.

A pivotal problem surfaces in regards to the hearers' interests. What if their interests are not what they should be? Should preaching be a means to help unspiritual people gratify unspiritual interests? Preaching must never be used to aid and abet unspiritual ends! Certainly this is much of what preaching is about these days – a means for how the gratification of selfish people can be achieved. The following perspective, though insightful, is ripe for abuse by many who preach today. The perspective is similar to this – you are interested in what you want. You are very interested in it. Everyone who hears you preach is just like you. They are interested in what they want. So, the only way to influence others is to talk about what they want and show them how to get it.[39]

Unfortunately, some preach in such a way which makes it obvious that they believe the Christian life is nothing other than a life of self-absorption, self-interest, and self-aggrandizement. To them, the Bible is just a guide to help one achieve a life of ultimate avarice. Somehow, they have come to believe that life is all about self! Such a view is a perverted view of life and preaching. A preacher who lives and preaches from this framework, thus engendering this deviant pursuit in others, is involved in the ultimate perversion of preaching!

In dealing with the interests of the hearers in a sermon introduction I am not trying to establish some hellish hybrid of expository preaching that seeks to explain the Bible and at the same time seeks to promote a self-achievement agenda! Expository preaching will not only bring greater understanding of God's Word to the hearer, but in the understanding of God's Word, the hearer's interests will be changed. This change will be according to the intention of God for His people that their lives will be marked by an increasing selflessness as they are sanctified by His Word. But a sermon introduction, like the Christian life itself, must move in a direction of where the believers are to where they need to be. A sermon introduction must be of personal relevance if it is to be interesting to the hearers. A sermon introduction that is designed to secure the interest of the hearers is not a threat to expository preaching, but an expository preacher who fails to secure the interest of his hearers will certainly be an uninteresting expositor.

Expository preaching cannot be threatened by an expositor that can interest his hearers from the earliest portion of the sermon, but it is marginalized by the expositor who preaches an uninteresting introduction to an expository sermon. There is at least a partial corollary between an ineffective salesman and an ineffective expositor. The following identifies the correlation:

> Thousands of salesmen are pounding the pavements today, tired, discouraged, and underpaid. Why? Because they are always thinking only of what they want. They don't realize that neither you nor I want to buy anything. If we did, we would go out and buy it. But both of us are eternally interested in solving our problems. And if a salesman can show us how his services or his merchandise will help us solve our problems, he won't need to sell to us. We'll buy. And the customer likes to feel that he is buying – not being sold.
>
> Yet many men spend a lifetime in selling without seeing things from the customer's angle.[40]

The same shortcoming is true of some expositors of the Bible. An expositor that people want to hear is one who can make a vital connection between the passage to be expounded and their lives. The hearers do hope there will be a connection between the preacher's exposition of Scripture and their lives, but this hope can dissipate quickly. A good introduction assures them that their hope will not be in vain.

The Results of Securing Interest

It is rightly asserted that 'A discourse without application would not be a sermon, but only a declamation – a monologue.... We are not merely to speak before people but to them.'[41] John Broadus says that application in preaching 'is the main thing to be done'. So it is, not just in some parts of the sermon but in each part of the sermon – each of the main points, the conclusion, and yes, even in the introduction – application must be involved. But how can there be application in a sermon introduction when the sermon body has yet to be preached? This question presupposes two things that must be refuted if sermon introductions are to improve: preaching does not happen in a sermon introduction; and, a sermon introduction is an irrelevant portion of a sermon. Both presuppositions must be understood as false.

Certainly, exposition of the text will not be taking place in a sermon introduction. So the preaching that takes place in a sermon introduction will not be expository preaching. Expository preaching will take place in the body of the sermon where the biblical text is explained. But preaching in the introduction will occur when the subject-matter of the text to be expounded throughout the body of the sermon will surface and receive personal, relevant treatment in the introduction. Preaching occurs in the sermon introduction when four elements are incorporated, each one helping to secure the interest of the hearers. These four elements are: positive and negative flesh and blood scenarios; vital questions; crucial assertions; and, a determinative projection of the subject-matter to the lives of the hearers. When these elements are part of the introduction content, the preacher will not only be preaching and, therefore, addressing his hearers in a personal, relevant way but, even more importantly, he will be introducing his sermon in such a way as to secure the interest of his hearers. When a preacher secures the interest of the hearers in the introduction, he is preaching. A preacher is preaching in the introduction when he secures the interest of the hearers. The personal relevance of the subject-matter to the hearers is the key to both preaching and securing interest in the sermon introduction.

A good sermon introduction enables a preacher to preach before he even begins to expound the text in the body of his sermon. The sermon introduction must indicate how the sermon itself will indeed have a bearing on the lives of the hearers, therefore the sermon introduction will cause the hearers to act. The resulting action caused by the application, or the bearing on life, in the introduction will be to cause the hearers to listen with earnest expectancy and understanding that the sermon they are about to hear will be life-changing. It is only when the hearers perceive the sermon may be life-changing that a preacher will sense that they are truly interested in what he is saying. As it has been suggested, 'The secret of man's being is not only to live but to have something to live for.'[42] If this is true, then the genius of the sermon introduction is to assure the hearers that the sermon will be of significant help in their journey.

In short, a good sermon introduction will demonstrate that the message they will hear holds vital information necessary to a life worth living. The interest of hearers will always be related to the lives they are living. The more a sermon introduction demonstrates that the sermon will have a substantial bearing on the lives of the hearers, the more interest the hearers will have in hearing the message.

With growing interest, attention grows, and with growing attention a preacher is able to accomplish more in his preaching. It is only when our hearers are truly interested in our subject-matter that we are working with maximum effectiveness in our preaching.[43] When attention is half aroused, concepts will be faint and fragmentary and thus inaccurate, fleeting, and useless.[44] In sequence, which comes first, attention or interest? Do we get attention in order to secure interest or do we secure interest in order to maximize attention? The answer is, we do both.

There are two phases of a hearer's attention that we must understand. There is an initial getting of the hearer's attention and there is a maximized attention or an achieved willingness of the hearers to be attentive to a sermon. In the middle of these two phases of attention is the securing of interest. The initial getting of attention is what the preacher does for the hearers very early in the sermon introduction. Through carefully crafted statements he causes his hearers to track with his thought process, to become attentive to the subject-matter he will be expounding from his text. The maximized attention is the achieved willingness of the hearers to be attentive to the sermon about to be expounded. Maximized attention is a commitment the hearers make to the preacher to listen carefully to his exposition of a biblical text. Maximized attention is the desired *final* outcome of an effective sermon introduction. In the middle of initial attention and maximized attention is secured interest.

The completed sequence of a good sermon introduction is as follows: there is an initial getting of attention which leads to the secured interest of the hearers, which then creates a maximized attentiveness of the hearers. The preacher must get the hearer's attention so as to secure their interest in the subject-matter he will be preaching. With secured interest in the subject-matter of his sermon, the preacher has achieved a willingness of his hearers to be attentive to the expository sermon he will preach as he explains a biblical text in order to enhance their knowledge of Scripture and change their lives through this enhanced knowledge. Since maximized attention follows interest it is folly to attempt to gain maximal attention without first stimulating interest.[45] This denotes the typical model of – getting the attention of the congregation (in the introduction), in order to secure the interest of the congregation (in the introduction), for the result of preaching to an attentive congregation for the duration of the sermon. The only other acceptable variation to this is to begin the introduction with an attempt to secure interest (remember, when interest is secured the preacher automatically has achieved initial attention) for the result of preaching to an attentive congregation for the duration of the sermon. In either scenario the point is clear – without securing the interest of the hearers in the introduction, a preacher will not be preaching to a truly attentive congregation – a congregation whose attention has been maximized. Therefore, interest must be secured and it must be secured in the sermon introduction!

Hindrances to Secured Interest
The results of securing interest are that we actually begin preaching in the sermon introduction to an attentive congregation that anticipates hearing the exposition of a biblical text. Before considering more fully the means of securing interest, we need to consider some major hindrances in the process of securing interest.

Three chief hindrances of securing interest in a sermon introduction, as well as maintaining attention throughout, are apathy, distraction, and uncertainty or lack of clarity in communication. Apathy, to some extent, is an automatic reality that awaits every preacher of any sermon to any congregation. This is *initial* apathy. Initial apathy is the very reason why interest must be secured. Initial apathy stands in the way of secured interest and, therefore, initial apathy must be overcome by secured interest. Initial apathy must die so secured interest can thrive. If interest is not secured, then *continued* apathy will be a reality for the sermon introduction and perhaps even turn into *escalated* apathy during the preaching of the sermon. Of course, this continued apathy is due to the hearers' inability to perceive the significance of the material being expounded to their lives. And, of course, continued apathy is proof of the preacher's failure on behalf of this congregation for the preaching of this sermon.

Distraction is the division of a hearer's attention between marginal issues and/or environmental circumstances around the hearers.[46] Each hearer will become distracted with his or her own wondering thoughts when they are not interested in what the preacher is saying, or when they were interested but the earlier interest begins to wane. Certainly, there may be external factors that will compete and eventually win out in the battle for attention of a disinterested hearer.

Another hindrance to securing interest and maintaining attention is lack of certainty regarding what is being said and/or lack of certainty of how what is being said is personally relevant. Even when we are very clear as to what we intend to say, there is no guarantee that our hearers will understand what we mean by what we are saying, and therefore they will miss the significance of what is being said. Such uncertainty is certain to curtail the interest of the hearers. In other words, the certainty with which a preacher preaches impacts his ability to interest his hearers. He must say what he means and mean what he says, and do this with a variety of repetition in order to get through to the majority of his hearers. Em Griffin makes the point for certainty of communication as he writes:

> There's an old story about three umpires who were talking shop. The first umpire said, 'Some are balls, some are strikes. I calls them as they is.' The second umpire wasn't so sure. He put it this way. 'Some are balls, some are strikes. I call'em as I see'em.' The third umpire felt the need to correct them both. He flatly declared, 'Some are balls and some are strikes, but they ain't nothing 'till I call them.'[47]

As Griffin continues he relates clarity in communication to repeating something in a variety of ways. He says,

> Words don't mean things, people mean things. And there's always the chance that the words we select to present our main point may mean something very different to our hearers than they do to us. That's why it's wise to state our case in two or three different ways. If the first one fogs by some of our listeners, the second or third blend of words may click in as we intended.[48]

So the preacher must make sure his hearers have ample opportunity to understand how the sermon will impact their lives. The preacher must provide various avenues for the hearers to be hooked by the introduction material. The attempt to reveal in the introduction how relevant and, therefore, significant the sermon will be cannot be left up to a single statement, illustration, assertion, or question. A plurality of any of these, and perhaps a combination of a plurality of these, will be needed to secure substantially the interest of the majority of one's hearers.

For interest to be secured the congregation must be impressed with the subject-matter of the text to be preached. A favorable regard for the subject-matter of the text can be created by the following:

1. by stating the advantages the hearers will receive by understanding the passage

2. by showing how significant problems and issues of the hearers are remedied or alleviated by the content of the preaching portion

3. by connecting the subject-matter of the text to historical situations where the subject-matter was either set aside and/or implemented previously

4. by demonstrating how the subject-matter will profoundly impact the quality of life or will measurably improve the validity of their service to the Lord

5. by raising false impressions, interpretations of the subject-matter and text which are misleading or harmful for one to hold.[49]

A favorable regard for the passage to be preached is important in order to secure interest, but what does a preacher do to secure the interest of his hearers, specifically? In other words, what must a preacher do to secure the interest of the hearers in a sermon introduction? What are the means by which interest is secured? The answers to these questions will be provided as we consider how interest is secured.

Consider the Following Questions

1. How are voluntary, involuntary, and nonvoluntary attention distinguished?

2. What causes nonvoluntary attention to occur and how is this accomplished?

3. What does balanced exposition, in design and delivery, provide for the hearer?

4. How is passion and compassion defined and which is more important for the sermon introduction and which is more often lacking in a sermon introduction?

5. How does an upgrade of the hearer's 'motivation quotient' relate to the preacher's challenge 'to dare his hearers not to listen to him' in the sermon introduction?

6. Respond to the following question: 'If God works through His Word, how could it be reasonable to dismiss expository preaching based on cultural and societal factors?'

7. What is the rationale for refuting the danger of a sermon introduction that is 'too good'?

8. What is the requirement of a preacher so that he will not present the sermon introduction in a dull or disinterested way?

9. What is it that Haddon Robinson calls 'the task of ministry' and what must happen for this task to be accomplished?

10. What is the difference between 'foolishness' and 'ignorance' of a preacher who cannot secure the interest of his hearers in the sermon introduction?

11. What is involved in the viewpoint of a preacher who commits the ultimate perversion of preaching?

12. How is it possible to be preaching in the sermon introduction before the text to be expounded is even considered? What four elements of securing interest material allow preaching to occur in the sermon introduction?

13. What are the two phases of attention and how do they relate to interest?

14. What are the three hindrances to secured interest and how are these described?

15. What are five ways by which a preacher, in his sermon introduction, can create a favorable regard for the subject-matter of the sermon?

Words to Live and Preach by

The Counsel of the Righteous Man

Proverbs 12:5 – The thoughts of the righteous are just, but the counsels of the wicked are deceitful.

Proverbs 13:14 – The teaching of the wise is a fountain of life, to turn aside from the snares of death.

Proverbs 15:1 – A gentle answer turns away wrath, but a harsh word stirs up anger.

Proverbs 15:28 – The heart of the righteous ponders how to answer, but the mouth of the wicked pours out evil things.

Proverbs 16:21 – The wise of heart will be called discerning, and sweetness of speech increases persuasiveness.

Proverbs 22:4 – The reward of humility and the fear of the Lord are riches, honor and life.

Proverbs 25:11 – Like apples of gold in settings of silver is a word spoken in right circumstances.

Proverbs 27:17 – Iron sharpens iron, so one man sharpens another.

Chapter Five

Securing Interest:
How Interest is Secured in an Introduction

The Means for Securing Interest

Interest is secured sufficiently when the content of the sermon introduction creates a net-effect that hooks the hearer so that he or she thinks to oneself, 'Hey! I need to hear this!'[1] If the content does not produce this result then the hearers are not interested to the level they should be. In other words, the preacher has failed them. He has not done for them what he needs to do in a sermon introduction. The preacher has failed his hearers in the sermon introduction in a two-fold way: a failure of inadequate content for a sermon introduction and a failure of inadequate conveyance of the sermon introduction material.

The means of securing interest are divided into *content* means for securing interest and *conveyance* means for securing interest. This will suffice as a general, two-fold answer to the questions asked above regarding what a preacher must do and what means are necessary to secure interest. In other words, the preacher must provide the necessary content means as well as demonstrate the necessary conveyance means in order for a good sermon introduction to be preached. The content means for securing interest are the specific matters that must appear in a sermon introduction in order for interest to be piqued. The conveyance means for securing interest are the more general matters of the preacher's communication of the sermon introduction content.

The key to developing the necessary content and the appropriate communication of a good sermon introduction is hard work. A good sermon introduction like a good sermon is not a product yielded conveniently as Paul Scherer insists when he writes, 'The first step toward a good sermon is hard work, the second step is more hard work, and the third is still more.'[2] It is soundly observed that, 'Probably sloth, as much as anything else, reduces ministry to levels of mediocrity and relative impotence. Sloth, indolence, a refusal to pay the disciplined price of effective servanthood, rob countless preachers of fulfilling their individual potential.'[3] Uninteresting sermon introductions are not the byproduct of diligent effort and conscientious preparation. But such is required for preaching and such is required for every component of a sermon, including the sermon introduction.

The sermon introduction must be considered as part of the sermon, not just a sermon preliminary. Roland Q. Leavell writes: 'The importance of preaching cannot be exaggerated. God-called preachers must fulfill their sacred missions in the pulpit if the kingdom of God is to be advanced.'[4] Many are the preachers who would stand by the force of this statement yet not agree that the sermon introduction is a matter of importance and deny its role in the advancement of the kingdom through preaching. Therefore, there are many men who preach sound messages preceded by introductions that are not commensurate with the messages they introduce. The unfortunate effect of this is that the messages are never as effective as they would otherwise be if accompanied by an equally sound introduction. For a preacher to do consistently good work in sermon introductions he will have to be concerned with more than just the body of the sermon, and a greater effort will be required in sermon preparation. Paying the price, long hours of diligent labor in sermon preparation must not be given to the body of the sermon alone!

Bible expositor Alexander Maclaren is an example of one who 'paid the price'. Maclaren (McLaren was the spelling he used for his name)[5] was known as 'The Prince of Preachers.' This was partly due to the fact that he expounded the Scriptures at Union Chapel in Manchester, England, for fifty-two years, reading the Scriptures daily in the original languages, and he believed that 'Any sermon worth hearing required sixty hours of labor a week.'[6]

James Black used to say, 'In the ministry of all places God has no use for a lazy person.' James Armstrong counsels: 'Be what you are called to be. Meet the demands. Pay the price. Offer yourself as a living sacrifice. Set about to learn truth, in every responsible way possible, that others might come to know fullness of life because of the integrity and vitality of your openness, growth, and faithful servanthood.'[7]

The example and advocacy of hard work in sermon preparation contained in the previous quotations are laudable indeed, but they must be applied to the preparation of the entire sermon, including the introduction! An effective sermon introduction is a logical necessity for, and a compatible component to, an effective sermon. Also, a good introduction is a great investment for a preacher to make to maximize the effectiveness of his time and effort spent in sermon preparation.

Securing Interest through Content Means

It almost goes without saying that a sermon introduction must gain the attention of the hearers and introduce them to the subject-matter the preacher will deal with in his sermon. Certainly a sermon introduction must do that. But, even more certainly, a sermon introduction must do far more than that – it must secure their interest. Preachers have been taught in their preaching courses, and in books on the preparation of sermons, that getting attention and indicating what the topic of the sermon will be is the majority of what a sermon introduction is to accomplish. Because of this, the resulting pedagogy and practice of introducing sermons is a dwarfed, insignificant, irrelevant salvo of words that precede a sermon. It is akin to sermonic morning dew which quickly dissipates, is forgotten, and affects the hearers only in a marginal way, if at all.

So what is needed to make substantial improvement? Substantially improved *content* is needed. Improved content is content that is abstract truth which becomes concrete truth by the supplementation of concrete images and depictions. The improvement lies in the fact that the truth presented abstractly does not remain abstract but becomes truth that is specifically depicted in the arena of everyday life. As James S. Stewart wrote, 'Truth made concrete will find a way past many a door when abstractions knock in vain.'[8] It is a substantial improvement for our preaching when we can demonstrate the truth in such a way that it enters the door of understanding rather than knocking in vain for such an entry. Truth made concrete is advantageous in every part of the sermon, especially in the sermon introduction.

Specific Content Means for Securing Interest
Substantially improved sermon introduction content is achieved when the following four content means are incorporated: when the subject-matter is seen concretely through *positive and negative flesh and blood scenarios*, so that the truth to be proclaimed in the sermon has been disobeyed with negatives implications, and the truth to be proclaimed has been obeyed with positive implications; when *vital questions* have been raised regarding the hearer's present obedience or disobedience to the truth illustrated by the flesh and blood scenarios; when *crucial assertions* are made regarding the immediate and long-term negative and positive

ramifications of disobedience or obedience to the truth; when there is ample assurance that what will be disseminated in this exposition will be a *determinative projection* of how well one may, or may not, live productively in this life. These four content means for improved sermon introductions are the same as the four elements of securing interest which allows a preacher to preach in the sermon introduction, referred to earlier in the previous chapter.

Now remember, all of this is still preliminary to the substantial exposition of a text, but one may well be understood to be preaching because a very definite connection is being made between truth and life. In other words, the truth that will be expounded in the body of the sermon is understood clearly in the sermon introduction to be a vital, relevant matter. As Faris Whitesell insists, 'the application may be considered the most important part of the sermon because it is the part that motivates the hearer to action. Without it the sermon fails, because Biblical truth is meaningless unless it bears on life.'[9] It is the sermon introduction which incorporates the content means of securing interest which shows the relevance of the truth to life and prepares the hearers to be motivated by the truth they will hear expounded.

In reference to the sermon introduction securing interest by means of the content, several postulates must be understood. We can boil it down to the following: First, preaching must be relevant; second, an irrelevant introduction makes for a disinterested congregation, as it has been suggested by the statement – 'The granite faces in our congregations are due to irrelevant preaching'; and third, relevant preaching requires that our preaching be personal.[10] A sermon introduction that is perceived to be personally relevant indicates that the sermon to be preached contains needed truth. Wayne McDill asserts:

> Getting their attention is just the beginning. The audience must have their interest in the subject awakened. They are interested in whatever touches their personal concerns. So the preacher must

show how his subject is relevant to the life of the hearer. This step is called the need step because the way to gain interest is to discuss some need in the hearer that you might meet. The common expression for this appeal is 'scratching where they itch'.[11]

The relationship between a sermon introduction and a sermon is a relationship that is bonded by the following: specific problems of man are depicted in the introduction, and the solutions to the problems are explained in the sermon; questions that really matter are raised in the introduction, and the answers are given in the sermon through the exposition of the text. Again, McDill is helpful as he observes:

> If the biblical truth concerns love, the need element may be conflict or loneliness. If the message is faith, the need element may be uncertainty and doubt. If the answer is salvation, the need element is alienation and guilt. The need element is to biblical truth what hunger is to food, what a headache is to aspirin, what fatigue is to rest. The need element can be seen in the hearer's assumptions, his symptoms, and the consequences in his life.[12]

If a congregation senses that the sermon will not provide needed answers and solutions for their lives, they will conclude that the sermon to be preached will be of little assistance to them, and therefore, will neither be sufficiently interested in the sermon nor very attentive to the preacher. The problems and questions raised in the introduction are to be resolved by the exposition of the text and the body of the sermon.

General Content Means for Securing Interest

Problems and Solutions
Much preaching today is nothing more than a simplistic 'how to' approach for every conceivable area of life. The unfortunate thing about such an approach is that it sets aside the significance of understanding the Scriptures as they were written, as well as setting aside the value of explaining the

Scriptures as they are soundly interpreted so that relevant exposition may be presented. Rather than this, the far too common procedure is to poach upon the Scriptures with the attempt to enslave a variety of texts to formulate a 'how to' grid to correct some selected problem or to accomplish some goal. I certainly would agree with these Scripture-poaching-preacher-practitioners that the Bible is a worthy guide for the practice of a faithful Christian life. I certainly believe that Scripture alone holds the abiding solutions to problems faced in this life. Although I am not in favor of an approach to preaching other than the exposition of Scripture, I do believe the problem-solution principle is valuable in the introduction of expository sermons.

The problem-solution approach in preaching has value to initiate momentum for learning. If the hearers can be presented with a problem that needs resolution then they will be interested sufficiently to put forth the effort necessary to grasp the knowledge essential to resolving the problem.[13]

An initial momentum for learning is a valuable derivative of the problem-solution method of teaching.[14] Such initial motivation for learning is never more of a premium than in the beginning of a sermon. To graphically depict a significant problem for which the information of the text to be expounded will be the resolution is of obvious merit. If the problem surfaced in the introduction will be resolved by the truths contained in the text to be expounded in the sermon, the hearers are likely to view the sermon as vital to one's immediate and/or future circumstances. Others may be interested simply because they have already personally experienced how the truth of the sermonic text has been a benefit to them. The point is this – though a source of genuine interest may be found in things that the hearers can relate to in their past, an even richer source of interest will be found in the relationship of the subject-matter to their future.[15]

Through the problem-solution relationship between a sermon introduction and the sermon body a preacher can maintain and exhibit the closest attention and genuine interest in the material to be expounded. This is beneficial to hearers and the preacher also. Through secured interest, not only will the ones hearing the sermon understand the significance of the sermon to be preached to them but the one who will be preaching the sermon will be encouraged to preach knowing that his hearers desire to hear his exposition of Scripture. Every preacher knows the real difference it makes to preach to a congregation who is interested in the sermon to come. Certainly a preacher should be interested in the sermon he will preach, but he is even more excited to preach when he knows that it will be received by attentive hearers. Whatever truly interests the preacher will impact those who hear him preach. Though it is important for the preacher to be interested in the sermon he will preach, it is disastrous if this is not the case. True enthusiasm is contagious but lack of enthusiasm is epidemic!

The value of the problem-solution approach in the sermon introduction is that it portrays the fact that the sermon will meet the needs of the hearers. As we think about the needs of humanity, we may think of them in two ways. We may think of 'need' in the sense of what is the condition in life of one who is a needy person in reference to that which is lacking in his life, the basis of his suffering, the cause and effect of his troubles, etc. Here the frame of reference is one's state of being – one who is needy. This is need in an internal, conditional sense. For example, in the internal, conditional sense, consider the need of a proud man. That which is lacking in his life is friends, people who care for him, respect and appreciate him. His hubris and self-concern drives people away from him, causing him to be lonely, friendless, and despised by many. The proud man is certainly a needy person in an internal, conditional sense.

However, we may also think of 'need' in the sense of that which will bring correction to what is amiss in one's life or the supply of what is missing. Here the frame of reference is a solution to a problem the individual has – what is needed. This is need in an external, corrective sense. Again, consider the need of a proud man, this time in an external, corrective sense. What is needed in the proud man is humility, the correct estimation of God as one who opposes the proud and exalts the humble. Additionally, the proud man needs to understand the true value and worth of others. The proud man is certainly a needy person in an external, corrective sense.

Every biblical concept has a corresponding need, either internal or external, in the life of humans which calls for its application. In the introduction a preacher must connect the subject-matter of his text to its corresponding need in the life of people. Wayne McDill writes, 'The need element is explicit in many texts and implicit in all. The gracious nature and activity of God is a constant in Scripture, as is the fallen nature of man. The causes, symptoms, and consequences of a failure to rightly respond to God all constitute the need element.'[16]

Most listeners are not in doubt about their need for biblical truth to bring correction into their lives and impact their present state of being. What is doubtful is whether the sermon they are about to hear will effect either of these. The sermon introduction must remove such doubt about the sermon they will hear!

A problem-solution depiction in the sermon introduction does much to secure interest from a congregation for a sermon they are about to hear. Bryan Chapell says the key to securing interest is to involve the listeners and he suggests the following ways to accomplish this:

> Involve their imaginations.
> Involve their sense of wonder.
> Involve their appreciation of the past.
> Involve their fear of the future.
> Involve their outrage.
> Involve their compassion.[17]

A problem-solution component may accomplish several of these.

Questions and Answers

All biblical truth supplies not only solutions to problems but also answers to questions. Questions vital enough to warrant time and effort to answer them hold additional ability to secure interest. In fact, it is said that 'The object or the event that excites no question will provoke no thought. Questioning is not, therefore, one of the devices of teaching, it is really the whole of teaching.'[18]

Questions raised in the introduction are of two types. There are questions that are answered immediately after they are raised and there are questions for which the answers will be suspended. Questions raised and answered immediately help to clarify the thinking one should possess at the initial point of investigation of a subject-matter. Though clarification through immediately answered questions is valuable for establishing a cognitive foundation for a subject-matter, it will do little to develop interest since answers to questions that seem to settle everything and end all questions end all thinking as well. However, such initial questioning and answering can be used to raise more important questions which call for important answers. And, of course, these more important answers are to be given in the body of the sermon through the process of expounding a biblical text.

After a truth is understood clearly, or a fact or a principle established through the use of questions and immediate answers, there still remains its consequences, applications, and uses. Questions can be asked which will be answered by the consequences and applications. Also, each fact and truth understood leads to other facts which renew the questioning and demands fresh investigation for additional insights.[19] These questions raised in the introduction to which the answers are suspended until the text is thoroughly examined create a need to know the information to be provided as the text is expounded. Therefore, interest for the exposition is enhanced by the postponement of needed knowledge.

Just as it is good to not answer too promptly the question asked, it is also serviceable to restate it variously. The various rephrasing of the question will provide greater force and clarity to the original question as well as providing a perception of the depth and breadth the answer will have. 'It must be remembered that knowing comes by thinking not merely [by] being told.'[20] The telling will take place but it will take place in the body of the sermon. Inquiry will take place in the introduction of the sermon which will secure interest from the hearers and cause them to desire to understand the sermon.

Securing interest in the sermon introduction is dependent upon both content means and conveyance means. The specific content means for securing interest include the incorporation of flesh and blood scenarios, vital personal questions, assertions regarding the immediate and long-term ramifications for disobedience or obedience to the truth, and assurances that the truth of the passage to be examined will be determinative as to the productivity of one's life of service for the Lord. General content means of securing interest include problem and solutions, as well as questions and answers.

Securing Interest through Conveyance Means

Knowledge

No preacher should fear that a thorough knowledge of his text and subject-matter will produce a cold, mechanical discourse rather than a warmhearted, enthusiastic exposition so much to be desired, admired and praised. True skill kindles and keeps alive enthusiasm by giving it success where it would otherwise be discouraged by defeat. An expositor's love for his work grows with his ability to do it well. Enthusiasm will accomplish all the more when guided by intelligence and armed with skill.[21] The preacher whose own mind glows with the truth, and who skillfully leads people to a clear understanding of the same truth, will not fail in inspirational power.[22] Knowledge, a thorough knowledge, of the text and the subject-matter of the text is essential for a preacher to preach in a way that will allow him to secure the interest of his hearers.

The teacher must know that which he would teach.[23] Here is a matter of significance for the preacher today. From the prophets he may learn that he may be profound and also simple, learned yet understandable, pious yet possessed of intellectual integrity. The ability to confuse by the vastness of one's erudition is not a necessary mark of learning. The power of the intellect can receive no better demonstration than the demonstration of such a successful discovery and formulation of the truth that it can be transmitted to the minds of others.[24]

Because the prophets did so well at providing a clear transmission of God's Word to His people, their ministries suggests a useful principle which every preacher ought to employ in the evaluation of one's preaching – intellectual clarity has a moral quality which is closely related to intellectual integrity. The prophet's understanding of the world from the standpoint of his vision of the God who called him, coupled with the incisive relevance of his presentation of this understanding, was more than a rational comprehension of reality. Upon these men rested a heavy obligation to know and to impart the Word of their God with all its ramifications for human existence.[25] Certainly the ramifications of truth for human existence are called for in the body of the sermon where application of the expounded text occurs. However, the hearers need to gain the conviction that the sermon to be preached in their hearing will be determinative in their lives – that it will have a bearing on every component of their being, impacting how they think, feel, and act in the light of biblical truth. But how will they be so impacted, and why would they be so impacted if the one preaching to them does not convey such significance of the truth to be proclaimed in the introduction of his sermon? If a sermon is to impact the hearer's mind, will, and emotions then the preacher must evidence the fact that the passage he will preach has already impacted his mind, his will, and his emotions. The greatest need for evidence of such personal impact of the truth in the preacher's life is found in the introduction of the sermon. As Howard Hendricks has written:

> All communication has three essential components: intellect, emotion, and volition – in other words, *thought, feeling, and action*. So whatever it is I want to communicate to another individual, it involves
> ... something I know,
> ... something I feel,
> ... something I'm doing.
>
> If I know something thoroughly, feel it deeply, and am doing it consistently, I have great potential for being an excellent communicator. In fact, the more thoroughly I know the concept ... the more deeply I feel it ... and the more consistently I practice it ... the greater my potential as a communicator.
>
> But all three components must be present.[26]

The sermon introduction is not exempt from the communication process. In fact, it is the pivotal point of our opportunity to communicate with our hearers. To think without feeling would be thinking with a total indifference to the object of thought, which would be absurd, and to feel without thinking would be almost impossible.[27] It is crucial that we communicate to our hearers that the truth we will preach is life-changing truth and we ourselves must be 'Exhibit A' in the body of evidence.

As preachers we go a long way in the direction of securing the interest of our hearer's as we know, feel, and are doing, or at least have already committed to practicing, the truth we preach. Interest will be highly probable when our preaching answers the following questions; questions which we ask ourselves and seek to answer through the sermon: What do I know that they must know about this passage? What do I feel about the truth of this text that they must feel? What do I do about the truth of this passage that they must do also?[28] Such evidence of thorough knowledge will encourage the hearers to want to know, feel, and do what the preacher has already personally discovered.

If an expositor truly desires his hearers to acquire knowledge of the text he will explain to them, it is reasonable to inquire about the kind of knowledge he desires for them to possess. The acquisition of knowledge may be of various qualities or levels of understanding. Knowledge is acquired in various levels which can be characterized by: (1) faint recognition; (2) the ability to recall for ourselves, or to describe in a general way to others, what we have learned; (3) the power to explain and prove readily what we have discovered as well as to illustrate and apply it specifically; and (4) modified conduct which results from truth that is so understood and appreciated in its deeper and wider significance that it forces us to act because of its importance.[29] In the sermon introduction we must indicate knowledge of the text to an extent that we can illustrate to the hearers the importance of the truth of the passage as well as convey the significance this truth has already had in our lives. To the degree this kind of knowledge is indicated, we garner secured interest. To the degree we fail to indicate this kind of knowledge of the text, we fail to garner secured interest. It is the third and fourth levels of acquired knowledge that commonly are not evidenced in a sermon introduction but hold the greatest potential for effectiveness in introducing a sermon.

A preacher will demonstrate from sermon to sermon in his preaching a varying degree of knowledge and beneficial insight as he moves from one text to another. Every preacher preaches at various levels of effectiveness from one sermon to another. The effectiveness or the lack of effectiveness of preached sermons is due in no small part to the preacher's knowledge of the passage. I am not affirming that no one can preach at all without fullness of knowledge; nor am I affirming that every one who knows his subject-matter thoroughly will necessarily preach well. But imperfect knowing must be reflected in imperfect preaching. What a man does not know he cannot preach successfully.[30]

As we think about knowledge of the truth, it is imperative that we understand that truth is known by its resemblances, and a truth can best be seen in the light of other truths. Instead of hearing the facts and descriptions about a subject-matter, the hearers must see it linked to a greater body of truth, in various fruitful relations. In other words, the subject-matter needs to be illustrated in several arenas of life so that the value and versatility of the subject-matter can be indicated. However, it must be understood that the power of illustrations comes only out of clear and familiar knowledge.[31] The inability of the preacher to illustrate, in the introduction, the significance of the sermon's subject-matter is a certain indicator that the preacher lacks the knowledge needed to introduce a sermon well.

The implications of a preacher's knowledge of his text and subject-matter are inescapable. In connection to the impact that his preaching will have on the lives of his hearers we have to realize that we cannot cause them to be interested in that which we have failed to understand in a significant way. The bottom-line is this – hearers follow with expectation and delight a guide who has a thorough knowledge of the field to be explored, but they follow reluctantly and without interest the ignorant and incompetent leader.[32] A sermon introduction that reveals that a preacher lacks a significant knowledge of the truth to be expounded invites disinterest of the hearers toward the sermon and disrespect toward the preacher of the sermon.

Developed Connection
All preaching must advance in some direction, not the least of which is the advancement in an acquisition of new insight. To merely teach what is already known and understood is to check the hearer's desire to obtain further knowledge and to

deaden the attention. It is a serious error to keep the hearers in the domain of the familiar under the assumed necessity of thoroughness. Old mines may be reworked if you can find ore at deeper levels, and old lessons may be worked over if new uses may be made of them.[33] The introduction needs to demonstrate that relatively familiar themes of Scripture have ramifications which have not been understood adequately or applied profitably. Of course, the introduction indicates that the much needed understanding of the seemingly familiar subject-matter will be explored in a fashion that will open new insights into that which has already been known, but known only in a partial or in a limited way.

The essence of preaching is to make the hearers become discoverers of truth.[34] This is the practice of a good expositor. He is one who arouses the spirit of inquiry in the minds of his listeners. This is true not only for the body of the sermon when the text is insightfully examined but in the sermon introduction where connections of the subject-matter to the Christian life are brought together and/or developed in a way that they have not been in their grid of understanding.

An active role in the process of understanding truth facilitates greater knowledge and greater interest. The one who is taught without doing any discovery for himself is like one who is fed without doing any exercise: he will lose both his appetite and his strength.[35] An introduction that basically indicates what the subject-matter of the sermon will be and perhaps how the subject will be treated as the text will be explained, simply puts the hearers in a passive mode. They are prevailed upon only to the point of understanding what the sermon will be about and the development the subject-matter will receive. This is stuff of very little consequence. It is also stuff that will be deemed as having very little interest.

An introduction that does not cause the hearers to want to know and need to know the truth of the text to be expounded is ineffective. It misses out on both of the two major factors of interest – personal curiosity and personal benefit. Personal curiosity is the love for knowledge for its own sake. The hearers must be made to become curious about the meaning of the text to be examined in the sermon and the implications of the understanding to their lives. The desire for personal benefit is a force which causes one to know for the sake of how the information gained may be used to bring about positive benefits and prevent negative effects in one's life. An effective introduction develops the connection between the hearer's desire to understand the passage to be preached and the hearer's desire to be benefited by the understanding of the passage as its truth is applied to life. A developed connection between the text to be preached and the hearers of the sermon must be distinct for the conveyance means of securing interest to be fully operational.

The final stage of the learning process is the discovery of the uses and applications of knowledge attained. No teaching is fully learned until it is traced to its connections with the great working machinery of nature and of life. Every fact has its relation to life, and every principle its applications, and until these are known, facts and principles are idle. The practical relations of truth, and the forces which lie behind all facts, are never really understood until we apply our knowledge to some of the practical purposes of life and of thought.[36]

The learning process demands this final stage and to this purpose and effort the preacher must constantly be directed.[37] Until truth is acted upon, the knowledge gained about the truth is really only potential knowledge, not actual, possessed knowledge. The intention of the preacher for his hearers to have the truth lived out in their lives is invaluable for him to be able to demonstrate in the sermon introduction the connection between biblical truth and daily living. Without this focused intentionality for the sermon, the introduction is bound to be lacking this much needed connection of life and truth. The effectiveness of a sermon introduction is, in part, due to a highly developed connection of the truth to be expounded and this truth as it is presently being obeyed or disobeyed in the lives of the hearers. The connection that must be developed is one of conceptual truth or the understanding of a subject-matter, and one of personal truth or the application of the subject-matter in life. When there is an obviously developed connection between conceptual truth and personal truth demonstrated in the introduction the hearer's interest will be secured more fully.

It is certain that the work of a preacher is to arouse the thinking of his hearers. In order to do this he must teach clearly and thoroughly, illustrate amply, and apply the truth to the lives of his hearers so that attention will be focused and interest will remain high. All of this must be done if the preacher is to be persuasive in his preaching. But a preacher cannot persuade hearers who have tuned him out because he failed to hook them or secure their interest regarding the truth he expounds. Persuasiveness is not an option. It is not enough for the preacher to know this and even to be committed to helping his hearers acquire possessed knowledge. His sermon introduction must indicate his commitment to his hearers to help them possess a personal, working knowledge of the truth. Therefore, preaching cannot be limited to the attempt to have the truth reproduced in the mind of his hearers. Howard Hendricks is right as he asserts that the task of all who teach the Word of God 'is not to impress people, but to impact them; not just to convince them but to change them.'[38] If a preacher desires to see his hearers changed by the truth he would preach, then his hearers must be interested in what he will say. A disinterested hearer cannot be persuaded about anything. As we shall see in fuller detail, if we are going to persuade our hearers we must first secure their interest.

Unction
What is unction? D. Martyn Lloyd-Jones defined unction as an access of power. To amplify his perception of unction Lloyd-Jones said it is 'God giving power, and enabling, through the Spirit, to the preacher in order that he may do

this work in a manner that lifts it up beyond the efforts and endeavors of man to a position in which the preacher is being used by the Spirit and becomes the channel through whom the Spirit works.'[39]

A simple understanding of unction is God's unmistakable presence attending and empowering the preaching of His Truth. Simply stated, unction is commonly referred to as the anointing of the Holy Spirit. Preaching with unction occurs because of the anointing of the Holy Spirit. But this simple understanding, as true as it is, might be understood in such a way to assume that the preacher bears no responsibility or liability for preaching with unction or the lack thereof. Without trying to curtail the sovereign work of God in anointing a preacher with His Spirit, there are some particular areas that a preacher must fulfill for there to be an unmistakable presence and empowering of the Holy Spirit in preaching.

Preaching that bears this presence of God is preaching that is according to His Word, and is spoken through His servant who is of His choosing and under His control, and therefore, speaks on His authority, by His power, in His conviction, with His passion, from His motives, for His purposes, and to His glory. To the degree that there is preaching with unction, there is to the same degree a man who is filled with the Holy Spirit so that nothing about that man is a cause to detract from preaching in the fullest possible enabling of the Holy Spirit according to the gifts he has been given by Him. Preaching with unction is accompanied by the perceptibly powerful presence of God that impacts the hearts of the hearers. Because there is preaching with unction there will be preaching with impact. The impact of the preaching will be determined by the will of God and the character of the hearers.

Unction was stated by Lloyd-Jones as 'the greatest essential in connection with preaching'.[40] Since this certainly is true, let's consider unction from the development of the eleven prepositional phrases found above.

Unction – Preaching According to His Word

Unction is the result of careful and diligent preparation having earnestly sought God in prayer for Him to do what He wills to do with the preparation that has gone forth. Careful and diligent preparation concerns both the messenger as well as the message to be preached, in other words, a subjective and an objective preparation. Certainly the preacher must spend time in personal reflection, prayer, confession, and personal commitment regarding the truth he has discovered. Unless he has made himself the initial audience of the sermon that he will ultimately preach to others, he will not preach with unction. This is the subjective preparation needed in order to preach effectively.

The point here, however, is the objective preparation and more specifically the results of the objective preparation – an exposition of a biblical passage, a message that is according to His Word. Expository preaching is not solely the endeavor of preaching a sermon to God's people on the Lord's Day or any other time. A sermon may be true in that all that is said does not nullify the teaching found in the Bible. The sermon may be insightful, encouraging, and of practical value. That does not constitute a message according to His Word. His Word is Scripture. The act of taking a biblical text and thoroughly explaining it, corroborating the explanation by other biblical passages, and applying the timeless truths derived from the passage is the closest thing a preacher can do to preach according to His Word. Much study will be needed to accurately interpret the text and be able to say, in effect, 'Thus saith the Lord,' in the process of expounding the biblical passage.

When, however, the appropriate work has been done to understand the passage to the point that its meaning can be communicated clearly, corroborated convincingly, applied profitably and the personal preparation of one's soul to preach the message to others has been accomplished, then one may know that he has not been presumptuous in his efforts to preach according to His Word. As Lloyd-Jones suggests, the right way to look upon the unction of the Spirit is to think of it as that which comes upon the preparation. An Old Testament incident which provides a good illustration which shows this relationship is the story of Elijah facing the false prophets of Israel on Mount Carmel. We are told that Elijah built an altar, then cut wood and put it on the altar, and that then he killed a bull and cut it in pieces and put the pieces on the wood. Having done all that, he then prayed for the fire to descend; and the fire fell. That is the suggested order.[41]

Carefully consider these questions for quite some time and reflect deeply upon the implications of them. Does it make sense to pray that God would bless the preaching of His Word when His Word will be replaced by the preaching of the preacher's sermon? If a preacher is involved in such a homiletical substitution, opting to preach a sermon rather than explain God's Word, can He expect that God would champion this effort? The more a preacher distances himself from the exposition of His Word the less confidence he may have that he will preach with unction. Unction aside, such a homiletical substitute will lack appropriate sincerity for preaching which is too common in preaching today.

Any message that is understood as God's truth rather than the preacher's sermon will be a message that will be marked by sincerity. How could it be otherwise? If a man is preaching according to God's Word, how could he not be in utmost sincerity in what he is saying? If however, he is preaching his sermon, only a man of hubris could preach from utmost sincerity.

Sincerity is the 'one thing without which all preaching is ineffective'. Sincerity manifests itself by the preacher's sheer honesty and authentic concern for God's truth and God's people.[42] Any preacher who truly bears concern for God's people would never substitute his sermon for God's Word. God is committed to blessing His Word, not a man's sermon. To the degree that a preacher's sermon is according to His

Word there is the prospect of both the empowering of the preacher and the using of that message for the benefit of God's people.

Unction – Preaching Through His Servant
Preachers do not naturally have unction. A preacher may naturally be very intelligent, or delightfully humorous, or shy and reticent, etc. Again, he may be a man who possesses a lot of charisma, and he may be a very forceful individual with a strong personality, and he may be a man who is thought of as being a strong natural leader, but this is not unction. Unction is not a natural commodity. It is a supernatural endowment. It is not possessed from moment to moment and from day to day. Unction is unique to the occasion of the preaching of His Word.

Preachers naturally have varying personalities and varying spiritual gifts. But one preacher who is called by God to preach, just as certainly as another preacher, may be used by God in his preaching in a dramatically different way and with dramatically different results. But both preachers can preach with God's unmistakable presence attending and empowering the preaching of His Truth. Both preachers, though God is well pleased to use them differently and is well pleased to provide varying results from their preaching, can equally possess unction. And both preachers, because they are both servants of the Living God, are required to give their best effort to their preaching. As it has been succinctly put,

> The ideal of preaching like the Old Testament prophets can be attained very rarely, if ever at all. But every preacher can commune with God like a prophet, can build character like a prophet, can pray like a prophet, can abhor sin like a prophet, can love souls like a prophet, and can try under the Holy Spirit to preach like a prophet.[43]

How many preachers view themselves and their calling as different from the prophets of old? How many men look at the biblical prophets and think, 'Now there is a man called by God, there is a true servant of God!' and then view themselves as a servant of God who is called by God to be involved in sermonizing and speechmaking? These men are destined to preach as though they are makers of sermons rather than a servant of God who is proclaiming God's Word.

I want to suggest that it makes a great deal of difference how a man views himself and his calling from God in regards to the unction that accompanies his preaching. As one prioritizes the significance of being one who is called by God to proclaim His truth, he will certainly want to serve Him well which means that he will have to have a strong grasp of the truth he will proclaim. A strong grasp of the message is important, but it is not enough. It is equally important that the message to be proclaimed has a strong grasp on the one who proclaims it. Preaching with unction is a matter of possessing a strong grasp of the truth and being possessed by a strong grasp of the truth. In other words, a preacher's feeling about the message has a lot to do with his communication of it.

Years ago someone asked Charles Haddon Spurgeon, 'How can I communicate like you do?' Spurgeon answered, 'It's very simple. Pour some kerosene over you, light a match, and people will come to watch you burn.'[44] That is about the only way some men in the pulpit would ever catch fire! Is God's Truth so exciting to you that it lights you up with excitement? Does it move you spiritually or is it simply cognitive content? If it does not move you, you may preach it, but you certainly are not ready to preach it because you have not allowed it to do in you and for you what it must do in you and for you in order to be a true messenger of the truth! If a preacher does not have a strong grasp of the message to be preached, and the message to be preached does not have a strong grasp on the preacher, how likely is it that he can preach with unction?

A Servant Of His Choosing. What makes a sermon interesting? Why do people listen to sermons, or what enables them to listen to them? No one can completely explain why we give our attention to a specific speaker of any kind, preacher or otherwise. Or, more especially, it is difficult to try to understand why some sermons are followed more intently than others. Although there are many factors involved, perhaps 'energy' would serve as a more adequate answer as any other explanation.[45] Though energy is helpful, perhaps enthusiasm is more descriptive. Enthusiasm, or the obvious demonstration that the preacher is convinced that he is involved in no small endeavor as he preaches God's Word, is absolutely crucial to preaching with interest and unction.

The greatest producer of enthusiasm for preaching comes from the enormously incomprehensible fact that one has been called by God to preach. Unfortunately, some men have 'gotten over' the incredible reality that God has called them to preach His Word just as some Christians have 'gotten over' the incredible reality that God has chosen them for salvation. A preacher who has grown complacent with his calling from God will preach complacently, and this kind of preaching will not be marked with unction! A preacher who, in effect, yawns at his calling is a preacher whose hearers will yawn at his preaching!

A preacher can not expect to be endowed with unction in his preaching and produce the interest that preaching with unction supplies if he is no longer resolute in fulfilling His God-given calling. Examine the Apostle Paul's words of testimony to the Ephesian elders regarding his relentless pursuit of completing the course God had set for him in the preaching of His Word. It is recorded in Acts 20:18-27 that Paul appealed to a testimony of proven zeal and unswerving commitment in proclaiming God's Word. He said:

> You yourselves know, from the first day that I set foot in Asia, how I was with you the whole time, serving the Lord with all humility and with tears and with trials which came upon me through the plots of the Jews; how I did not shrink from

declaring to you anything that was profitable, and teaching you publicly and from house to house, solemnly testifying to both Jews and Greeks of repentance toward God and faith in our Lord Jesus Christ. And now, behold, bound in spirit, I am on my way to Jerusalem, not knowing what will happen to me there, except that the Holy Spirit solemnly testifies to me in every city, saying that bonds and afflictions await me. But I do not consider my life of any account as dear to myself, in order that I may finish my course, and the ministry which I received from the Lord Jesus, to testify solemnly of the gospel of the grace of God. And now, behold, I know that all of you, among whom I went about preaching the kingdom, will see my face no more. Therefore, I testify to you this day, that I am innocent of the blood of all men. For I did not shrink from declaring to you the whole purpose of God.

The Apostle Paul had no doubts about his being chosen by God to preach His Word and that is why he was able to preach as he did. Paul's preaching was not marked by complacency but rather by solemn, bold, testifying and declaration. The weightiness of a man's preaching is commensurate to the weightiness of his calling from God and this contributes to his ability to preach with unction.

A Servant Under His Control. Preaching with unction occurs because the one preaching is controlled by God. Since unction comes from God, only one who is under His control will preach with God's unmistakable presence attending and empowering the preaching of His Truth. One who is under God's control will be one who is without corruption and will demonstrate an integrity that is essential for persuasion in preaching. Give attention to the words of Fenelon as he was convinced that a preacher, to be worthy of persuading others, ought to be an incorruptible man. According to Fenelon, 'it is mandatory that a preacher have an incorruptibility that will withstand everything and serve as a model for all. Without it he will not appear to be convinced of what he says, and, as a result, he will not be able to persuade others.'[46]

A preacher under God's control will preach with his emotions and passions aided and influenced by the presence of God in his life, by whom he is not only possessed but filled with the Holy Spirit. The only way one may preach under His control is to be controlled by, that is, filled with the Holy Spirit. To the degree to which one preaches without the filling of the Spirit, one will not preach under the control of the Spirit and forfeit the anointing of the Spirit. Lloyd-Jones is correct as he asserts that the element of pathos and emotion, that is, the reality of being moved, should always be very prominent in preaching. True preaching, after all, is God acting upon the preacher so that God is using this man rather than just a man uttering words. Therefore, the preacher is being used by God and he is under the influence of the Holy Spirit. This is what Paul referred to as preaching 'in demonstration of the Spirit and of power' (I Cor. 2:4). And that is always an essential element in true preaching.[47] True preaching, the preaching of a servant under God's control, will never be partial preaching – light without heat or heat without light. Again, Lloyd-Jones is instructive when he insists that, 'You must have light and heat, sermon plus preaching. Light without heat never affects anybody; heat without light is of no permanent value.'[48] When a man preaches as a servant of God who is under the control of God, his preaching will be attended with unction – preaching with heat and light.

Unction – Preaching On His Authority
Preaching by its very nature assumes authority – 'Thus saith the Lord.' If a preacher does not assume this authority he cannot escape a more subtle assumption and absolute corruption of authority – 'Thus saith the preacher.'[49] What the preacher says on his own authority will not be marked with unction. It may be characterized by a speculative tone or an arrogant assurance but it will not be possessed by God's unmistakable presence attending and empowering the preaching of His Truth.

> The preacher should never be apologetic, he should never ... be tentatively putting forward certain suggestions and ideas. That is not to be his attitude at all. He is a man, who is there to declare certain things; he is a man under commission and under authority. He should always know that he comes to the congregation as a sent messenger. Obviously this is not a matter of self-confidence; that is always deplorable in a preacher.... It means that you are aware of the solemnity and the seriousness and the importance of what you are doing. You have no self-confidence, but you are a man under authority, and you have authority; and this should be evident and obvious.[50]

It is not preaching God's authoritative Word with unction that should be of concern to a preacher and those who hear preaching. What should be of great concern to both the preacher and his hearers is the possibility of preaching in any way other than this.

Unction – Preaching By His Power

Though unction is not automatic so that it will be present every time a preacher preaches, it is true that a preacher can preach with unction consistently. There are preachers whose preaching is characterized by unction from sermon to sermon throughout the years. John MacArthur and David Jeremiah are two examples of preachers whose preaching is consistently empowered by God. The author has listened to these excellent expositors of God's Word preach for many years and has been impressed with the consistent excellence and powerful preaching of these men. Yet, I have been able to detect times when each of these men has demonstrated exceptional or additional unction beyond the level to with which they normally preach. In hearing these men preach one of their typical sermons a hearer will be impressed regarding the obvious empowering of these men as they preach. Unction is readily discernable. But occasionally, you hear them preach with an empowering that is atypical even for them and, as a hearer, you are aware of an uncommon level of empowering demonstrated in this sermon. Thus, unction may be consistent, and consistently demonstrated in great degree, only to be demonstrated at an even higher level from time to time. The bottom-line is this – they commonly preach with unction and occasionally preach with great unction!

For any preacher unction is a relative reality. Every preacher preaches with a common empowering of God in their preaching. But the common level of empowerment is replaced with a level that is above and sometimes below the norm. Even in the preaching of a John MacArthur or a David Jeremiah, having heard them preach in a few rare instances, my concluding evaluation of their preaching was something to the effect of, 'That was a good message but that is not as good a message as he normally preaches.' This is stated not to discredit these two incredible expositors but only to be perfectly honest about the reality of preaching in regard to unction – there is the usual level of unction, there is the greater-than-usual level of unction, and there is the less-than-usual level of unction. And such is the case for all who preach!

God produces the power and provides the enablement to preach powerfully. When unction is demonstrated, God and His will, His ways, His work, and His word are exalted and His people are impacted spiritually by the preaching of God's Word. When one is preaching with unction, only those who are spiritually dead or spiritually insensitive will fail to hear such a sermon with interest!

Unction – Preaching In His Conviction
Preaching must be done in great conviction. Desperate conviction gets hold of an audience. People listen in the presence of authentic conviction. The accent of conviction leaves the impression that something tremendous is at stake.[51] Conviction concerning the veracity and vital nature of the truth, not courting the approval of the hearers, is to be the concern of the preacher. Many hearers would be helped immeasurably to appropriate the following counsel:

> Consult yourself if you would know whether the speakers you hear are doing well. If they make a living impression upon you, if they render your mind attentive and sensitive to the things they say, if they warm you and raise you above yourself, then you may believe without fear that they have reached the goal of eloquence. If instead of moving you or inspiring strong feelings in you, they only act to please you and to make you admire the brilliance and the nicety of their thoughts and expressions, tell yourself that they are false speakers.[52]

The weakness of some preaching is that it does not affirm anything vital. It has no note of authority and imperativeness because it has no roots. Nothing is more pitiful than a preacher without deep-seated convictions. Someone has obviously exaggerated the case in picturing a preacher who said meekly in one of his sermons, 'If you do not believe, as it were, and repent in a measure you will go to hell, so to speak.'[53]

Preaching without conviction is an indictment on both the message and the messenger. A sermon that can be preached without conviction is a sermon that should have never been preached at all. A preacher without conviction is a public display of hypocrisy! Whatever the preacher is saying in his objective message to his hearers is being overridden by his subjective message to his hearers. His subjective message to his hearers is this – 'Don't believe anything I am telling you since it is obvious that I sure don't believe it!' A preacher without conviction is not a preacher who can preach with unction. When there is the preaching in true conviction there will be an obvious unction in that message. Conviction 'is the surest proof of the power of a ministry' and the incredible thing about the preaching of John the Baptist is that his preaching convicted even the Pharisees.[54] 'There is a contagion and power in personal conviction that cannot be equaled in any other approach.'[55] An uninteresting preacher will always be a man who lacks conviction and, therefore, lacks unction.

Unction – Preaching With His Passion
The first condition of an interesting sermon is that there is a fused interest for the truth being proclaimed by the preacher as well as the congregation. He may be on fire with what has little interest for them – result: heat in the pulpit and coldness in the pews. A preacher will never be on fire with a message unless it gets hold of him entirely. A congregation will not respond unless the truth reaches them.[56] It has been said that 'Nothing great is ever accomplished in this world without passion.' There must be urgency as well as clarity in our preaching. 'A packed head may make the people amazed, but a hot heart will make them act.'[57]

Preaching with passion is the result of the truth being preached profoundly impacting the heart of the preacher. Passion is also key to a preacher being used by God to impact those who hear him preach.

Passion is not a luxury item but must be viewed as a basic commodity in preaching. And why would this not be the case? In preaching, a preacher is not simply imparting information, he is dealing with souls, he is dealing with people on the way to eternity. A preacher deals with matters not only of life and death in this world, but with eternal destiny. Nothing can be so terribly urgent.[58] When one preaches it should certainly be evident that he understands the significance of his work. To the degree that he does, he will preach with passion.

Passion in preaching, or the preacher's obvious felt significance for what he is saying, has always been viewed as a priority. Even Jonathan Edwards viewed preaching with passion positively as he wrote:

> I think an exceeding affectionate way of preaching about the great things of religion, has in itself no tendency to beget false apprehensions of them; but on the contrary a much greater tendency to beget true apprehensions of them, than a moderate, dull, indifferent way of speaking of them.[59]

Securing Interest: How Interest is Secured in an Introduction

Edwards went on to conclude that, 'Our people do not so much need to have their heads stored, as to have their hearts touched' and the real need of our hearers is 'that sort of preaching, that has the greatest tendency to do this (to touch their hearts).'[60] Passion in a preacher, which is evident even in the movement of the body and facial expressions, is a painting of the thoughts of his soul.[61]

The most legitimate way an expositor can impact the emotions of those who hear him preach is by appropriate preparation so that his own heart is gripped by his understanding of the passage. 'This is a matter of feeling one's message. Nothing touches the emotions of people more effectively than for a preacher to feel his message.... The fire in his own heart will invariably strike fire in the hearts of others. They will be convinced that he really believes what he says.'[62] In order to preach with unction one must be passionate in the preaching of God's truth.

Unction – Preaching From His Motives

If a preacher does not preach with passion, which suggests a lack of sense of urgency, since he is there between God and men speaking between time and eternity, then he has no business to be in the pulpit. The pulpit is no place for calm, cool, scientific detachment in significant temporal issues and eternal matters. Calm, cool detachment may possibly be acceptable in a philosopher or an educator, but it is unthinkable in a preacher because of the unique situation in which he is involved.

Preaching must always be characterized by persuasiveness. An appropriate motivation in preaching is to persuade people. The preacher does not just say things with the attitude of 'take it or leave it'. He desires to persuade them of the truth of his message; he wants them to see it; he is trying to do something to them, to influence them. He is not just providing a learned discussion on a text, he is certainly not giving a display of his knowledge; he is dealing with the lives of people and he wants to move them, to take them with him, to lead them to the Truth. That is his whole purpose. So if this element is not present, whatever else it may be, it is not preaching.[63] Fenelon stated the case for passion in preaching through the preacher's motive to move his hearers by the very truth that moves the preacher in the act of preaching. To preach with passion and cause others to become passionate about the truth proclaimed is the height of eloquence. 'Eloquence consists not only in proof but also in the ability to arouse the passions. In order to arouse the passions, it is necessary to portray them. Hence, I believe that all eloquence can be reduced to proving, to portraying, and to moving. Every brilliant thought which does not drive towards one of these three things is only a conceit.'[64]

According to Fenelon, the true significance of preaching lies in the ability of the preacher to persuade his hearers. Anything that does not make a contribution to persuade is to be condemned for preaching. As viewed by Fenelon, the most basic motive of a preacher is to persuade them to subscribe themselves to the truth proclaimed in the sermon.

> Solid and well-expounded proofs are unquestionably pleasing; the lively and natural movements of the speaker have much charm; faithful and animated portraitures enchant. Thus the three things which we make essential to eloquence give pleasure; but they are not limited to this effect. I praise in a discourse all the pleasing traits which minister to persuasion; and I reject all the pleasing traits provided by a speaker to exhibit himself and to amuse his hearers with his wit, rather than to absorb them utterly in his subject. Therefore, I believe it is necessary to condemn all those things which serve only for sparkle, and which have about them nothing substantial and nothing conducive to persuasion.[65]

A passionate preacher does not preach with passion simply because he knows that the truth he proclaims can make a vital difference in the lives of the people who hear him. Additional passion will be evident to the degree that the preacher has compassion for those to whom he preaches. 'Compassion carries with it a great feeling for the afflicted and an active effort to help bear the load and relieve the pressure.'[66] When the hearers can sense that the preacher is not just offering truth that is valuable to them but he offers them valuable truth because he earnestly desires their ultimate well-being, they will attend the sermon with increased interest. The discernable compassion of the preacher provides refreshment through the ministry of the Word from one who has a heart for those who hear him preach. This refreshment provided to the hearers enables the hearers to listen with greater interest to the one who is preaching to them. Unction is due to a passionate preacher who has great compassion for his hearers so that they can be benefited by God's Word.

Unction – Preaching For His Purposes
Certainly a major consideration for the energy of a sermon is the preacher's personal interest in the truth he will be expounding and, consequently, his desire to preach the sermon. Obviously, if one is about to preach yet without a compelling desire to do so, not only will unction be conspicuously absent but his purpose for preaching this sermon is deficient of divine prerogatives. Consider these comments regarding purposeful preaching:

> He must impress the people by the fact that he is taken up and absorbed by what he is doing. He is full of matter, and he is anxious to impart this. He is so moved and thrilled by it himself that he wants everybody else to share in this. He is concerned about them; that is why he is preaching to them. He is anxious about them; anxious to help them, anxious to tell them the truth of God. So he does it with energy, with zeal, and with this obvious concern for people. In other words a preacher who seems to be detached from the Truth, and who is just saying a number of things which may be very good and true and excellent in themselves, is not a preacher at all.[67]

But what is it the preacher is absorbed in doing? What purposes possess him if he is to preach with unction?

Paul Scherer's assessment of a good sermon establishes a well-balanced, multi-faceted criterion for assessing all sermons. He affirmed that a sermon worthy of the name is to a greater or lesser degree a combination of preaching that is doctrinal, expository, ethical, pastoral, and evangelistic. He said that a sermon without exposition, with nothing which leads to a clearer understanding of God's Word, is without its highest sanction. A sermon without doctrine, with nothing which leads to a clearer understanding of the cardinal tenets of the Christian faith, is without foundation. A sermon without the ethical is pointless. A sermon without the pastoral is spiritless. A sermon without the evangelistic is Christless and useless altogether![68] Unless a preacher is compelled to preach by the same purposes God has for the preaching of His Word, he cannot preach with unction.

Unction – Preaching To His Glory
An expositor's great opportunity to proclaim the gospel of Jesus Christ is the regular worship services of the church.[69] Even though he may be preaching to the membership of the church, there is never warrant to assume that everyone who hears the message is a Christian. A pastor must edify God's people and, as a true shepherd, he must feed the sheep with the Word of God. However, unbelievers do not need to be edified. They need to be saved. Just as the believer needs to be being sanctified through the preaching of God's Word, the unbeliever needs to be justified by faith in Jesus Christ. Since the only need of an unbeliever is a relationship with the Lord Jesus Christ, it means that we must proclaim the gospel if we are to serve them at the point of their need.

The only message that will save the world is contained in the Word of God. Any message proclaimed from God's Word must not be without the message of salvation. Roy Short provides a helpful challenge for fervent gospel preaching when he writes: 'Let the preacher meditate upon it until it grips his heart. Let him ponder it until it flames in his soul. Let him turn it over in his mind until its glory and eternal freshness so sweep over his spirit that his lips burn to speak, and his whole being is crying out 'Woe is me if I preach not the Gospel."[70]

Otto Baab was not at all reticent to prescribe the prophetic Word as that which is needed in our culture, and this need for our culture was addressed by him in 1958. Though it was undoubtedly needed then, how much more so now? Baab wrote:

> The preacher has one imperative obligation – to make known with fervor and conviction the independence of God and the ultimate authority of the One who subjects human motives and actions to the searching scrutiny of his holy will. More preaching on the theme of God as judge will restore to the gospel the moral quality which it once had in its biblical setting. Such preaching will also serve to identify plainly the ways of God so that they cannot be confused with the ways of man.[71]

I do not believe that a pastor should have to decide whether his sermon is to be for the cause of edification or for evangelism. It should be intended to accomplish both. There are only two types of people in the world and in the church – believers and unbelievers. God's Word is the solution for the needs of both. God is glorified as believers are sanctified by the explanation of His Word just as He is glorified as unbelievers are converted by explanation of the gospel. The man who preaches with unction is one who realizes that his preaching is for God's glory.

Preaching with unction as detailed above is not as commonplace as it should be because many factors are necessary for it to be a reality. There are many reasons why it is absent or not sufficiently present as one preaches. The crux of the matter, as suggested by the eleven references to the pronoun 'His' in the previous subtitles, is that the measure of a preacher's unction is an indicator of one's humble dependence upon God for one's highest pursuit in this life – to be a faithful ambassador of the living God.

Persuasion

A sermon and a lecture are two entirely different things. A lecture primarily is intended to instruct and, to a lesser extent, may even be intended to entertain. An expository sermon must teach and certainly should be interesting, but it ultimately, as with any true sermon, seeks to persuade as the principal objective.[72]

All learning begins at the feeling level. People accept what they feel disposed to accept, and they reject what they feel disposed to reject. If their attitude is positive, they tend to embrace what they hear. If their attitude is negative, they tend to walk away from it.[73] If hearers have negative feelings about the one preaching to them they will probably reject what he is saying, since they reject him. If the hearers like the one preaching to them, or if they believe the one preaching to them is genuinely interested in their benefit, then he can be used mightily to get them to believe and act differently than they were believing and acting before he preached to them. Dale Carnegie has written: If a man's heart is filled with discord and ill feeling toward you, you probably will not win him to your way of thinking. People can't be forced or driven to agree with us but they may be led to agree with us.[74]

When a person says 'No' and really means it, his entire organism – glandular, nervous, muscular – gathers itself together into a condition of rejection. There is, usually in minute but sometimes in observable degree, a physical withdrawal, or readiness for withdrawal. The whole neuromuscular system, in short, sets itself on guard against acceptance. Where, on the contrary, a person says 'Yes,' none of the withdrawing activities take place. This person is in a forward-moving, accepting, open attitude. Hence the more 'Yeses' we can, at the very outset, induce, the more likely we are to succeed in capturing the attention for our ultimate proposal.[75]

Socrates is honored as one of the wisest persuaders who ever lived. His technique, now called the 'Socratic method', was based upon getting affirmative responses from questions he would raise. He would ask questions with which his opponents would have to agree. He kept on winning one admission after another until he had an armful of yeses. He kept on asking questions until finally, almost without realizing it, his opponent found himself embracing a conclusion that he would have bitterly denied a few minutes previously.[76]

J. Pierpont Morgan observed that a man usually has two good reasons for doing anything: one that sounds good and the real one.[77] In our preaching of God's Word to His people it must always be the case that we appeal to motives that are biblical and therefore God-honoring, and that we challenge the hearers to live according to the truth expounded from God's Word. Someone has captured the essence of persuasion as they wrote, 'The fool tries to convince me with his reasons, the wise man persuades me with MY OWN.'[78] However, such a view of persuasion is faulty even though it is prevalent in much preaching today. This view of persuasion is antithetical to expository preaching.

In expositional preaching, a wise man and a faithful expositor will persuade men by describing and corroborating God's reasons for every thought, attitude, motive, or action to be taken up or set aside. Expository preaching, then, becomes the method by which people can be persuaded by God's reasons so thoroughly that His reasons become their own. Is there really a need for such an agenda of persuasion for people to own God's reasons for their own? Well certainly there is from an ethical and moral perspective. That is obvious. But it is needed for a very pragmatic reason as well, that is, because fallen man does not naturally do that which is in keeping with God's reasoning. And believers, though equipped with the Holy Spirit of God and are therefore enabled to do what the reasoning of God would require of them, may need to be informed or reminded of God's reasoning.

Basically humans tend to do what they desire to do. Obviously there are limiting factors, but in the final analysis the fact remains that we do not do many things we don't want to do or don't choose to do for one reason or another. People are constantly pushed and pressured to do or not do many things, but still they usually decide their course of action on the basis of some dominant need, want, or desire.[79] Ralph L. Lewis suggests that a preacher must excite some desire or passion in the hearers and satisfy the hearers that there is a connection between the action to which he will persuade them and the gratification of the desire or passion which he excites.[80]

It is possible for one to influence others and control their behavior only as one affects the desires and purposes of others. Persuasion can be viewed as the process of revitalizing old desires, purposes, and ideals or persuasion can be viewed as the process of substituting new desires, purposes, and ideals in the place of old ones.[81] Expository preaching accomplishes both since it can revitalize and substitute the desires, purposes, and ideals that God would have them to hold.

It is said that Lacordaire, the famous French Dominican preacher of the nineteenth century, once visited a village and listened to the preaching of the local priest – a saintly soul with a wonderful pastoral gift but no talent for oratory. The villagers expressed their astonishment that so great a man should dare to listen to one who was so inferior to himself as a preacher. But Lacordaire replied, 'When I preach people crowd the churches, and even sit on the top of the confession boxes to hear me; but when your saintly priest preaches they go into the confessionals.' It may be that, after all, the obscure priest was the better preacher, for he knew how to touch the conscience.[82] Eloquence is nothing but the art of instructing and persuading people by moving them.[83] The exposition of Scripture is the platform from which the greatest persuasion can be accomplished since it brings the hearers to a more insightful instruction of God's Word which the Holy Spirit will use to persuade them to obey.

However, it is suggested that, 'If reason fails to change a man, know that if you touch the lever of his affections, you move his world. There is no motion without emotion.'[84] While I agree that there is no motion without emotion I would suggest that to move a man's world through the lever of his affections that have been touched without his reason being substantially instructed and informed is nothing other than manipulation. It is through expository preaching that manipulation is avoided because the affections are justly moved as they should be moved, in response to truth which has been understood for the first time or understood as it has never been understood before. Through the exposition of Scripture hearers can understand the true significance of the truth of Scripture. The affection that is vital is the desire to live consistently with that which is deemed truly important. As it has been rightly asserted about the cause and effect relationship of preaching, 'The motive must be worthy of the deed; the result must be worthy of the effort, and the suggested action should lead to the desired result.'[85] However, the motives, deeds, actions, and results must be consistent with Scripture as it is understood through a clear and thorough explanation of its meaning. This entails expository preaching.

Lewis suggests six faith-based promises: success, satisfaction, integrity, sympathy, duty, and love. He also suggests six fear-based threats: failure, suffering, guilt, indignation, insecurity, and selfishness.[86] In a very real sense all of our daily actions are predicated upon, are motivated by either a promise of benefit, pleasure, reward, and well-being or they are overshadowed by a threat of judgment, pain, punishment, and shame.[87] It is only legitimate to show the hearers how good it will be if they follow the counsel of Scripture as well as warn the hearers how bad it will be if they refuse to do so.[88] This is the extent of persuasion an expositor can and must exert upon his hearers. God's Word is not an 'It doesn't matter whether it is obeyed or disobeyed' matter. Any preacher who believes that it is ought to never preach again! And any preacher who rejects such an idea ought to reflect it in his preaching!

Any true definition of preaching must say that it is accomplished by a man who is there to deliver a message from God, a message from God to people. To use the language of Paul, he is 'an ambassador for Christ'. That is what he is. He has been sent, he is a commissioned person, and he is standing there as the mouthpiece of God and of Christ to address people. In other words, he is not there merely to talk to them. He is not there to entertain them. A preacher is there to do something to all of those who hear him preach. He is there to produce results of various kinds but he is there to influence people. He is not merely to influence a part of them; he is not only to influence their minds, or only their emotions, or merely to bring pressure to bear upon their wills and to induce them to some kind of activity. He is there to deal with the whole person; and his preaching is meant to affect the whole person at the very center of life. Preaching should make such a difference to a man who is listening that he is never the same again. In other words, preaching is a transaction between the preacher and the listener. It does something for the soul of a man, for the whole of the person, the entire man; it deals with him in a vital and radical manner.[89]

Preaching is designed by God to address us in such a manner as to bring us under judgment; and it deals with us in such a way that we feel our whole life is involved, and we go out saying, 'I can never go back and live just as I did before. This has done something to me, it has made a difference to me. I am a different person as the result of listening to this.'[90]

We have been thinking about preaching with unction and preaching persuasively. These will be a reality only if there is an authoritative declaration of Scripture. In the absence of an authoritative declaration of God's Word, a declaration motivated to explain and apply the God-intended meaning of the passage, unction is subject to be replaced by showmanship and persuasion is prone to become manipulation. An authoritative declaration of Scripture will occur only if one believes that Scripture is authoritative and it is to be declared in keeping with its nature, which is God's Word to man. Additionally, an authoritative declaration occurs only as the expositor preaches consistently with his belief system so that the sermon he preaches is not so much his sermon as it is God's Word explained clearly, persuasively and mandating an appropriate response from the hearers. It is futile to try to separate an authoritative declaration of Scripture from the true purpose for preaching which, according to J. I. Packer, is 'to inform, persuade, and call forth an appropriate response to the God whose message and instruction are being delivered.'[91]

Authoritative Declaration
Much of the approach and theory of preaching at present is dedicated to the inductive approach. The last three decades of the twentieth century were inundated with books advocating the inductive methodology and decrying deductive preaching, especially expository preaching, because it is rampantly deductive. Actually, the noxious weed of inductive preaching began to sprout three decades into the twentieth century. Though its faulty rationale was being advocated incipiently, it was soon championed precipitously decades later by those of the same theological bent, holding a weak view of Scripture. Consider the following quotation,

> As a matter of strategy, if for no other reason, the new preaching must be inductive in its emphasis and approach. Inevitably so, because the whole spirit and method of thought in our day is inductive, and if we are to win the men of today to the truths of faith we must use the method by which they find truth in other fields. In the old days the text was a truth assumed to be true, and the preacher only needed to expound its meaning, deduce

its lessons and apply them. Often enough a text was a tiny peg from which a vast weight of theology depended, and so long as men accepted both the text and the theology all went well. Of course, the old formula, 'The Bible teaches, therefore it is true; the Church affirms, therefore it is valid,' is still sufficient for those who accept such authorities. But in an age of inquiry, when the authority of the Bible and the Church is questioned by so many, such an appeal does not carry conviction.[92]

This is perhaps the most valuable statement one may discover about inductive preaching! It is the way of preaching for the man or the woman (preachers of the inductive camp do not think twice about the illegitimacy of women pastors and preachers) who does not hold to the authority of Scripture and the veracity of biblical texts! This statement is serviceable to affirm the opposite – as long as people accept the truthfulness of the text and the authority of the Bible, 'all went well' with preaching as an attempt to expound the text, deduce lessons and apply them to life.

One other statement needs to be uncovered regarding the purported merit of inductive preaching, which I believe only serves to condemn it.

> The inductive method is indispensable in teaching the genetic truths of faith, doubly so in an age when a spongy texture of mind deplores all dogma and loves disembodied ideas that float in vapory phrases in the air, binding us to nothing positive.[93]

I don't see how a greater condemning blow could be voiced to the inductive method than those intended to commend it. If one is really seeking to make a ministry of suggesting 'disembodied ideas that float in vapory phrases in the air, binding us to nothing positive', then one could do no better than to champion inductive preaching.

I will have to admit that if I did not believe in an authoritative, infallible, and inerrant Bible I would be an inductive preacher! Why not? If the Bible is in error, if the

Bible is not a sound guide for faith and practice, if the Bible does not truly represent God and His revelation, if the Bible does not contain timeless truth, then I would not bother with it, submit to it, or proclaim it deductively by expounding the meaning of its passages! Under such conditions, I would be interested in and advocate my views of subjective, relative reality, situational ethics, the opinions, speculations and theories of worldly people. Why not? If it is not authoritative, infallible, and inerrant, what do you have to lose by setting it aside? Oh, but since it is authoritative, and since it is infallible, and since it is inerrant, why would one do anything less than give it the clearest, most definitive explanation possible as one declares what God has given to us to guide our faith and practice?

People are quick to assert as fact that preaching is broken and therefore needs to be fixed. The rationale goes something like this. 'Preaching is broken since it does not work. It does not work because lost people are turned off by it and Christians are bored by it. Therefore, you can't grow a Church by dealing with the Bible in a serious or substantial way.' Well, something certainly is broken, but what is broken is not preaching. Preaching is not broken, it has never been broken, and it never will be broken. When lost people are convicted by the truth of God's Word, then preaching works! When people who profess to be Christians are bored by the preaching of God's Word, the problem may only be the disinterest in spiritual things by those who claim to love God yet who do not care for His Word!

There are people who are in the Church and they call themselves 'Christians', but are really only interested in themselves and their sins. These people desire preaching that allows them to exist as they are and maintain the interests they have without any interference from preaching. They desire to be comforted by sermons that will affirm the lives they are living rather than the proclamation of truth that will confront them, convict them and call them to a corrected way of living.

Therefore, these people are disinterested in any message that carefully clarifies the claims of Scripture as it is faithfully proclaimed. To do so would be immediately threatening to their existing status. Why would unrepentant, sinful, religious people who say they are Christians, or true Christians who are abiding in sin, have a great desire to understand the Bible? Such people are not in the market for a man who can and will expound the Scriptures in uncompromised exactitude. When these people hear such preaching, they are quick to claim that preaching doesn't work, preaching is ineffective, preaching is broken. But is this true? No, not at all! If such people are not interested in preaching that explains and proclaims the Word of God, then the problem is not God's Word or God's messenger but the people who desire the things of the world more than the things of God! But when these worldly people hear the truth of God's Word explained and they suffer distress because of the truth they have heard, truth that makes it painfully clear that they must confess and repent of sin, then preaching works! The purpose of preaching is not, and never has been, intended to placate people in their sin. Just the opposite is true. The claim of the ineffectiveness of preaching cannot be validated by sinful hearers who do not want to be challenged by it. Preaching is not broken and it does not to be fixed. A great proof of that fact is evidenced by sinful people who dread it because it works so powerfully when they are exposed to it!

The truth is simply this – people who do not desire earnestly to be exposed to the truth of God's Word, to understand God's Word, and make whatever personal changes that may be necessitated by God's Word in order to be in line with it are not reputable sources to judge preaching! A weak view of the Word of God and an unimpassioned desire to live the truth must be challenged rather than facilitated by those who preach it! The purpose of preaching is not to wed together Holy Scripture and an unholy world so that Scripture is viewed as means to reconcile the precepts and priorities of the world to the Kingdom of God. Jack Sanford addresses this responsibility for preachers not to be 'the world's reconciliators'. He writes:

> The world's reconciliators would water down the gospel ethic, whitewash sin, and seek a compromise between the sons of God and the children of Satan.... The world and the Christian are entirely different, and the clash they have with each other is inevitable.
>
> How can the preacher, as a herald of God, deal honestly with this terrible ethical delimma? Can he hope to present a first-century, ethical system as a pattern for life to men struggling to get along in an atomic-hydrogen age? Is the rigid standard of life as portrayed in the Sermon on the Mount really only an 'interim ethic,' presented for that handful of fishermen who expected the kingdom of God to be brought to a quick, triumphant climax? Have modern sophistication and intellectualism made the Carpenter's demands obsolete and impossible? Are the tensions and pressures of modern living beyond the scope of Christian ethics? Is the demand of the Lord that his people shine with the brightness of purity really beyond the ability of human achievement? Are the ethics of Jesus realistic and to be taken seriously by modern men? These, and many more kindred questions, must be answered by the preacher in his pulpit ministry of the gospel of Christ. The answers he gives dare not be 'other worldly' with the emphasis upon the by and by; but they must be honest, straightforward answers, applicable to life as it is lived now.
>
> The world would dismiss, rather than answer, these pressing questions by simply ignoring them as irrelevant and idealistic. Self is first with the world, so there is really no ethical problem at all. By its own actions, the world has been saying for centuries that man has moved far beyond the foolish and senile assertion of the Sermon on the Mount. We live in the era of science, the time of practicality, the age of the Big Me, when men are concerned only for what they can profit for their own person.[94]

Sanford is right. Preachers must not place themselves in the impossible situation of trying to feed believers who desire spiritual growth through the exposition of Scripture and make this palatable and non-offensive to unbelievers or those who call themselves Christians but have no appetite for spiritual truth.

Even as we content ourselves to preach uncompromisingly the truth of God's Word, we must understand that few sermons demand the entire attention of the hearers. The demand that the sermon makes upon the hearer in order to understand and follow the sermon is a significant factor which may inhibit or accentuate attention. The hearer's attention may be diminished if the demand is too great just as it may be diminished if it is not sufficiently demanding. Too often an intelligent, spiritual listener does not need more than half his mind half of the time to follow the typical sermon. This will cause them to be inattentive out of a boredom that is furnished by the preacher. On the other hand, if the sermon demands an over-strained attention to complicated textual detail this may cause them to become inattentive, having given up the effort to follow the preacher's exposition.[95] The needed balance is established through movement or, as will be discussed in chapter eleven, the progression of the sermon and the advancement of thought in the sermon. The most dependable interest factor is movement, movement of developing thought. As long as a sermon is going somewhere the congregation will go with it.[96]

The sense that the message is going somewhere is aided by good structure for the sermon, in other words, a good sermon outline. Sermon structure will be considered in the second part of this book. For now it is sufficient to understand that interest is affected by a structured sermon as opposed to a sermon that is preached without any discernable development or progression of thought throughout the delivery of the message.

Securing interest in the sermon introduction is dependent upon both content means and conveyance means. The specific content means for securing interest include the incorporation of flesh and blood scenarios, vital personal questions, assertions regarding the immediate and long-term ramifications for disobedience or obedience to the truth, and assurances that the truth of the passage to be examined will be determinative as to the productivity of one's life of service for the Lord. General content means of securing interest include problem and solutions, as well as questions and answers. The conveyance means for securing interest in the introduction include knowledge of the text and subject-matter, a developed connection of the subject-matter and new insights for the hearers, unction, persuasion, and authoritative delivery.

Consider the Following Questions

1. What are the three postulates germane to securing interest through means of content?

2. How are the internal, conditional needs of a hearer distinguished from the external, corrective needs of a hearer?

3. What is the bottom-line regarding a hearer's willingness to follow a preacher as he preaches? What does a preacher with insignificant knowledge invite from his hearers?

4. What does a sermon introduction need to demonstrate when familiar passages are to be preached?

5. What does the practice of good expositors, or the essence of preaching, accomplish for the hearer while the Scriptures are being expounded?

6. How does an effective introduction affect the hearer's sense of personal curiosity and personal benefit?

Words to Live and Preach by

The Acquisition of Wisdom

Proverbs 1:5 – A wise man will hear and increase his learning, and a man of understanding will acquire wise counsel,

Proverbs 3:7-8 – Do not be wise in your own eyes; fear the Lord and turn away from evil. It will be healing to your body and refreshment to your bones.

Proverbs 4:13 – Take hold of instruction; do not let go. Guard her, for she is your life.

Proverbs 4:20-3 – My son, give attention to my words; incline your ear to my sayings. Do not let them depart from your sight; keep them in the midst of your heart. For they are life to those who find them and health to all their body. Watch over your heart with all diligence, for from it flow the springs of life.

Proverbs 7:1-4 – My son, keep my words and treasure my commandments within you. Keep my commandments and live, and my teaching as the apple of your eye. Bind them on your fingers; write them on the tablet of your heart. Say to wisdom, "You are my sister," and call understanding your intimate friend;

Proverbs 9:10 – The fear of the Lord is the beginning of wisdom, and the knowledge of the Holy One is understanding.

Proverbs 14:6 – A scoffer seeks wisdom and finds none, but knowledge is easy to one who has understanding.

Proverbs 15:14 – The mind of the intelligent seeks knowledge, but the mouth of fools feeds on folly.

Chapter Six

Stating the Purpose: An Indication of a Passionate Preacher

The Predominance of Unintentional Preaching

'Sir, why are you preaching this passage?' If you want to stump most preachers, or cause them to be almost speechless, then ask them that question just before they deliver their sermons! Many preachers would either be without a clue in trying to provide an appropriate answer to the question or they would respond to the question with an answer that would only serve to indicate how unintentional they are in their preaching. After a pause accompanied by a most incredulous look, you might hear something like: 'The Lord led me to preach this passage' or 'I'm paid by the church to preach, among other things, so they expect me to preach every Sunday' or 'Because I'm preaching through the book of Romans and this is the point at which I left off last week, so this is the next passage to be expounded' or 'I believe we really need to understand this passage of God's Word.' Such responses would only evidence the plight of so much preaching today – it is predominantly unintentional!

All of the above responses are good ones, as far as they go, but they do not go far enough to instill a man with the kind of intentionality that will be a driving force in his preaching.

Obviously, we want to believe that God would approve our preaching of the text to be expounded. Certainly, we want to be worthy and responsible pastor who exalts preaching as a priority in ministry and, thus, fulfill the expectations the church has for him. How admirable it is to systematically preach through consecutive verses of entire books of the Bible. Of course we desire people to understand every passage that will be the focus of our exposition. However, not one of the previous responses constitutes a sufficient basis of intentionality for preaching a passage of the Bible.

In his book, *Teaching to Change Lives*, Howard Hendricks relates an experience which illustrates the importance that purpose was discovered to have for preaching. He writes:

> I once went to preach in a church on the West Coast, and as I got up to speak I found this sign facing me on the lectern: 'What in the world are you trying to do to these people?' It nearly derailed my message.
>
> Afterward I asked the church's pastor about the sign. He said, 'Hendricks, I've been preaching for twelve years without an objective, and it finally dawned on me one day that if I didn't know what I was doing there's a good possibility they didn't know what they were supposed to do. So I've started coming into the pulpit with clear-cut objectives.'[1]

Have you made such a discovery about your preaching? The pastor was correct. If you have not understood your purpose for preaching the sermon, neither will your hearers.

No enterprise should be as intentional as the preaching of God's Word. The absence of such purpose in preaching is a weakness but it is one that can and must be corrected. J. H. Jowett writes persuasively for the correction of a common fault in preaching, which is preaching without a clear purpose. Reflect at great length over Jowett's well-stated words.

> Let us put it (the purpose) into words. Don't let it hide in the cloudy realm of vague assumptions. Let us arrest ourselves in

the very midst of our assumptions, and compel ourselves to name and register our ends. Let us take a pen in hand, and in order that we may still further banish the peril of vacuity let us commit to paper our purpose and ambition for the day. Let us give it the objectivity of a mariner's chart: let us survey our course, and steadily contemplate our haven. If, when we turn to the pulpit stair, some angel were to challenge us for the statement of our mission, we ought to be able to make immediate answer, without hesitancy or stammering, that this or that is the urgent errand on which we seek to serve our Lord today. But the weakness of the pulpit is too often this – we are prone to drift through a service when we ought to steer. Too often 'we are out on the ocean sailing,' but we have no destination: we are 'out for anywhere,' and nowhere in particular. The consequence is, the service has the fashion of a vagrancy when it ought to be possessed by the spirit of a crusade.[2]

Of this we must be certain – a sermon that does not reflect a definite purpose reflects a purposeless preacher.

The Need for Purposeful Preaching

All preaching must be purposeful, and this applies to expository preaching as well. Much is needed to be done in the lives of the hearers every time God's Word is proclaimed. As C. H. Spurgeon said, 'Some are dead, you must rouse them; some are troubled, you must comfort them; others are burdened, you must point them to the burden-bearer. Still more are puzzled, you must enlighten and guide them; still others are careless and indifferent, you must warn and woo them.'[3]

Certainly one of the things needed for better preaching 'is a new appreciation of how sermons gain, not lose, their power, subtlety, and effectiveness by starting with direct, plain thought about what a preacher wants to see happen and why.'[4]

What a preacher should want to see happen is that his hearers understand why he is preaching his sermon and that they be resolute in incorporating the truth of the text into their lives. Stephen Olford designates the purpose of the sermon as the 'burden of the message'.[5] It is the burden of the message that makes it clear to the congregation why the message is being preached. As the burden of the sermon, the purpose statement then requires that the preacher has understood the critical nature the passage to be expounded has for those who will hear it. The critical nature of the sermon is expressed through the burden of the sermon.

When the purpose for preaching the passage has been discovered and can be written out carefully, it will be clear to those who hear the sermon that it is of utmost importance to the preacher that the message be declared, and that the message be embraced. The preacher will not be viewed as a detached voice, sounding a message with neutrality. It will be apparent that he knows the value of the truth he declares, first of all because it is God's truth, but also because of the benefits of that truth in the lives of those who respond as God requires.[6]

The listeners, because of a clearly articulated purpose statement, can sense that the preacher, himself, views the preaching of the sermon as a vital matter. In so doing, the listeners will understand that it is vital for them to listen attentively to the sermon and respond to it appropriately. In other words, the preacher's burden becomes the hearer's burden. They, then, become as concerned that the truth of the text becomes part of their lives as he is concerned that it becomes part of their daily experience.

In his 1875 Yale Lectures on Preaching, John Hall said, 'Have an aim in each sermon. Do not enter on it because you must preach something. If anyone should say to you, "What are you driving at?" you should have no hesitation in answering.'[7] A. T. Pierson is unequivocal in his connecting purposeful preaching with powerful preaching as he insistently remarks:

Stating the Purpose: An Indication of a Passionate Preacher

If we are to have a new era of power in preaching, we must have a more definite result, toward which all else moves. An essay may be ingenious, and an exposition original and yet lack oratorical power; as Whately said, the man 'aims at nothing, and hits it.' Above all others, the preacher needs the power of an engrossing purpose.[8]

Not only is it important that the preacher has a purpose for the sermon, but more importantly the purpose of the sermon must have the preacher.

In order for this to be so, the purpose must be closely related to the subject-matter of the message. G. Campbell Morgan said 'the introduction should be characterized by pertinence to the subject' and in the introduction there must be 'always an indication of what is proposed to be done'.[9] The preacher's grasp of the sermon's subject and the objective of the sermon are 'the greatest aid to homiletic power'.[10]

If this is true, then the purpose of a sermon is not just one additional element among many other elements a preacher needs to incorporate into the sermon. The sermon's purpose works to galvanize the sermon's proposition and its attending structure into a significant assessment of the text. The sermon's purpose strengthens the essential unity of the sermon. In his book, *The Preacher's Workshop*, John Wood captured the role that the sermon's purpose statement makes toward the unity of the sermon:

> In respect to the purpose statement of the sermon it is true that the preacher should aim to say one thing only, and to say it well. Any material that does not ultimately further his objective should be ruthlessly expunged from the sermon – no matter how attractive it may seem to him. He is out for a verdict, and he cannot afford to send his people down interesting cul-de-sacs while en route to his ultimate destination.[11]

The sermon structure establishes a *rational* unity for the sermon, yet the purpose of the sermon establishes a *relevant* unity for the sermon and a consistent tone for the sermon. R. C. H. Lenski depicts well the relationship between the parts of the sermon, or the various points of sermon structure, and the consistent tone of the sermon that is accomplished by the single purpose of the sermon. He makes his point very adeptly:

> Take as an illustration a dining table. It is made to place dishes and food on, for us to sit at and to eat from. That is its purpose or aim. It has legs, an upper frame, and a flat top. These are the parts. They harmonize in regard to the aim. They are thus one in tone, though each part is different from the other. Every sermon with essential unity aims at one great purpose, for it is one sermon, not two sermonettes, or more. Its natural parts are all there, and all agree, though quite different from one another. Aiming to accomplish one thing, their tone naturally is one.[12]

A clearly defined purpose not only enhances the unity of the sermon through a distinct and consistent tone for the message, but an obviously elevated intensity in the manner of sermon delivery will result as well.

By virtue of the fact that the preacher has understood how the text of Scripture and, therefore, his sermon preached from that text must impact his hearers, his manner in preaching will be marked by his intentionality for preaching the message. A well defined purpose for preaching supplies an appropriately intense manner in preaching.

Though an appropriate intensity is a lacking commodity of much preaching today, the lack of an appropriate intensity in preaching is a deficiency that is not new. Even in days when preaching was sufficiently stout in substance, quite unlike much preaching of today, sermons were lacking the intensity that comes from a clear purpose for preaching the sermon. Shedd writes, in 1876, about preaching as being inadequate in terms of the manner of preached sermons as lacking 'a depth and seriousness of view'. Regarding this apparent weakness he believed that 'The principal lack in the current preaching is not so much in the matter, as in the manner.' By this he meant that preaching was not so fused with the speaker's personal convictions, and presented in such living contact with the hearer's fears, hopes, and needs, as to make the impression of stern reality. Of course this is even more indicative of preaching done in pulpits today. As he quite insightfully continued he said that 'The pulpit must become more intense in manner' or it will lose its power.[13]

If the preaching of the nineteenth century lacked intensity, I can only imagine how shocked Shedd would be to hear preaching in the twenty-first century, especially in the West. This weakness in preaching, which is still present in many current sermons, not only needs to be corrected but needs to be corrected as of the sermon introduction.

When one preaches without a definite purpose for the sermon, one's preaching will be weakened immeasurably. If a hearer is listening in vain for a preacher's purpose statement, the sermon will be marked by a mysterious, enigmatic quality rather than representing a serious, straightforward communication. Spurgeon recounts having heard sermons with no apparent purpose or design. The preaching of such sermons only caused him to wonder why they were preached at all.

> I have often wondered why certain sermons were ever preached, what design the preacher had in concocting them. I would not suspect the preachers of wishing to display themselves; yet what else they were doing I do not know. Caligula marched his legions, with the beating of drums, and sounding of trumpets, and display of eagles and banners, down to the seashore, to gather cockles! And there are sermons of that sort: beating drums, and sounding trumpets, and flaunting flags, *and cockles!*[14]

For one to preach with no obvious purpose is just as great an indictment as if one were to preach for the sole purpose to exalt oneself in the process of preaching. Spurgeon continues:

He must preach as though eternal realities were suspended on the passing hour. This is a thought which ought to be deeply inwoven with the preacher's views and emotions. I have often asked myself why it is that a congregation assembled for the worship of God are, for the most part, less interested in a discourse from the pulpit, than a jury are interested in an argument from the bar! It is not because the bar is always more eloquent than the pulpit, though it often is so; nor is it altogether because the pulpit speaks of unearthly things, and the bar of things earthly. It is mainly because the speaker and the hearers in the courts of law speak and hear with the view of coming to a present decision on the subject submitted to their consideration. This responsibility rests upon them, and they may not be listless. Let but the thought be present to the mind of the preacher and the hearers, that in the progress and at the close of his discourse decisions are to be made that will affect the destiny of men, for weal of for woe, through interminable ages, and the listless hearing, and this insensate preaching, will exist no longer.[15]

Since preaching deals with issues far more significant than any court, preachers must reflect this reality through purposeful preaching. Purposeful preaching will not materialize unless the preacher can write it out clearly, in his study, long before he enters the pulpit to preach.

The validity of preaching has been vindicated rightly through the following questions and assertion: Does the sermon have a valid function in disordered days like these? Can it communicate truth and interpret hard-to-accept dimensions of reality to people who are bogged down in quagmires of disillusionment, anger, materialistic self-centeredness, and personal defeat? Preaching alone is valid to provide needed instruction for life in this world as long as the sermon is an actual representation of life as it is in light of biblical truth.[16] The sermon will be vindicated to the degree that it emphasizes a thorough dealing with the text and an accurate interpretation of the text for the ultimate purpose to bring to the hearers the 'mandates for radical change'[17] in keeping with the truth of the text which has been dealt with thoroughly and accurately.

Sermonic Purpose and Expository Preaching

Many years ago the purpose of a sermon was stressed more than is common in today's homiletical treatises. A. T. Pierson was an example of one who wrote with great conviction on the subject of purpose in preaching. So strong was Pierson's advocacy of the sermon's purpose that he insisted that it must be the controlling element of the sermon if it were to be 'properly a sermon'. If this were not the case, he surmised that either the text or the subject would control the sermon. If the text controls the sermon, then an exposition or an exegesis is the result. If the subject controls the sermon, then an essay or a discourse is the result.[18] I believe Pierson may have oversimplified the distinction between a proper sermon, with the purpose as the controlling element, as opposed to an exposition with the text as the controlling element. The inference he suggests is that an expository sermon is less than what it should be because the text is so dominant and controls the sermon. The additional inference is that it is sufficient for a preacher to champion the purpose of a passage as his purpose for preaching, yet without having to deal with the passage to the extent that the explanation of the text does not become dominant. However, if one sees expository preaching as the approach to be taken in preaching rather than a less-than-the-best approach to be taken in preaching, then one can allow the text to control the sermon, yet at the same time allow the purpose of the text to be achieved through the exposition of that text.

A controlling text that achieves the purpose of the text is the combination to be sought in preaching – a combination that constitutes a proper expository sermon. Nevertheless, Pierson is correct in his insistence that preaching should be marked by a resolute purpose and his counsel toward that end is articulated well.

However, since we are dealing with expository preaching it must be understood that expository preaching requires additional effort for the expositor to process a passage thoroughly and be purposeful at the same time. Here is the caution that must be honored – the expository preacher must be careful not to lose the thrust of the sermon amid a massive amount of commentary. One cannot preach effectively and at the same time pursue a thorough investigation of every exegetical insight. The essential process of selection of material will be enhanced by retaining what is most valuable for clarifying the meaning of the text so that the purpose of the sermon may be achieved in the allotted time provided for the sermon.[19]

The hearers must not lose track of the purpose of the sermon. A wise discrimination by the preacher regarding the amount of material to be incorporated into the sermon helps the hearers to stay abreast of the purpose for the sermon. The hearers bear their responsibility too in understanding the purpose of the sermon.

Jay Adams instructs hearers of sermons to be better listeners by expecting to hear a life-changing word from God. His counsel is not only beneficial to those who hear sermons but also to those who preach them. Listen carefully to Adams's penetrating words:

> The whole point is this: when you go to hear a sermon, you must be concerned about one thing: what does God have to say to me? Focus on God. See preaching as a transaction not merely between yourself and the preacher, but between yourself and God. The preacher is a means to that end. Go expecting to hear a Word from God that, when obeyed, will change your life. Lesser expectations will not do.
>
> I have sat in the pew long enough to know it can be irritating when the sermon is halting or superficial, but if you are an alert listener who is anxious to receive a message from God, you will rarely go away disappointed.[20]

This is excellent counsel but it does not negate the preacher's responsibility to be purposeful in preaching. Even when preaching before the most well focused congregation, a preacher must have a purpose for the sermon and be able to state it clearly in his sermon introduction. They should not have to wait longer than the completed introduction to understand what he will be driving at.

If listeners follow Adams' advice, and they should, then preachers should certainly be able to state for them in the introduction exactly what God would have them to do in response to the sermon to be preached and how this sermon will be life-changing if they will comply with God's purpose for this portion of His Word. This is predicated upon the fact that the preacher can discern God's purpose for the passage of Scripture from which he preaches and that the preacher can be so discerning of that purpose as to articulate it in a clear purpose statement in the sermon introduction.

It is possible to discern God's purpose for a passage if the text has been understood. God's Word is not without purpose! When one preaches it is not enough to give careful consideration to the context, grammar, syntax, words or the passage, and crucial cross references to the passage from which one preaches. These things must be done in order to explain the biblical text in one's preaching so that the preacher constantly focuses upon a passage of Scripture in his preaching. If one's preaching does not focus upon a passage of Scripture then his sermon will become a poor substitute for, and an obstacle to, biblical exposition. And, of course, this will not do! Jay Adams provides a faithful reminder of the authority of, benefit of, and commitment to biblical preaching when he contends:

> Preachers today have no authority for preaching their own notions and opinions; they must 'preach the Word' – the apostolic Word recorded in the Scriptures. Whenever preachers depart from the purpose and intent of a biblical portion, to that

extent they lose their authority to preach. In short, the purpose or reading, explaining, and applying a portion of Scripture is to obey the command to 'preach the Word.' In no other way may we expect to experience the presence and power of the Holy Spirit in our preaching. He did not spend thousands of years producing the Old and New Testaments (in a sense, the Bible is peculiarly *His* Book) only to ignore it! What He 'moved' men to write He now motivates us to preach. He has not promised to bless our word; that promise extends only to His own (Isa. 55:10, 11).[21]

This is an incredibly valuable insight made by Adams. Preaching is not about the preacher's sermon as much as it is about God's Word! The preacher must be concerned about expounding a proper understanding of His Word and projecting an accurate statement of what God intends to accomplish in their lives having understood His Word. Therefore, preaching the Word must include explaining the content of a biblical text but also establishing the intent of the biblical text.

Preachers who explain a text to God's people without enforcing the purpose of the text upon them ultimately fail to serve them because they have not fully, and faithfully, preached His Word. Having a purpose for preaching a sermon is not a nuance for, but a necessity in, the preaching enterprise. Purposeful preaching is not a sound and sensible objective, but a solemn obligation, for a Bible expositor.

To preach purposefully, that is, to establish a clear purpose statement for each sermon, a preacher must be guided by, and consistent in, incorporating two related presuppositions regarding the truth he will marshal in his sermon. God's Word is given to us to do more for us than to change our thinking about a subject-matter. God's Word is given to us to change how we feel and how we act in accordance with a subject-matter.

The preaching of Jesus Christ in His Sermon on the Mount is a perfect example of preaching that is intended to do much more than inform the thinking but also to impact the feeling and to direct the will of His hearers. As Jesus concludes his sermon He warned His hearers as to the significant matter of acting upon or failing to act upon His instruction. 'Therefore, everyone who hears these words of Mine, and acts upon them, may be compared to a wise man, who built his house upon the rock' (Matt. 7:24). 'And everyone who hears these words of Mine, and does not act upon them, will be like a foolish man, who built his house upon the sand' (Matt. 7:26).

The issue of compliance to the truth was the central issue, not a peripheral issue in His preaching. The feeling of peace and security for acting upon His words is both obvious and intended just as much as the feeling of fear and insecurity for not acting upon His words. Jesus has been depicted appropriately as 'a master communicator because he not only spoke from his own heart, but he also directed his speech to the hearts of others. He changed minds by touching hearts. More than anyone else, Jesus demonstrated that the way to connect with people was to give them more than just information.'[22] In light of the Lord's procedure and purpose in preaching, one would do well to do as He did, that is, purpose to change how people think, feel, and live.

Jesus purposed to speak to the hearts of people and purposed to change the temporal lives and eternal destinies of those who heard Him. This still is, and will always be, the most effective way of communicating God's truth today. One cannot settle for aimless preaching, preaching without a purpose, and be following the example of the Lord's preaching. Expository preachers, especially, need to be determined to preach as intentionally as Jesus did. As Andrew Blackwood correctly remarks:

> The man who prepares a sermon ought to start by defining his objective. This he should state as clearly and specifically as he knows how. Expository sermons fall short in this respect more often than in any other. At the very beginning such a sermon

should reveal a clear objective to guide the speaker and the hearer in every step of the way toward a lofty goal.[23]

The unity and relevancy of a purpose statement announced in the sermon introduction, attended to throughout the body of the sermon, and achieved in the sermon conclusion will remedy the criticism 'that the average expository sermon has neither beginning, middle, nor end. Like a ball of twine it simply unwinds.'[24]

As unfortunate as this criticism is, I believe it is a correct and well justified assessment of the typical expository sermon. Bible expositors can certainly be the most purposeless of preachers. This must change!

Purposeful Expository Preaching and Forceful Delivery
Having a well defined, clearly stated purpose will have positive implications for the delivery of the sermon. When a preacher has a purpose etched in his mind and heart he will preach with greater forcefulness because he will be persuaded of the significance the message will have, or should have, upon the hearers.

When biblical truth has been understood so well that the preacher can see how the sermon will impact the lives of the hearers this causes the sermon to be weighty in his own estimation. A forceful preacher must have a message, he must know how the message will be of worth to those who hear it, and he must know that the sermon will be indispensable. Even if a preacher knows that his sermon is composed of truth, biblical truth, but his own estimation of that truth is 'So what?', he can never really preach it, to say nothing of preaching it with passion, authority, and urgency.[25]

The purpose helps to concentrate the weightiness of the message in a forceful statement which may get across to some who, otherwise, would remain hardened toward the message. Through the perceived weightiness of the purpose statement the message that gets across is that the sermon will be of genuine personal worth. As one author stated it, rather convincingly:

> A hammer may weigh 50 pounds, but if it is put together as loosely as a bale of hay, it may not be useful in driving a carpet tack into soft pine wood; but even though the hammer may weigh but a few ounces, if it is of compact, blue steel, it will be useful to drive a 20-penny nail into hard oak.[26]

Every sermon needs a purpose because every sermon is designed to persuade the listeners to comply with the truth discovered in a given passage. Preaching requires more than just informing the hearers of the meaning of the passage, but informs them of the personal meaning the passage should have for their lives, or put in other words, 'the sermon aims to sway listeners to do something'[27] in keeping with the intended meaning and purpose of the passage.

Expository preaching, which only aims at a correct, thorough, and clear interpretation of a text, is certainly preaching. However, an expository preacher does not distinguish himself by preaching sermons that are without purpose and practical benefits for his hearers. His sermons must be purposeful and practical just like any other preacher. The only difference should be that the expository preacher's purposeful and practical messages are soundly established in, and supported by, a text of Scripture that is being explained to his hearers. Alfred Garvie's assessment and indictment of expository preaching that tends only to be information oriented is well deserved. He writes, 'There is an expository preaching, in which the scholarly interest is allowed to predominate, and the preacher seeks only to inform and instruct regarding the Bible without any practical purpose or evangelical appeal. It is altogether doubtful whether the ambassador of Christ has any right to be content with doing this only.'[28]

In preaching from any portion of the Bible, a preacher must ask and be able to answer the question, 'Why was this material recorded in Scripture?' Walter Liefeld writes: 'We reverently ask God, "Why did you put this here?" I am not only asking what the teaching *is* but *why* it is given here.'[29] At times the answer will be very clear from the context preceding and following. Sometimes the passage itself speaks so loudly that there is no ambiguity. There are other times, however, when one must exercise careful judgment based on what is known of the general direction of a book and of the purposes for which God inspired Scripture as a whole. Here, 2 Timothy 3:16-17 is very helpful: 'All Scripture is God-breathed and is useful for teaching, rebuking, correcting, and training in righteousness, so that the man of God may be thoroughly equipped for every good work.'

Again Liefeld states:

> At the risk of over-emphasis, we must remind ourselves that unless we have made a sensitive, compassionate, forceful, and unmistakable application, we have merely done exposition, not expository *preaching*. We must constantly be asking ourselves not only *what* we are preaching, but *why*. We need to ask ourselves repeatedly what the *goal* of our exposition is.[30]

The true expository sermon will combine a faithful explanation of the passage in proper balance with, and in proper relationship to, its application. The key again lies in the context of Scripture. What are the facts? What is the life situation? What are the moral, ethical, and doctrinal issues? What was the intent of the Holy Spirit and the inspired human author in producing this text?[31]

By means of a purpose statement you, as a preacher, are 'able to say, in a single sentence, what you want the sermon to accomplish in terms of your people's behavior, feelings, or experience.'[32] This statement must be articulated in the introduction of every sermon.

Purposeful Preaching and Pastoral Responsibility

In his *Nine Lectures on Preaching*, R. W. Dale provided a sound responsibility and rationale for being intentional in calling people to comply with biblical truth in pastoral preaching. As a pastor, unlike a missionary or evangelist, one preaches to a congregation largely composed of people who confess the authority of Christ's Lordship over their lives. Therefore, 'you will have to instruct your churches in religious truth and duty.'[33] In order for a man truly to be a pastor, 'he must learn how to teach.' Dale explained the teaching role of a pastor through the following clarification:

> I do not mean that sermons addressed to Christian people should be simply didactic. The formation of right moral habits and the discipline of the spiritual life should be the supreme objects of pastoral preaching; but ethical and religious knowledge is worth having for its own sake, and in the absence of it we have no reason to look for the development of the higher forms of moral and spiritual character.[34]

As Dale points out, real preaching must do more than provide knowledge of what was unknown; it must also enforce that which is known and has been known for a long time. The pastoral responsibility of a preacher is addressed as he writes:

> Where moral duty is recognized it is not always discharged, even by Christian people. Through force of habit, perhaps unconsciously, they distinguish between duty and duty. One duty they dare not neglect, another they neglect constantly without any keen compunction. Sins of one class they suppose to be utterly inconsistent with loyalty to Christ; sins of another class they have come to regard as being mere infirmities – infirmities to be regretted, infirmities which mar, no doubt, the perfection of Christian character; infirmities for which they need God's forgiveness; but still mere infirmities, which may be tolerated.... Some habits their consciences condemn only occasionally; weeks and months go by and these habits are unrebuked.... It is certain – we may learn it from observation, we may learn it from our personal experience – that the Divine life which comes to a man when he is regenerated does not at once transform the whole

character. He may be guilty of many moral offences which his conscience does not condemn; or the authority of his conscience may be feeble, and he may make no serious effort to escape from moral habits which he knows are sinful. In our ethical preaching we must deal both with moral ignorance and with the want of moral earnestness.[35]

If we are to 'deal with' such offenses in our preaching, and indeed we should, the sermon's purpose statement should indicate that this will take place, and in what specific way correction is needed for believers to live in keeping with God's Word.

However, for such a suggestive purpose statement to be uttered the preacher must first have no reticence about asserting his role of a faithful pastor and a relevant expositor of God's Word. He is there to wield the sword of God's Word which will perform corrective surgery in the lives of some hearers. The preacher must have the courage to fulfill his role and lovingly proclaim truth that may be offensive to some hearers. A faithful expositor must be more fearful of not being straightforward with the truth of God's Word than he is fearful of man's response to the spoken Word of God. Jack Sanford asserts that the preacher needs to have courage if the Word of God is proclaimed with relevance and purpose. Consider carefully his insightful perspective which will provide a much-needed remedy to the typical sermon, if applied consistently in one's preaching.

> The only way the preacher can preach the ethics of Jesus is to preach them as he did – plainly, without any embellishment or theory. The same sense of divine sanction which gave Jesus unusual power and courage, must be felt also by the preacher if he is to properly lay the claims of the Bible. This means that he must be without fear in his enunciation of the ethical demands of the Lord.
>
> Ethics cannot be preached truthfully nor effectively with an attitude of apology or a spirit of fear. It is necessary that the

preacher be without fear, for he will soon discover that he is at crosscurrents with the men to whom he preaches if he is true to the teachings of Jesus. This grim fact must be alive in the preacher's mind at all times, just as it was uppermost in the mind of the Master. In fact, Jesus was never unmindful of the harsh attitudes shown him by his contemporaries. Indeed, his soul was sorrowful unto death on many occasions, when people whom he had come to save rejected him because his demands were far beyond their ability to meet. Yet his course was laid out for him, his face resolutely set toward the cross, and his principles unchanging. He had a standard of righteousness which would not be compromised, even if it meant rejection by the crowd and death at their hands. It is at this very point that the preacher is faced with an ancient stone of stumbling.[36]

Pastoral responsibility is fulfilled in part by purposeful preaching. Purposeful preaching is neither automatic nor is it consistently accomplished without the preacher's desire to help those who hear the Word preached and the preacher's dependence on God's power to preach it for His glory and pleasure.

Purposeful Preaching and Persuasion
When a man preaches with a clear purpose for the sermon, the listeners will be able to perceive the potential, if not a promise, for personal benefit from the sermon. Obviously, the preacher will have to make good on this perception through the preaching of the message but, as of the sermon introduction, the hearers should have a distinct understanding that the preacher will be a bearer of valuable, personally relevant, and life-changing truth for them in the text to be expounded. Because the hearers can discern that the preacher has a clear purpose for preaching the sermon, he will already begin to make headway toward becoming what every preacher must become in order to be effective – a persuasive preacher.

A purposeful preacher, being viewed by the hearers as one bearing a measure of persuasiveness, stands a good chance to be a well received preacher before any congregation. The words of an unknown author capture the essence of purposeful preaching and preachers.

> There's a man in the world who is never turned down
> Wherever he chances to stray;
> He gets the glad hands in the populous town,
> Or out where the farmers make hay;
>
> He is greeted with pleasure on deserts of sand,
> Or deep in the aisles of the woods;
> Wherever he goes there's the welcoming hand
> For the man who delivers the goods![37]

Yet, the inescapable and unfortunate reality is this – preaching is not nearly as persuasive as it should be because of the preacher's purposelessness. As long as preaching lacks in purpose it is worthy of censure. The culpability of attempting to preach without a vital purpose is echoed by John Oman's indictment:

> The trouble with your calling is that you have often to speak when you have not found anything faintly resembling a burden of the Lord requiring to be uttered; and that, even on what you have to say, you have not had time and quiet to muse till the fire burns with any clearness of flame. Then you may fall into what has been described as 'the dreary drip of desultory declamation'.[38]

The final effect of your preaching should be before you from the start, and every word you utter should be directed towards it. The final effect of your preaching must be more than one of the main points of the sermon or a word of exhortation at the end.[39]

For a preacher to preach with a purpose requires that the sermon he will preach will be, in some measure, a persuasive speech. In a persuasive speech, there should be no doubt in the minds of the hearers exactly what the speaker intends for them to think, feel, and do.⁴⁰ It has been stated that the preacher must do two things, namely, instruct the hearers in order to enlighten their intellects and move the hearers by appealing to their wills.⁴¹

The Purpose Statement as a Persuasive Proposal

The purpose statement of a sermon implies that the hearers will be called to a definite response by the preacher according to the understanding of the biblical text he has set forth. The purpose statement is actually a proposal of what the preacher desires to achieve in the lives of his hearers through the exposition of a biblical passage. A well structured purpose statement meets three required criteria: it is required that the proposal be seen as *achievable*, it is required that the proposal be *desirable*, it is required that the proposal be *advisable*. In other words the hearers must be brought to the point where they conclude – I can do this, I want to do this, and I will do this! When this is the case, the expositor has been a persuasive preacher!

Therefore, the purpose statement, as a persuasive proposal, should be characterized by three qualities: living, not dead; forced, not avoidable; momentous, not trivial. If the purpose statement, as a persuasive proposal, is one that the hearers can actually do something about, then it is a living proposal, not a dead proposal. The purpose statement, as a persuasive proposal, must be a forced proposal, not an avoidable proposal. It is a forced proposal if the hearers are given a challenge they cannot shrug off or avoid. A purpose statement is a persuasive proposal if it is deemed as momentous by the hearers, not a trivial one. A momentous proposal is one that conveys a depth of real significance about the subject-matter to be treated as well as the response of the hearers to the subject-matter which is understood to be required of them and understood to be vital to them if they will only comply with the truth.⁴²

The Role of Explanation in Persuasion

Preaching must explain and prove. The preacher must convince his hearers that his explanation of a passage's meaning is in fact what the passage means. But beyond this, the preacher must persuade his hearers to act in accordance to the Scripture's meaning they now possess. In his book, *Sacred Eloquence*, Thomas J. Potter describes persuasion as the ultimate aim of all preaching:

> It is one thing to convince a man that he ought to change his life; it is another to persuade him to make this change. This latter, this persuasion, is the ultimate aim of all preaching, the end which the preacher necessarily proposes to himself. All his instruction, all his argumentation, all his previous efforts, are simply intended to lay the foundation on which to build persuasion. It is well, it is necessary, to triumph over the intellect by conviction, but what result has the Christian preacher really attained if he has not also moved the will, gained the heart – in one word, persuaded his hearers.
>
> Many preachers take great pains to instruct and to prove – in other words, to speak to the intellect of their hearers; but, unfortunately, it is not the intellect which is sick, but the heart, which is the victim of evil passions; and the heart is not to be reached by cold and logical reasoning. It must be touched, it must be moved, it must be persuaded to embrace and put in practice that truth which the intellect has presented to it. Through the influence, and by the aid, of those passions by which it is so deeply moved and governed it must be gained to the side of virtue. The sinner must be brought not only to believe, but to practice.
>
> To attain this great end is the aim and object of persuasion, or the art of moving the will, and persuasion is the only way of attaining it.[43]

To change the behavior of people is a legitimate effect of preaching. But changed behavior is a legitimate effect of preaching only if behavioral change is effected through a conscience that has been changed by an accurate understanding of Scripture.

Stating the Purpose: An Indication of a Passionate Preacher

This requires an explanation of its contents. Behavioral change based upon a coerced conscience, a conscience that is compelled to act without a biblical rationale, is manipulation not persuasion. One who is coerced to act without sufficient reason is not an individual who has been persuaded, but rather, an individual who has been manipulated.

Explanation, though indispensable for true persuasion, does not automatically produce persuasion. A sufficient rationale for behavioral change does not effect behavioral change until the conscience has been moved. Only God can change the conscience of an individual. Certainly, God uses preachers who may be viewed by men as powerful and persuasive proclaimers of truth, but they are only human instruments God is using to accomplish His will.

This much is clear – a man cannot affect the consciences of his hearers independent from the power of God working in their hearts. In fact, a preacher cannot even affect their intellects through his exposition of the truth independent from the power of God. A preacher can pray much, study well, and gain a great amount of understanding of a passage to be preached. He can carefully and prayerfully prepare a thorough exposition that will accurately explain the meaning of the passage. Yet, his prayer, study, personal understanding, careful preparation, and clear exposition of biblical truth does not produce understanding in the minds of the hearers independent from the power of God! He is not able to produce increased understanding in the minds of his hearers any more than he was able to produce increased understanding in his own mind regarding biblical truth. God produced the increased understanding of His truth in the mind of the preacher as the preacher faithfully studied and prayed. God, not the preacher, was responsible for his own increased understanding of biblical truth just as God, not the preacher, will be responsible for increasing the understanding of his hearers as he preaches the truth he has now come to comprehend. The preacher is responsible to pray, study, and preach but he is not responsible to effect his hearer's understanding of the truth, their change of conscience in light of the truth, their change of character through submission to the truth, or their changed behavior by complying with the truth.

Still, a preacher must prepare and pray so that he may be used, by God, as a human instrument by which God may effect these things in the lives of his hearers. As God is well pleased to use preaching in the lives of men, it will certainly start through the explanation of His Word. Understanding God's role in preaching does not cause us to misunderstand the significant effect of persuasion in preaching. Again, Potter is helpful in reminding us of the more completed results of persuasion that go beyond, but yet are based upon the explanation of Scripture. I was refreshed to read Potter's words extolling the value of moving hearers through the Word of God as it is preached. He writes:

> A discourse which leaves our hearers cold and insensible, which does not move the most hidden depths of their souls, and inspire them with strong, fervid, and efficacious resolutions, may sparkle with gems of rhetoric, and be beauties of composition; but, most assuredly, it will be neither a good nor a useful sermon.
>
> On the other hand, if a preacher succeeds in moving his hearers, if he succeeds in acting upon their hearts, all is gained. He is certain to please, since he who moves always pleases, and the more he succeeds in moving the more will he please. His arguments will produce their full effect; for the intellect will no longer seek to withhold its assent from the truth when the heart has been already gained, and thus the victory is assured.
>
> The strength, then, of a preacher lies much more in the power of moving than in reasoning. It is by gaining their hearts that the preacher influences and turns men to his purpose, rather than by convincing their intellect, although this too is necessary. Hence the great and wonderful effects produced by some sermons, which, although in no wise remarkable for composition, are

delivered with that unction, that real earnestness, that burning zeal, which, springing from a heart that is all on fire with a desire for God's glory and the honor of His holy name, acts with such irresistible force on the souls of men.[44]

Although persuasion must begin with explanation, explanation that is clear and is understood to be a correct interpretation of the biblical text, persuasion is not equivalent to a rational understanding of the truth alone.

Persuasion must be viewed as understanding that moves people to act in accordance with that which has been understood. To go from a cognitive enlightenment of the truth to a personal implementation of the truth requires a change in how one regards the truth in a most personal way. In a word, 'feeling' must be affected if one is truly persuaded about any truth in God's Word.

Certainly, the very idea of denoting significance to such a highly personal, subjective, impression-oriented domain as one's feelings is to encroach upon dangerous terrain. Feelings can be given a prominence and priority that will most assuredly usher in gross error. Nevertheless, to deny the appropriate and necessary inclusion of the feelings in the process of persuasion is not only dishonest but will prevent one from understanding true persuasiveness in preaching. To oppose error with an equal yet opposite error will never allow one to arrive at the truth. When one has been persuaded by the truth of any passage of Scripture, one's feelings will be affected. Again, Potter is helpful in understanding the necessary inclusion of the feelings in the process of persuasion.

> Feeling is the soul of eloquence, and it is pathos, the expression of that feeling, which, humanly speaking, is the moving power in the preaching ministry. It is through pathos of thought, of word, and of expression, that a preacher wields his greatest power in preaching. The sermon which does not apply itself to the heart, which does not move and gain it, is devoid of the greatest and noblest result which should characterize every sermon.[45]

How can an expositor of the Word of God explain the great truths of God's revelation to man, of which he is a guardian, and do it coldly and without feeling? What greater contradiction can be conceived than an expository preacher who can speak God's truths without feeling in his voice, without emotion on his countenance, calmly and coldly as if he did not believe them, as if he were merely treating insignificant peripheral issues instead of truths which are determinative of life?[46]

The necessity of being able to affect the feelings of the hearers with the truth as the truth is explained in order to be a persuasive preacher is addressed convincingly by the following:

> A man may be a great philosopher without the faculty of persuading and of influencing the will. He may be an accomplished lecturer, although he may not know how to strike one chord of the human heart, or touch one string of the human soul. But, if it be true that persuasion is the ultimate end of all our preaching , if it be true that a sermon is essentially a persuasive oration, then it follows that, unless he possess this great faculty, whatever else a man may be, he will never be a preacher.[47]

A preacher is one who has gained a personal understanding of a biblical passage, has been personally persuaded about the significance of the passage, intends to be used by God to bring a change of understanding, conscience, character, and behavior to his hearers, and is able to articulate in the introduction what he is intent upon seeing God do for them through the preaching of His Word.

Persuasion is the art of influencing the will by appealing to the passions. Persuasion, which must be based upon clear instruction and solid proof, is the fruit of successful appeal to, and moving of, the passions of the human heart. Passions are those affections of the soul which awaken the will to embrace that which will be personally beneficial and to flee from that which will be personally detrimental. Persuasion is the result when one accepts an appeal for one's personal good based upon objective truth as explained from the Scripture. Here then is the critical connection for persuasion – it is the connection between scriptural truth and personal good.[48]

Truth is the object of the intellect, good is the object of the will. A person will not act except for the attainment of something perceived to be a good; something which will be instrumental for one's happiness, for the perfection of one's nature, for the development of one's being. To make one believe, it is enough to demonstrate and corroborate the truth. To make one act, it is required to demonstrate that the action will satisfy some pertinent end. Nothing can be considered a pertinent end which does not gratify some affection. In order to persuade one to attain that end, a preacher must necessarily appeal to the affection which is to be gratified by its attainment. Hence, without an appeal to the passions there will be no persuasion.[49]

Direct and Indirect Persuasion

A preacher's appeal to his hearers' passions is both direct and indirect. A preacher directly appeals to his hearers' passions by the mere force of his own evident passion, which finds expression in his words, his voice, his eyes, his facial expressions, and his gestures. In this way, a preacher immediately and directly appeals to the hearts of his hearers and inspires them with the same feelings with which he is so deeply penetrated, and which he expresses with such power and strength.[50] Thus, a preacher can only purpose to achieve in the hearts and lives of his hearers what has already occurred in his own heart and life as he has studied the passage from which he will preach.

A preacher indirectly appeals to his hearer's passions by his explanation, illustration, and application of the truth. From the consideration of such matters, he appeals naturally and indirectly to the hearer's volition to act according to the truth of the text.⁵¹ Although a preacher cannot, by direct volition, excite or allay any sentiment or emotion, he may, by direct volition, provide material to impact understanding with such thoughts as shall indirectly operate upon the feelings and affections of the hearers.⁵²

It is in the sermon conclusion where the strongest direct and indirect appeals are made to the hearers. If the preacher's purpose for the sermon is achieved in the lives of his hearers, it must either be achieved cumulatively by the time he concludes the message or it must be achieved solely in the conclusion itself.

However, the sermon introduction must exhibit a definite, discernable purpose for preaching the sermon. The purpose must propose to affect the lives of the hearers in a significant way. The sermon introduction must begin to demonstrate direct and indirect appeals for persuasion. In the introduction of the sermon the preacher's passion must be perceptible, thus demonstrating his own estimation of the sermon's worth for himself and for his hearers. Also, the sermon introduction must present substantive content which suggests to the hearers that the sermon to be preached to them will be indeed be worthy of their time and attention.

Earnest Preachers and Persuasive Preaching

It is in the introduction that the essential quality of a persuasive preacher becomes obvious – that he is deeply moved by his subject and introduces the sermon as a man who is inspired by the sermon he will preach because the sermon has already been beneficial to him. It is the heart that has been moved already that is able to move the hearts of others. The sermon introduction must evidence the moved heart of a preacher. The passion of a speaker is a crucial factor for the effectiveness of public declaration, which is not limited to, but certainly includes the declaration of a sermon by a preacher. Cicero said:

I have tried all the means of moving. I have raised them to the highest degree of perfection which was in my power, but I candidly confess that I owe my success much less to my own efforts than to the force of the passions which agitate me when I speak in public, and which carry me out of myself.[53]

In like manner Quintillian said:

'We aspire to move others strongly.' Let us first feel in our own hearts those sentiments with which we seek to animate them. How shall I soften others if my own words prove that I myself am unmoved? How shall I inflame the hearts of my hearers if I myself am cold? How shall I draw the tears from their eyes if my own are dry? It is impossible.[54]

And the reason for this is plain. When the preacher is profoundly penetrated with, and moved by his subject, his interior emotion imparts to his words, his looks, his gestures, his whole bearing, a warmth and feeling which exercise an almost irresistible influence upon his hearers.

This is the influence that is to be exhibited in the introduction by a preacher, so that, even before the hearers have heard his discourse they begin to think as he thinks and to will as he wills. We have a striking instance of this in St. Ignatius Loyola. Although Loyola preached with the utmost simplicity of language, he did so with such an unction and emotion that, even those among his audience who did not understand the language in which he spoke were, nevertheless, moved to tears by the very tones of his voice, by the earnestness and burning zeal which appeared in his every gesture and look.[55] Francis de Sales wrote:

Preaching must be spontaneous, dignified, courageous, natural, sturdy, devout, serious, and a little slow. But to make it such what must be done? In a word, it means to speak with affection and devotion, with simplicity and candor, and with confidence, and to be convinced of the doctrine we teach and of what we persuade. The supreme art is to have no art. Our words must be set aflame, not by shouts and unrestrained gestures, but by inward affection. They must issue from our heart rather than from our mouths. We must speak well, but heart speaks to heart, and the tongue speaks only to men's ears.[56]

If a preacher does not feel in his own heart those sentiments with which he seeks to inspire others, it is vain to make a pretense of possessing them since the heart appeals to the heart and that the tongue only speaks to the ears.[57]

James Stalker, in his book *The Preacher and His Models*, makes a helpful insight regarding a preacher's earnestness in preaching:

> It is the truth which has become a personal conviction, and is burning in a man's heart so that he cannot be silent, which is his message. The number of such truths which a man has appropriated from the Bible and verified in his own experience is the measure of his power. There is all the difference in the world between the man who thus speaks what he knows from an inner impulse and the man whose sermon is simply a literary exercise on a Scripture theme, and who speaks only because Sunday has come round and the bell rung and he must do his duty.[58]

Stalker rightly asserts that there will be a clear difference between a preacher who is earnest and one who is lacking earnestness. Even more, he is perceptive in relating the preacher who is not earnest as one who is motivated by nothing more than the duty he bears to preach, simply because it is time to do so.

There is not an automatic reciprocity, but there should be an actual reciprocity between preaching with purpose and preaching with earnestness. It is not automatic that an earnest preacher will have a specific, hearer-directed purpose for preaching his sermon. As desirable as it is that an earnest preacher would have a specific hearer-directed purpose for preaching, this simply is not the case. Yet, a preacher who is possessed by a vital purpose for preaching the sermon will be affected by this beneficial reality. The purpose of the sermon contributes greatly to the earnestness of the preacher.

No preacher, however, will become earnest simply by trying to be so. The preacher must not aim at earnestness but he must aim at his object, to do some spiritual good to his hearers. After all, is the preaching of an expositor any different than the preaching of a prophet? Certainly, the preaching of a prophet and an expositor are the same in this aspect – the messages from both the prophet and the expositor are messages from God and messages to men.[59] This general aim of preaching a message from God to men will be accomplished as the preacher seeks to accomplish a more specific aim, accomplishing the purpose for preaching a specific sermon for a specific spiritual end in the lives of the people who hear him preach. Earnestness is a product from being captivated by a compelling, specific reason for preaching the message.[60]

Earnestness in the preacher creates earnestness in the hearers. The more a preacher loses himself and is lost to himself in true earnestness, the more earnestness he communicates to his hearers. Whatever is powerful enough to absorb and possess a preacher has at least a prima facie claim of attention on the part of his hearers. The most authoritative persuasiveness, however, is that which is drawn from the personal trait of an earnest moral nature evident in the life of the preacher.[61]

This earnestness of the preacher is not in conflict with, nor exclusive of, the working of the Holy Spirit in the preacher's life. The opposite, however, is true. A Spirit-filled preacher will be one who is possessed by great earnestness in his preaching. The Lord Jesus Christ said, 'The Spirit of the Lord is upon Me, because He anointed Me to preach the gospel to the poor. He has sent Me to proclaim release to the captives, and recovery of sight to the blind, to set free those who are downtrodden, to proclaim the favorable year of the Lord' (Luke 4:18-19). Beyond the obvious fulfillment of Isaiah 61:1 which refers to the ministry the Messiah would have, one cannot miss the connection between His anointing of the Spirit and the specific objectives for His proclamation of God's Word.

I certainly agree with Broadus who wrote, 'After all our preparation, general and special, for the conduct of public worship and for preaching, our dependence for real success is on the Spirit of God.'[62] P. T. Forsyth is correct as he asserts that spiritual power and authority of the pulpit is a personal authority, but it is not the authority of the preacher's person. The personal authority of the pulpit is the authority of the divine Person whose burden is the Word.[63] What Forsyth did not believe but must be stated, especially in the context of expository preaching, is that the authority of the pulpit is through the proclaimed Word of God by a preacher who is empowered by the Holy Spirit of God. One must not attribute authority to the person of the Holy Spirit of God but then withhold authority from that which He inspired, the Word of God. Forsyth took great pains to separate authority from the truth of Scripture itself as he wrote:

> What does not go unsaid, what needs saying, is that the preacher's authority is not the authority of his truth. In the region of mere truth there is no authority. Mere truth is intellectual, and authority is a moral idea bearing not upon belief but upon will and faith, decision and committal. It is not statements that the preacher calls on us to believe. It is no scheme of statements. It is not views. It is not a creed or a theology. It is a religion, it is a Gospel, it is an urgent God. In the region of mere theology we may be bold to say there is no authority; the authority is all in the region of religion. The creed of the Church should have great prestige, but not authority in the proper sense. Belief, in the region of theology, is a matter of truth or truths; it is science, simple or complex. And science knows no authority.[64]

But the truth, God's Word, is authoritative! It is authoritative because it is inspired by God. God cannot be viewed as authoritative and, at the same time, His Word not be viewed as authoritative. His Word bears the very authority He possesses. Therefore, when His Word is expounded the authority of His Word will be perceptible. It should be perceptible! The authority that is perceived comes, not from the preacher. The preacher cannot add to the authority of the Scriptures and he will not detract from them if he will only preach them! And this will inevitably be the case because the authority comes from the Word of God and the God of the Word! Just read what Howard Hendricks has to say about the authoritative declaration of Scripture which is boldly presented in the fullness of one's being. Hendricks says:

> As Christians who believe in the authority and inspiration of Scripture, we have a body of truth given by revelation, truth that is to be communicated with the world. So we don't have to manufacture the message. We have only to declare it. This is our greatest asset, and yet it also tends to be a particular communication problem in the evangelical community.
>
> Why? Because most of us settle for communicating the message with the intellectual component only. We rely too heavily on words alone. We're convinced that if we tell people the right thing, it will automatically solve their problems. We're too weak in communicating through the emotional and volitional aspects – the feeling and action components – because it threatens us out of our socks.[65]

The pulpit is without rival in authority when the Word of God is expounded from it. In contrasting the authority of the press and the pulpit, Forsyth notes that the press is for information or suggestion at most but it is not there for authority. But the pulpit is there with authority. The press may offer an opinion as to how the public should act, but the pulpit is there with a message as to how people must act in obedience and trust. The press may be an adviser, but the pulpit is a prophet. The press may have a thought, but the pulpit must have a gospel, and a command.[66]

Jowett is perceptive as he says, 'When, for any cause, we are separated from the Lord our speech lacks a mysterious impressiveness. We are wordy but we are not mighty. We are eloquent but we do not persuade. We are reasonable but we do not convince.'[67] All such statements finding hearty approval, nonetheless, the working of the Holy Spirit of God will be evidenced by a preacher who is purposeful in his preaching. He will not be preaching simply for the dissemination of information. One endowed with the unction of God in his preaching will be about accomplishing the function of God's Word in the lives of those who hear him preach. Like the uneducated but intuitive preacher exclaimed, 'I can't tell you what unction is, but I can tell you when it ain't!'[68] And what unction definitely is not is a man who preaches without a purpose.

When unction is evidenced it will be accompanied by a preacher who has a specific and worthy purpose for preaching his sermon. When unction is absent you will discover that the preacher apparently had no greater purpose for preaching the sermon than to simply preach the sermon. Even if such a sermon is deemed to have been a good one, it still was not as effective and powerful as it could have been if the preacher would have had a specific objective for preaching the sermon.

Earnest Preachers and Purposeful Preaching
Having a specific purpose for preaching a sermon allows the preacher to be volitionally earnest – he *is* about accomplishing something worthwhile in the lives of his hearers as he preaches the sermon. Furthermore, having a specific purpose in preaching a sermon allows the preacher to be visibly earnest – he *appears* to be about accomplishing something worthwhile in the lives of his hearers as he preaches the sermon. The only way to appear earnest is to be earnest. And one cannot preach earnestly or be perceived to preach earnestly unless he is trying to achieve something great through the preaching of the sermon.

Bourdaloue, the great Catholic preacher, said of the sharp screaming voice of another, 'He grates upon the ears, but he rends the hearts.'[69] It has been rightly asserted that earnestness in preaching makes a vital difference in one's preaching. Draw encouragement and confidence for the task of preaching by taking to heart the following precepts. 'To be a powerful and effective preacher, it is not necessary to be a polished speaker, a graceful orator, or adept in the excellency of men's speech.... Let him be downright earnest, with a heart burning with charity, and let him speak as he feels, and not one word he utters will fall idly to the ground.'[70]

It was a very clear, albeit a corrupt and detestable purpose, that caused Adolf Hitler to be the vocal ambassador of Hell in his day. His formula for impassioned speech was uncomplicated and serviceable for any communication opportunity – "(1) Have something to say. (2) Say it simply. (3) Make it burn.'[71] His belief in the efficacy of impassioned speech is captured in his assertion, 'Only a storm of burning passion can turn people's destinies, but only he who harbors passion in himself can arouse passion.'[72] Certainly he was correct concerning the influence of a speaker upon his hearers since it is understood that fervor on the part of a speaker is basic in arousing the enthusiasm of the listener. And, unfortunately, he moved a nation with his impassioned speech directed by purposes originating from the pit of Hell.

Purposeful preaching is essential for preaching with true earnestness. Earnestness vitally impacts and empowers preaching. Phillips Brooks said, 'He who lacks emotion lacks expression.'[73] 'Without passion no pulpit can be a throne of light,' wrote Raymond Calkins.[74] Charles S. Horne declared, 'When I read our Lord's infinitely moving lament over Jerusalem, or His impassioned indignation against religious hypocrisy, I marvel that we can ever imagine Christian preaching to be admirable that is not deeply penetrated with emotion.'[75] Horne further suggested, 'Nobody ought to ever go into a pulpit ... without profound emotion and passion.'[76]

It is preaching with some specific purpose which the preacher trusts God to effect in the lives of his hearers that constitutes authentic preaching. The preacher not only believes that the preaching enterprise makes a difference in the lives of people for time and eternity, but each time he preaches he does so with a specific targeted change that is to be made in the lives of those who hear the sermon. Raymond Calkins writes:

> Preaching ... is never vague, generalized, impersonal. It is direct, near, intimate, and deals always with the realities of daily experience. It is the bringing to bear the realities of eternal life upon the realities of daily life. There is where much modern preaching goes for nothing. It does not focus on the real spiritual situations in which men and women find themselves. But all Bible preaching focused on a real situation. It brought a message from heaven but it laid it right next door to some concrete situation here on earth.[77]

Preaching always purposes to have God's Word actualized in the lives of people in some specific fashion. The preacher who is resolved to be used by God as a choice instrument in the lives of his hearers will be a man who believes that true usefulness in preaching takes place as he gives himself to the task of explaining the meaning of Scripture, sermon after sermon, through the years of his ministry. I like what Raymond Calkins says:

> Hundreds of preachers, not gifted in many other ways, but good, devout men, by their intimate and loving familiarity with the Bible, and by their earnestness in expounding the Bible ... have strongly gripped the congregations of their churches.... It is the Bible preacher, always finding in it inexhaustible spiritual treasure, who keeps himself fresh year after year and never fails to satisfy the human hunger and thirst for God.[78]

Calkins continues and indicates the need for preaching that is not only understood intellectually, but experienced personally and proclaimed passionately. He writes:

Stating the Purpose: An Indication of a Passionate Preacher

The truest and the most fruitful ministry is one that is born out of the 'eternal elements of experiential religion.' And the finest preaching is that which gives utterance to these realities. The preaching for which we wait here in America is that which is the fine blend of both mind and heart; which is truly rational, and at the same time is truly prophetic and evangelical, in that it issues from a heart itself in the grip of the Christian experience so that others may feel and know it.... There is to be found in the best Scotch and English preaching an evangelical fervor, a spiritual passion, a prophetic mood and purpose which grip the heart and make it feel the full impact of the Christian evangel.

Here in America, however, too often we have either the one or the other. We have intellect without passion, or we have fervor without intellect. The weakness in American preaching today is the rift between knowledge and prophecy, between intellect and evangelism, between scholarship and passion.[79]

The corrective for this must begin the expositor's study or it will never be corrected in the pulpit. If all the insight and understanding accrued from his study of the passage cannot be synthesized into a specific statement of purpose for preaching the passage, then his exposition will lack an earnestness it otherwise should have possessed.

Consider the Following Questions

1. How many of the last ten sermons you have preached had a purpose statement as part of the sermon introduction? Was it articulated clearly? Was it the burden of the sermon and a driving force for you as you preached the sermon?

2. How is it that the hearers are more concerned that the truth of the text becomes part of their lives because of a clearly articulated purpose statement?

3. How does a purpose statement contribute to the unity of the sermon?

4. How does a clearly defined purpose increase the intensity of the sermon as it is delivered?

5. What did Spurgeon identify as the reason that a jury listens with greater interest to the arguments from the bar than do congregations as they listen to a preacher?

6. In expository preaching, which is to control the sermon: the text from which the sermon is preached or the purpose for the sermon? Explain your answer.

7. What two presuppositions must a preacher possess in order to preach purposefully? How does the Sermon on the Mount reflect the purposeful preaching of the Lord?

8. What is the rationale behind the assertion that a clearly defined purpose has positive implications for the delivery of the sermon?

9. Does every sermon need to have a purpose? Explain.

10. What is it that a preacher must not be reticent to do in order to be a faithful pastor and a relevant expositor of God's Word? What does this require of the preacher?

11. Why is it that purposeless preaching turns into 'the dreary drip of desultory declamation'?

12. What are the three required criteria of a purpose statement if it is to be a persuasive proposal? What three qualities characterize a purpose statement as a persuasive proposal?

13. How is it that exposition of Scripture factors into a legitimate behavioral change in the lives of those who hear a sermon?

14. Though explanation is indispensable for behavioral change, why is explanation not sufficient for behavioral change? What else is needed and how is this supplied?

15. What is needed in order for a hearer to go from a cognitive enlightenment of the truth to a personal implementation of the truth?

16. In order for persuasion to occur, what is the critical connection that must be made? Identify and explain.

17. How does a preacher appeal to the passions of the hearers directly as opposed to indirectly?

18. How does a preacher's earnestness affect persuasiveness?

19. How can there be an actual but not automatic reciprocity between earnestness and persuasion?

20. What are the means by which earnestness is produced?

21. What is the rationale for the authority of Scripture as equal to the authority of God?

22. How is volitional and visual earnestness related to purposeful preaching?

Words to Live and Preach by

The Pleasure of God

Proverbs 3:1-4 – My son, do not forget my teaching, but let your heart keep my commandments; for length of days and years of life, and peace they will add to you. Do not let kindness and truth leave you; bind them around your neck, write them on the tablet of you heart. So you will find favor and good repute in the sight of God and man.

Proverbs 3:33-5 – The curse of the Lord is on the house of the wicked, but He blesses the dwelling of the righteous. Though He scoffs at the scoffers, yet He gives grace to the afflicted. The wise will inherit honor, but fools display dishonor.

Proverbs 5:21 – For the ways of a man are before the eyes of the Lord, and He watches all his paths.

Proverbs 11:1 – A false balance is an abomination to the Lord, but a just weight is His delight.

Proverbs 11:25 – The generous man will be prosperous, and he who waters will himself be watered.

Proverbs 16:2 – All the ways of a man are clean in his own sight, but the Lord weighs the motives.

Proverbs 16:7-8 – When a man's ways are pleasing to the Lord, He makes even his enemies to be at peace with him. Better is a little with righteousness than great income with injustice.

Proverbs 16:11 – A just balance and scales belong to the Lord; all the weights of the bag are His concern.

Chapter Seven

Stating the Purpose:
An Indication of a Significant Sermon

Biblical Authority and Purposeful Preaching
In an effort to dissuade preachers from focusing upon insignificant issues, one writer of the nineteenth century exclaims, 'The pulpit is not the place for raising questions to which an authoritative answer cannot be given.'[1] The giving of an authoritative answer? How wonderfully strange such counsel sounds in the present-day context of homiletical instruction and practice. The prevailing homiletical advice is for preachers to divest themselves of anything that might be imagined by anyone as bearing a message that could be perceived as authoritative. But this advice, the present-day fleeing from anything that hints of authority, fails to recognize that biblical preaching comes with a 'sure note of authority'. Albert Mohler is correct in his comments regarding preaching and the authority of the Bible:

> Teaching assumes authority. After all, we have to know what it is we are to teach. Far too many preachers think this is an authority that is personal.... But there is only one authority that is the preachers' authority, and there is only one authority that undergirds and justifies his teaching ministry, and that is the authority of the Word of God. This Word is inerrant, infallible,

authoritative, and trustworthy. It is that Word, and that Word alone, that is our authority; and it is not only the foundation, but the substance, the content of our teaching and preaching.[2]

Though it is true that the Bible is authoritative, it is also true that some preachers who would profess to believe that the Bible is authoritative preach in such a way that they contradict their profession. In other words, they preach as though the Bible is not authoritative! They refuse to assert biblical truth! They traffic in speculation and suggestion and relativism! They will fog that which is clear! They will question that which is certain! They will suspend that which must be enforced – an immediate and complete compliance to the truth of God's Word!

Though this is tragic, it is not new. This timorous seed was possessed by Erasmus during the reformation period as he preferred to not make assertions and suspend judgment about difficult doctrines of Scripture. Luther found this disposition intolerable:

> When Erasmus said to Luther, 'I would prefer not to make assertions,' Luther became **apologetic**. He said, 'You would prefer what? You don't want to make assertions? Take away assertion, and you take away Christianity. The very mark of the Christian is that the Christian boldly makes assertions before the world.' Then, in his passion, Luther said, 'The Holy Spirit is not a skeptic. And the things that He revealed are more certain than life itself. Away with the skeptics!'[3]

Certainly there is wisdom in not being dogmatic on truly difficult doctrines and passages of Scripture. To traffic lightly upon such matters is not only sound procedure but reflects humility. What I am referring to are not difficulties of text and doctrine but the unwillingness to be assertive with certain truth. The non-assertive spirit predominates preaching today. The non-assertive seed of Erasmus is reflected in a homiletical harvest that is producing a famine of the Word in the church!

Stating the Purpose: An Indication of a Significant Sermon

When you examine the preaching of preachers illustrated in Scripture you find, in the vast majority of instances, men who were certain of the truth they proclaimed and were certainly assertive in the truth they proclaimed! The preachers of the Bible are telling things which they know. Their knowledge is positive because it rests on a personal experience of God. In writing about the preaching of the prophets and apostles, Hugh Thomson Kerr asserted:

> Indeed, a prophet is one who speaks of another. The Apostles, too, were prophets. They were extremely anxious to disclaim any credit for their message. They deliberately shied away from any responsibility for that message. They wished no one to think well of them, to praise them, to applaud them for their services or their sermons. They did not desire to be thought of as either eloquent or educationally or theologically equipped or endowed with personality sufficient to explain the results of their preaching.[4]

It is because some people want a message with authority behind it that they love their Bibles and a forceful exposition of Scripture. And for the same reason, these people are dissatisfied with much modern preaching. They are looking for someone who can speak with the certainty of personal conviction. But it is not evident that such conviction belongs to many preachers of today. If a preacher does not have an understanding of a passage and is not involved in explaining the meaning of a passage, he will not wield authority in his preaching. Without this note of spiritual authority, a sermon may possess all else – introduction, exposition, illustration, application, and conclusion – but it has lacked the one thing which gives a sermon carrying power – the breath and message of the Almighty God.

The wisdom of the Puritan preachers was epitomized by the belief that, 'You will only preach that sermon well which first you preach to your own soul.'[5] It has been wisely suggested that:

Unless the preacher's own soul has been troubled, no one else's will be. Except the preacher has first trembled at the voice of the Lord, no one else will tremble at the sound of his voice. Wherever you have a preacher burning with his message and delivering it as well as a good singer sings, or as a good writer writes, the people are eager to hear.... People do love to hear preachers who mean what they say.[6]

This outlook does not cause the preacher to preach authoritatively. It merely allows the preacher not to be an inhibiting factor of the authority of God's Word. The authority of God's Word may become imperceptible because of a preacher's failure to understand the truth, or a failure to be convicted by the truth, or a failure to see the implications of the truth in his life and the lives of those who will hear him preach, or even a failure to intentionally compel the listeners to comply with God's Word.

An expository preacher ought to be shamelessly bold and blatantly purposeful in his preaching. And why should this not be the case? He speaks with authority, as long as he is explaining God's Word and demanding and compelling people to conform to it. But this requires the preacher to understand the simple nature of his responsibility – to disseminate God's truth.

The truth that must be disseminated is what the text means and what the text requires of them based upon its meaning. The understanding of the passage as well as the application of the passage must be clarified and enforced by the expositor. It is the authority of the Scripture that allows a man to affirm, 'This is what it means' and 'This is what you are to do about it.' Too often clear explanation (even the very attempt to labor in explanation) and assertive application are absent in preaching because the authority of Scripture is not a settled issue in the mind of the preacher! If the authority of Bible is not the compelling, controlling basis of one's preaching then the content, the motive, and the result of preaching cannot be what it should be. The substance will not be the Word of God but the opinion of the preacher. When this is the case, the motive cannot be to please God but rather to please men in the act of preaching. The result is that the preacher is not a true spokesman for God. Don Kistler writes:

> Pastors must deliver God's Word to His people in such a manner that the majesty and authority of it is preserved.... Why do preachers often act as if what they are saying is simply their opinion? Preachers are not there to give their opinions, they are supposed to be giving the people the very mind of God! Failure to do so was a mark of the false prophets in Jeremiah's day. 'The prophets prophesy on their own authority; and My people love it so.' The people love it when no one is in charge. They love it when the pastor is on the same level as they are. They love it when they share; they don't love it when pastors preach.[7]

The preaching of God's truth, if it is in fact preached, will be authoritative and will be perceived as such. This will inevitably be the case because the Word of God is authoritative. A preacher is not responsible to protect God's people from the authority of God's Word any more than he is responsible to produce the results of God's Word in the lives of his hearers. This gives him a true sense of humility and selflessness. He is, after all, just a messenger of the King. In addressing the humble, selfless preaching that characterizes a faithful shepherd of God's people, John MacArthur writes:

> If you want to be used mightily by God, get yourself out of it. Learn to see yourself as a garbage pail, or in the words of Peter, clothe yourself with humility. It's not you; it's not your personality; it's the Word of God. He doesn't need the intellectuals. He doesn't need great people, fancy people, or famous people. Because the people aren't the power. The power is the message![8]

His task is to faithfully discharge the message of the King. He need not consider himself as anything other than the vocal extension between the King and His subjects. He is there to make sure the King gets a hearing. This is first and foremost. Of secondary interest, is that the subjects respond to the King's Word as they should. However, it is a correct response to God's Word that will be productive for his hearers but this is beyond the preacher's power to control. The preacher must pray that his hearers will respond to God's Word but the preacher must make sure that it will be God's Word, as it has been expounded to them, to which they are called to respond.

What must never become a concern to the messenger is the hearer's response to him, having brought to them the King's Message. Self-concern on behalf of a preacher can only interfere with a bold, purposeful proclamation of God's truth. A self-interested preacher is a divided man. A self-interested preacher cannot be concerned with personal receptivity from the hearers and absolute fidelity to God's Word at the same time. A flattering ministry is an enemy to authority, for when a preacher is inclined to 'sing placebos and sweet songs, it is impossible for him not to betray the truth.'[9]

One who will truly speak for God, not occasionally but consistently through years of preaching, must die to self-interest and must prefer to speak accurately God's truth, regardless of any personal reprisal that may come to him for having done so. In other words, he must make sure that God is heard; he desires that God's people will submit to God's Word; but he must not care for himself in the process of speaking for God.

Courage, not self-concern, has always been, and will always be, the hallmark of one who speaks for God. In regards to the prophets who spoke for God,

> They forgot themselves in their message. The fire of God in their bones would not permit them to hesitate. Whether it was a frowning king or an infuriated mob the prophet had to be brave, he set his face like a flint. Comfort, reputation, life itself might be at stake; but he had to speak out all that God had told him.[10]

Stating the Purpose: An Indication of a Significant Sermon

In reference to the Apostle Paul's being constrained by the Word, it is noted:

> It was not he who had the Word; the Word had him. Into his preaching Paul was thrust by the constraining power of a great conviction. This phrase vividly suggests the ideal condition and experience of a real preacher. All true preachers have this sense of urgency behind them. Martineau used to go to hear Spurgeon preach. A friend asked him why he did: 'You do not believe a word he says.' 'No,' replied Martineau, 'but he does.'[11]

It is the 'personal electricity', the 'live feeling', born of courage and a personal experience of God in the understanding and proclamation of His truth which the preacher directs to the realities of human experience which makes a real sermon – a message marked with integrity.

The evidence of genuine sincerity and passion keeps a preacher from forfeiting the confidence and responsiveness of those to whom he speaks.[12] He is seen as a messenger that believes what he is saying, and is convinced about that which he would have them to believe and practice. As the saying goes, 'If you want people to bleed, then you have to hemorrhage!'

It is purpose which causes a sermon to be pointed or incisive, without which a sermon cannot be truly excellent. It is when a man intends to speak for God and intends for those who hear him to comply in some specific way to the Word of the God, for whom he speaks, that a preacher will be purposeful. It will be evident that this kind of a preacher believes that God has spoken in His Word and His Word is not irrelevant to the lives of men. When he preaches God's Word he will not be preaching a message that is marked by irrelevance, but rather, one that is marked with purpose. R. L. Dabney, a former preacher and preaching professor, wrote about the necessity of a 'pointed effect' in preaching:

> The pointed or incisive discourse may be likened as to its framework to the ancient warship. Its weapon of offence was its

beak. Let us suppose that the architect had left the ponderous mass of pointed metal which formed this beak lying in some accidental position amidst the timbers of the ship, and all those timbers a disorderly heap of rubbish merely thrown together and set adrift upon the sea as a raft. The impact of this shapeless pile, instead of piercing the opposing trireme, would only have dissolved itself into fragments and the intended prow would probably have sunk out of sight without even coming into the feeblest contact with the enemy's hull. The architect, therefore, commits no such folly. He places the beak at the forefront of his structure. He causes the chief beams of his framework to converge to its base, and frames them into it. He adjusts the ribs and braces to support these in turn, so that there is not one piece of timber in the whole ship which does not lend its strength, either directly or remotely, to sustain the prow immovably in its place. And now, when the triple banks of rowers raise their chant and strain at their oars all in concert, they launch the pointed beak into the adversary's side with the momentum of the whole ship's weight. In like manner, the impression made by an oration depends upon its point.... Many sermons are deficient in point. They either have no valuable and practical truths of cardinal weight, or these are not made to stand out to the apprehension of the hearers. No decided impression can be expected from such addresses. No lodgment is made in the conscience of the people; they go away with the vague feeling that they have been only listening to a strain of goodish but aimless talk.[13]

Dabney continues,

> This failure of pointed effect ... is often the result of weakness and confusion of thought. And this, in turn, proceeds from indifference of heart. Earnest purpose and desire are always pointed. The distressed beggar needs no rhetoric to teach him how to make the point of his petition prominent.... Let the preacher, then, cultivate that faith which makes the ruin and the rescue of sinners dread realities to him; let him share the constraining love of Christ in its power; let him feel a consuming zeal to save souls. Then he will not go into the pulpit aimless. He

will have a definite and absorbing purpose, a message to deliver, and a result to effect, which he cannot leave unaccomplished without grief. This holy passion, and this alone, will give his sermon true point. The true cause of the vapid and aimless discourses, which are heard from so many pulpits, is that the preachers are not under the active influence of faith and love for souls. Thus we learn again that true and fervent piety is the prime qualification for sacred eloquence.[14]

A sermon with sufficient 'point' comes from a purposeful preacher who has been more than marginally impacted by the truth of the Scriptural passage from which he preaches. And when he preaches, he requires of his hearers the same response to the truth that he demanded from himself.

It is because of biblical authority that a faithful and courageous expository preacher can wield sufficient pointedness in his purposeful preaching. To unleash the authority of God's Word by explaining its meaning and enforcing its practical and personal responsibilities upon the hearers, though required by God, may not be received well by those who hear truly pointed preaching. Such preaching is certain to be rejected by those who do not regard the Bible as authoritative. Nonetheless, the expository preacher must be undaunted by the erroneous assumptions some may hold regarding biblical authority and preach it as it is, because of what it is – The Very Word of God! And when this is done, the expositor must be ready to stand up under the resistance that some will have toward the Word of God that he has faithfully stood up for in the exposition of its content. Albert Mohler stresses this point:

> Furthermore, this line of work has a nasty way of getting you into trouble. It seems that the more faithful one is in preaching, the more trouble one encounters. Why? There is conflict and controversy. You preach the Word. You did not come up with it. This is not your opinion, and it is not something you came up with in order to offend people. You are simply preaching

the Word. After all, that is your assignment. So you preach the truth, and the next thing you know... (someone) is up in arms over whatever you said. Conflict and controversy are always hard, and they again tend to be correlated to faithfulness in preaching.[15]

Even more insightful are his statements that:

> Indeed, I will go so far as to assert that if you are at peace with the world, you have abdicated your calling. You have become a court preacher to some earthly power, no matter how innocuous it may appear. To put it straight: you have been bought! If there is no controversy in your ministry there is probably very little content to your preaching. The content of the Word of God is not only alive and active, it is sharper than any two-edged sword, and that means it does some surgery. It does some cutting, and that leads to bleeding.[16]

The expository preacher must anticipate that the authority of God's Word will be pointed for his hearers as he preaches the text just as the expositor found the truth of God's Word to be pointed in his study of it the previous week. The pointed expository preacher is, in effect, a surgeon who is used by God to perform surgery in the lives of others before he is fully recovered from the same exact surgery which God has recently performed on him. The expositor must be willing to be an equally good surgeon as he was a patient!

The Cognitive and Volitional Unity of Purpose
Purpose, which is a distinguishing trait of a sermon, terminates in the volition of the hearer so that it passes through the understanding into the motives of the soul. In order to secure the sermon's purpose, or the single practical effect of the sermon, the preacher must be able to distill from the various implications of the passage to be expounded the overarching, dominant, practical effect intended to be produced upon the hearer's will.[17] This is the volitional unity of the sermon.

Stating the Purpose: An Indication of a Significant Sermon

Just as a sermon has a cognitive unity, a single proposition which unifies a variety of more specific theological principles, so must the sermon have a single practical effect that the sermon is intended to achieve. The sermon's purpose is attained through the agency of understood theological principles, derived from and corroborated by the exposition of the text, as well as the various practical implications derived from the exposition of the text. Having heard a purposeful exposition of Scripture, the hearers should perceive a single, dominant, practical response that the preacher demands *from* them based upon the exposition and application of the text preached *to* them.

The sermon's purpose and proposition will always be related but they must always be distinct. The proposition helps the hearers to grasp the overarching understanding of the passage but the purpose helps the hearers to come to terms with the overarching implications of the passage. The purpose must never be limited to an 'understanding' of the text to be expounded. This is a given! To fail to provide an understanding of the passage is complete failure for an expository preacher. The expositor must provide understanding of the passage, but even more so, he must provide a personal, practical, responsible understanding of the passage which is the living out of the truth of the passage in their lives.

Expository preaching must effect an enhanced understanding of Scripture and an enhanced living in conformity with Scripture. The expository preacher explains the text to provide comprehension of God's Word but he ultimately explains the text to provide compliance to God's Word. The purpose statement relates to how one specific way of compliance to God's Word can be achieved. The purpose of the sermon, stated in the introduction, must always be directed to the listeners, not the proposition. The purpose of the sermon, stated in the introduction, must always be worded in such a way to target the listener's compliance to the truth, not just their understanding of the truth.

The purpose of the sermon is typically larger and more general than any of the various implications or applications of the passage. Yet each of the various applications of the passage takes its place in making a contribution to how the purpose is to be achieved in the lives of the hearers. However, the purpose of the sermon may be more precise and specific than any of the various implications or applications of the passage. When this is the case, the applications of the text radiate from the text as a star radiates light waves. The purpose of the sermon is like a lens which collects the various light waves and concentrates them into one burning focus. The text, like a star, emanates various rays or applications. The purpose of the text, like a lens, collects the various rays or applications to provide a clear, focused, vision as to what is to be done about the truth and the implications of the passage expounded.[18]

The sermon's purpose, clearly defined and articulated, provides unity for the sermon just as a good sermon proposition and structure provide unity. Sermonic unity requires not only the discussion of one dominant subject, but also the disclosure of one practical impression or the one practical effect intended to be produced upon the hearer's will.[19]

A Three-fold Criteria for Purposeful Preaching

What is the basis for having a purpose in the introduction of a sermon? The basis for a sermon purpose is a thorough understanding of the passage to be explained in the process of expository preaching. It is in the introduction of the sermon that the listeners must understand with no uncertainty that the message to be proclaimed to them will be of great personal relevance. The purpose statement not only bears out the fact that the sermon will be relevant but it encompasses the ultimate responsibility they must shoulder in order to live in compliance with the truth to be expounded in the sermon.

Former United States President, Woodrow Wilson, remarked about the preaching he had heard in his lifetime.

'I have heard a great deal of preaching and I have heard most of it with respect; but I have heard a great deal of it with disappointment, because I felt that it had nothing to do with me.'[20] This indictment must not become a legacy to preaching, in general, and especially not expository preaching.

Preaching must have very much to do with the lives of the hearers. It must be obvious to the hearers early in each sermon, in the introduction, that the sermon will indeed have a great bearing upon them. The personal relevancy of the sermon is more than the preacher's promise to the congregation. It must be perceived by the congregation that the preacher's driving purpose for preaching the sermon is to change their lives in some specific way, according to the claims of the text to be expounded.

The previous chapter began with four potential responses that a purposeless preacher might provide to an inquirer if asked his reason for preaching a passage. You may recall the responses as: 'The Lord led me to preach this passage' or 'I'm paid by the church to preach, among other things, so they expect me to preach every Sunday' or 'Because I'm preaching through the book of Romans and this is the point at which I left off last week, so this is the next passage to be expounded' or 'I believe we really need to understand this passage of God's Word.'

Only the fourth response had a hearer-directed reality, and this was directed only at their cognition. A purpose statement must fall in line with three criteria. To begin with, a purpose statement *is a hearer-directed not a preacher-directed phenomenon*. Additionally, a purpose statement *must reflect how the message preached will impact the lives of the hearers, how they live, not just how they think*. Also, the purpose statement *must be in keeping with the purpose which God designed for this passage*.

In other words, a purpose statement indicates the overarching relevance the passage must have for the hearers' lives, once the passage is expounded clearly and understood thoroughly, because this has always been in keeping with God's design for this portion of His Word. A purpose statement reflects the timeless design of God for the truths to be expounded from the passage. The purpose statement, then, indicates the application of the truth that must be incorporated by the hearers. Therefore, the purpose statement suggests the relevance that the forthcoming exposition will have in the lives of the hearers before the text is even expounded.

Through a well defined purpose statement, declared in the introduction of a sermon, the hearers understand that the message to be preached will be personally relevant and they can understand the demands and the benefits that this portion of God's Word will bring into their lives. The ultimate perception of the hearers is that the purpose statement declared in the sermon introduction reflects God's purpose for this passage of Scripture in their lives.

The Components for Purposeful Preaching
In order for purposeful preaching to take place there must be a purpose statement that incorporates three components – precise terminology, specific intent, and accurate understanding.

Precise terminology
It is crucial that the purpose statement be very precise and accurate in the terminology it contains. You may find it hard to cast your purpose statement into one simple declarative sentence, but it must be done every time you preach. As one author put it:

> It's necessary because we ordinarily tend to hem and haw, toss in lots of verbal filler, and rob our ideas of power by using cop-out qualifiers like sort of, kind of, perhaps, rather, and maybe. When we finally do finish, we aren't sure at all that what we've said is what we actually meant. And our audience isn't even

certain what we've said. For both their sake and ours, we need to present our main thrust in a single line.[21]

Such indecision is always detrimental to preaching but it must be most strenuously avoided in the introduction of a sermon, and especially so when articulating the purpose of the sermon. An ill-stated, imprecise purpose statement reflects the fact that the preacher will be driving at something in this sermon, but it will also be obvious that he has not yet figured out what it is precisely. This is only marginally better than having no purpose at all. Make no mistake about this point, preaching without a purpose indicates a degree of indifference a preacher has for the whole enterprise of preaching!

Specific intent
A preacher is never in a more perilous condition than when his urge to preach is diminished by the slow corrosion of indifference, so that he experiences a lessened agony of mind and spirit in his preparation and preaching of God's Word. He goes on preaching, or perhaps we should call it talking, simply because it is a habit and, after all, it is his means of livelihood. But he becomes less and less diligent in preparation, more casual in delivery, and more convinced that an increasingly perceived futility of preaching is due entirely to the congregation and not at all in himself. 'Such a man cannot really preach and should not pretend that he can. The fires have gone out.'[22]

Through the overarching application of the sermon, indicated in the purpose statement of the sermon introduction, a preacher is focused in his preaching because he is preaching for some vital, significant effect. Through the application of the sermon indicated in the purpose statement, a preacher begins preaching in earnest far sooner than one would if he were unintentional. If Spurgeon's dictum, 'Where the application begins, there the sermon begins' is given merit, then the intentional preacher begins preaching, or at least establishes a foundation for preaching, before the introduction is completed. This causes the introduction to be a vital component that is actually the initial portion of a sermon rather than a flimsy precursor for the sermon!

Through the application of the sermon indicated in the purpose statement, a preacher begins to convey that the introduction of the sermon and the sermon to be preached will consist of personal, not perfunctory, matters. Daniel Webster was reported to say, 'When a man preaches to me, I want him to make it a personal matter, a personal matter, a personal matter!'[23] A good introduction, bearing a well-defined statement of purpose, begins to satisfy those hearers who want to know that the sermon will be of personal relevance to them. The purpose statement of the sermon introduction assures that the message will be relevant because it promises 'a practical bearing'[24] of the truths to be expounded.

Accurate Understanding
It is crucial to indicate the practical bearing the sermon will have just as it is crucial to indicate the subject-matter of the passage to be preached. Determining the subject remains only half-done when the preacher has discerned what the biblical writer was saying. We do not fully understand the subject until we have also determined its reason or cause. Consideration of a message's theme ultimately forces us to ask, 'Why are these concerns addressed? What caused this account, the facts, or the recording of these ideas? What was the intent of the author? For what purpose did the Holy Spirit include these words in Scripture?'

Until we have determined a passage's purpose, we should not think we are ready to preach its truths. Yet, as obvious as this advice is, it is frequently neglected. Preachers often think that they are ready to preach when they understand the subject of a passage and how the subject is developed in the passage, though they have not yet determined the text's purpose.[25] A sermon introduction must be viewed as faulty if it does not provide the hearer with a clear understanding of the object of the sermon just as it would be viewed as faulty if it failed to provide the hearer with a clear understanding of the subject of the sermon. The objective of the passage is just as discernable as the subject-matter of the passage to the careful student of Scripture.

We do not have to guess that there is a purpose for the text. The Bible assures us there is a reason for every passage it contains, and it clearly tells us the basic nature of this purpose. The apostle Paul writes, 'All Scripture is God-breathed and is profitable for teaching, for reproof, for correction, for training in righteousness; that the man of God may be adequate, equipped for every good work' (2 Tim. 3:16-17). Paul indicated that God intends for his Word to complete us. That is why the translators of the King James Version interpreted verse 17 of the passage to read, 'that the man of God may be perfect.' God intends for every portion of his Word (i.e., 'all Scripture') to make us more like Himself. Paul writes, 'Everything that was written in the past was written to teach us, so that through endurance and the encouragement of the Scriptures, we might have hope' (Rom. 15:4). The corrupted state of our world and our being require God's aid. He responds with his Word, which focuses on some facet of our need in every portion of His Word.[26]

Obviously, there may be more than one perceptible purpose identified for a text, but a sermon's unity requires the preacher to be selective and ordinarily concentrate on the Scripture portion's main purpose.[27] Donald Miller correctly insists, 'To use biblical passages for purposes not in harmony with those which prompted the writing of them is to misuse them.'[28] His instruction, therefore, is as follows: 'In determining the purpose of an expository sermon, the controlling principle should be that the purpose of the sermon should be the same as the purpose of the scripture on which it is based.'[29]

The purpose of the sermon must be in harmony with the original purpose of the preaching text. I use the word *harmony* advisedly in order to indicate that the purpose of the sermon cannot always be exactly the same as that of the text because we live in different times and circumstances than the original recipients of the text. One must always honor the original purpose of the text by remaining in harmony with it, but one may extend that purpose from its original Old Testament or New Testament setting to its contemporary setting. But the purpose of a given passage of Scripture is timeless, rising above cultural specificities, and can be principlized because any Scripture has always had only one meaning which is instrumental in effecting God's purpose for that passage.

Since biblical texts have become part of God's progressive revelation, rigid identity of their purpose may subvert the fact of God's progressive revelation of Scripture. For example, if the specific purpose of Genesis 17:9-14 was to have God's people circumcise all males as a sign of God's covenant, then in light of Acts 15 that can no longer be the purpose for the New Testament congregation. Similarly, if, in the context of prevailing customs, the specific purpose of I Corinthians 11:2-16 was that praying and prophesying women wear a veil, in the light of contemporary customs that original, specific purpose no longer holds. This complexity does not mean that these texts can now be set aside as antiquated; rather it means that their original purpose of acknowledging the covenant in the one case, and propriety in worship in the other, ought to be extended in a manner appropriate for this day and age. Such extension of purpose to our day naturally brings with it a requirement to discern the true meaning of a passage, and in the absence of this, will inevitably bring about the subtle temptation to impose one's own purpose on the text. That is why the deepening or expansion of the purpose of any biblical passage must be rigorously controlled by a wrestling with the real aim of the original writer.[30]

We must be purposeful in our preaching. We must make our purposes the same, in principle, as those of the scriptural texts we preach. When necessary, we may go beyond the immediate intention of the biblical writers in applying or deepening truth, but we must never contradict or twist that original purpose. The Scriptures must control all unbridled subjectivism in the enlarging, adapting, and applying of truth to the ever-changing needs of modern life.[31]

God's Glory – The Ultimate and Incessant Purpose

James W. Cox, in his book, *Preaching: A Comprehensive Approach to the Design & Delivery of Sermons*, asks a tragically flawed and misdirected triad of questions as he writes regarding the purpose of a sermon. Cox asks: Do we preach to carry out the purpose of God and thus get glory for Him, or do we preach to do something good for those who hear us? Is preaching an end, or is it a means? Is it irrelevant to human need, or is it relevant?[32]

Unfortunately, Cox asserts an unnecessary and unnatural either/or depiction of preaching. To begin with, there is no tension between preaching to glorify God and preaching to be of a benefit to those who hear the Word of God preached. It is a given that both things should take place every time the Bible is expounded. As a pastor I had the following statement printed on the top of the church stationery: 'Proclaiming the God of the Word through the Word of God.' When the Bible is expounded, those who hear the exposition should not only understand God's Word better and be challenged by the implications of the text, but they should also understand more thoroughly the God who inspired the biblical text.

The accurate understanding of God through any and every passage will result in His glorification. God cannot be understood and, at the same time, not glorified. It is the lack of understanding of God that causes one to fail to glorify God. As He is understood, He will be glorified. Obviously, I cannot appreciate Cox's either/or proposition regarding the glorification of God or the helping of those who hear us preach. It is always crucial to show our hearers why God is great and greatly to be praised. How God is to be praised by those who are in compliance with His Word will always be appropriate and helpful as well. It is a both/and, not an either/or reality, regarding God's glory and man's benefit in our preaching.

Moreover, do we preach and dare not desire to earnestly bring glory to God? May it never be! Preaching for God's glory is the perpetual intention for every sermon we preach. Read carefully John MacArthur's conviction regarding one's incessant purpose in preaching.

> Begin by focusing on the reality that your sermon is an offering to the Lord. Be driven by the truth that the Lord is your highest judge. Then your consciousness will compel you to deliver the truth as a holy offering to Him. This gives you the proper frame of mind for your solemn responsibility.
>
> What your colleagues or congregation may think or say is not your major concern. Know that delivering the message the Lord has given you is your service to Him for His satisfaction. That is why Paul charged Timothy 'in the presence of God and of Christ Jesus' (2 Tim. 4:1) to preach the Word. Let your thoughts after preparation and before delivery dwell on the Lord and His response to your expositional offering to Him. In the hours immediately before you preach, face the serious reality that you must deliver up a sacrifice that will be acceptable to the divine author of Scripture.[33]

Not only is the glorification of God in our preaching not an option, but as MacArthur points out, it is to be a passion in our preaching and pursuit in our preparation for preaching.

Next, Cox ponders the role of preaching, as to whether it is an end or if it a means. Preaching is God's appointed means to give mankind the greatest help for his greatest needs. But preaching must, first and foremost, serve as an end to bring glory to God!

The Believer's compliance to God's Word
Preaching that substitutes the preacher's opinions for an exposition of God's revelation of Scripture, and preaching

which imposes the preacher's agenda on his hearers rather than disclosing God's purpose for the passage, makes preaching impertinent and irrelevant. However, such 'preaching' should not even be viewed as true preaching. At least it is not expositional preaching! The exposition of God's Word can be irrelevant only if its author, God, is irrelevant. I think not! Cox inquires, 'Why explain, narrate, or examine some details of the text if they contribute nothing to the sermon's dominant goal?'[34] My question is, Why have a dominant goal in preaching to which the details of the passage can make no contribution? The preacher's goal is obviously not in-line with the text he will be abusing by using it to achieve his purpose for preaching.

Every worthwhile sermon touches our lives directly or indirectly, immediately or in the long run. But it is the sermon whose relevance is obvious that gets the best hearing. A common way in which preachers practically apply the truth of the sermon is to tack on an application or a moral at the end, but there is a much better way. The sooner the hearers realize that they have a stake in what the preacher says, the sooner they will begin to listen. The place for the application to begin is in the introduction, and application ideally should be carried through *to* and *including* the conclusion.[35]

Certainly, application in the sermon introduction will only constitute an obvious relevance that the passage to be expounded will have in the lives of the hearers. As we have already stated, true application cannot begin until a portion of the text has been explained. Until truth has been established there is no truth to be applied. But a certain indication of the relevance the passage will have in the lives of the hearers, once it has been explained, is not out of place or premature in the sermon introduction.

It is the purpose statement of the sermon introduction that not only assures the hearers that the message to be preached will be relevant, but it discloses how the truth of the text must be accommodated in their lives. As John Stott has rightly stated, 'If there is no summons, there is no sermon.'[36] Through the purpose statement in the introduction of the sermon the hearers should understand that a sermon will certainly be preached because the summons of the sermon can already be detected.

Distinction between a Sermon's Object and Subject

The statement of the purpose of the sermon is not the ideational content of the sermon. The ideational content of the sermon is established through the sermon proposition. The *purpose* statement describes *what you want to have happen* with the sermon. Borrowing the language of education, the purpose should describe a 'behavioral objective' of the sermon.[37]

Fortunate is the man who discovers early in his ministry that every sermon should have a specific purpose and the clear aim should be taken to achieve that goal. Otherwise he will fall into the habit of aiming at nothing and hitting it! For it is tragically easy to hit nothing. And no matter how brilliant or clever or packed with content a sermon may be, if it does not have a clear purpose in view, and if everything in it is not directed to the fulfillment of that purpose, it can be nothing but a 'tragedy of aimlessness'.[38]

There is a premature readiness that can be assumed by a preacher when he believes that he is well prepared because he has an outline and sermon proposition that rightly represents the meaning of the passage to be preached. As significant as this is, it is not enough. The subject of the text and, therefore, the sermon has been understood, but the objective of the text and the sermon to be preached from that passage must be understood just as thoroughly. Until this is done a preacher is not ready to preach. As indicated earlier, the object of the sermon and the subject of the sermon are related but distinct.

Confusion will inevitably occur regarding the distinction between the sermon's theme and purpose, or aim. Miller is helpful in distinguishing clearly between the two:

Stating the Purpose: An Indication of a Significant Sermon

The theme involves the particular truth to be set forth in a sermon; the aim consists in what we desire that truth to do to the hearer, or what we desire the hearer to do in response to the truth. The theme is the subject; the aim is the object. There may be times when theme and aim are so closely related that it is difficult or impossible to distinguish between them. But there are many occasions when our preaching will be given a keener cutting edge if we keep clearly before our minds what we want the truth of our sermon to accomplish.... The purpose, therefore, differs from the theme as the surgeon's instrument differs from the outcome of his operation. He uses the instrument not merely to cut; he cuts in order to heal. The aim is to be distinguished from the theme as the lecture on heart disease differs from the cure of the heart patient.[39]

If a sermon is to accomplish anything, it must accomplish something. Therefore, a sermon should be like a microscope whose function is to concentrate attention on a very narrow range of vision in order to enlarge and clarify this limited area so that many things about it which were previously unnoticed are brought to light with inescapable significance. Limitation means concentration.[40]

A focused concentrated objective for the sermon is missing in much preaching today. R. W. Dale wrote that 'many young preachers, when they sit down to prepare a sermon, start like Abraham, who "went out, not knowing whither he went".' He continues: 'The preacher who has a definite end to reach, rarely loses any of the time which he gives to preparation; he sees in the distance the point to which he has to travel and he either finds or makes a road to it.'[41]

In his book, *The Divine Art of Preaching*, A. T. Pierson elevated the role of the sermon's purpose as he argued for the equal significance of the parallel elements of the 'germinal and terminal laws in preaching'. By the germinal law of the sermon, he meant 'the theme and the essentials of its treatment' for a scriptural text. By the terminal law of the sermon, he meant the 'certain end, or terminus, to be kept in view'. This terminus depicted 'the definite aim, or result, in the convictions, affections, and resolutions of the hearer.' The terminus 'gives the goal of the sacred discourse'.[42] The purpose statement makes clear in the minds of the hearers what the sermon will be about.

The Overt Declaration of a Sermon's Purpose Statement
The purpose statement cannot be too overt. The problem with the purpose statement for the sermon, provided the preacher has one, is that it is either not discernable, or it is known generally but the listeners never hear a statement that they can identify as the specific purpose for the sermon. Ken Davis advocates a highly discernable statement of purpose as he writes:

> Don't be afraid to let your audience know what to look for. Near the beginning of almost all my presentations I will make a statement like this: 'Today I have one purpose in stepping before you, to give you three reasons why you should commit your life totally to a loving Christ.'
> Now they know the purpose of my talk and the method I am going to use to persuade them: I am trying to convince them to commit their lives to Christ, and I am going to give them three reasons why they should do so. This kind of message makes the listener look forward with anticipation to hear what the reasons might be. Even a hostile person will listen so that he might refute those reasons.[43]

It is only when a preacher has a clear sense of his directed purpose for the sermon that he can communicate best and lead others most effectively.[44] As it is in any area of life so it is in preaching. Failure in every department of life is linked, inextricably, with uncertain aims and unclear goals.[45]

General and Specific Purposes
For our preaching to be as good as it can be we must have sermons which our guided by objectives, specific objectives,

for the sermons we preach. No matter how specific the purpose of the sermon, the sermon's purpose must affect the needs of the hearers. The content of the sermon must be an explanation of the biblical text with an obvious relevance to the lives of those who hear the sermon. According to Skinner, 'A congregation set afloat on a vast sea of thought, equipped with everything but a rudder and a sense of destination, will not only fail to complete the voyage but will also find the experience frustrating and enervating.'[46]

It has been said that preaching is like shooting quail. If you aim for all the birds, you hit none, but if you aim for one, you are likely to get several. It is quite likely, therefore, that in aiming at specific, individual needs, we shall come nearer to meeting the needs of the whole group to whom we preach. This is true not only because the basic spiritual needs of men are quite the same, so that if we really lay bare the soul of one man his neighbor is likely to say, 'That speaks to my need, too.' It is true also because, quite often, the needs of individuals are best met in crowds.[47]

Brown, Clinard, and Northcutt distinguish three objectives or purposes for preaching: a total objective, a major objective, and a specific objective. The total objective of the sermon is exactly the same for every sermon: 'to bring life to the people.'[48] The major objectives are based upon the needs of the people and are suggested to fall into one of six categories. According to the authors: people need to be saved – the evangelistic objective; people need to grow in devotion to God – the devotional objective; people need to develop more mature understanding of God's truth – the doctrinal objective; people need to live in better relationships with others – the ethical objective; people need to serve God in a more dedicated way – the consecrative objective; and people need to find strength and comfort in trouble – the supportive objective. A preacher must understand which of these basic needs of people the sermon will meet.[49]

The specific objective or purpose of the sermon is defined by the authors as expressing in 'a positive or affirmative statement the response the pastor desires from his congregation as a result of one particular sermon.'[50] Several clarifications of Brown, Clinard, and Northcutt's assessment of the major and specific objectives may be helpful to the expositor.

First of all, the evangelistic purpose must not be considered as one of six possible major purposes for a sermon. The evangelistic purpose must be an unstated purpose for every sermon, unless it is an evangelistic passage that is being expounded. An expositor must understand, or at least assume, that the people who hear him preach represent the ultimate division of mankind – the lost and the saved. The one thing, among other things, to be done in the *conclusion* of the sermon is to present Jesus Christ to those who are unbelievers. The expositor must realize that the truths of the passage directed to believers for their edification cannot be appropriated by unbelievers and these truths are outside of the unbeliever's only need – to be saved from their sins through faith in Jesus Christ.

The evangelistic objective is a given, it is automatically a part of every sermon that is a true sermon. Can one be said to be a minister of the gospel and fail to declare the life, death, burial, and resurrection of Jesus Christ when he preaches? I think not! The role of evangelism in preaching seems to be too much of an all or none practice in preaching. Some pastors view the proclamation of the gospel to be the dominant purpose and dominating content of their preaching. Other pastors view the proclamation of the gospel to be the task of the evangelist, not the pastor-teacher, so they believe they are free to delete it since they are preaching for the edification of believers.

In his discussion on the philosophy of preaching, A. J. F. Behrends provides good analysis of the preachers who believe the gospel is the sole purpose for their preaching.

> One large, earnest, aggressive section of the Christian Church, whose piety and consecrated zeal are beyond dispute, maintains that preaching should not only be evangelical, but evangelistic. The preacher is simply a herald, and the substance of his message is the proclamation of the free forgiveness of sins, and the heritage of eternal life, through the mediation of Jesus Christ. The message of the pulpit is mainly to the unconverted.... To save souls is said to be the preacher's business, and the salvation of the soul is associated with some definite, formal, and public act of confession and committal. The preacher, therefore, should incessantly urge men to immediate and pronounced decision. The normal life of the Church is assumed to be one of perpetual revival, in the restricted sense of that phrase. Under such a theory, preaching becomes hortatory. It never passes beyond the rudiments of religious instruction. It may make use of the Pauline epistles, but it cannot move in their deep and broad grooves. It is constantly tempted to discount and discourage thorough and systematic training in Christian intelligence, and to make numerical increase the standard of ministerial efficiency. It counts the converts, it neglects to weigh them.[51]

The need to proclaim the gospel must not become a reason to keep pastors from quality exposition of the Bible any more than the need to expound the Bible must not prevent pastors from a serious proclamation of the gospel in the conclusion of their sermons. Edification of the believer and evangelism of the unbeliever are not mutually exclusive responsibilities for a Bible expositor. Both are germane to his task. The evangelistic objective must be accomplished in every sermon. But one must not think that doing expository preaching, verse-by-verse through entire books of the Bible, equates an explicit preaching of Christ. Sinclair Ferguson sounds a needed caution to this assumption:

> We must never make the mistake of thinking that any system of consecutive exposition of Scripture absolutely guarantees the preaching of Christ.

It is possible naively to assume, because we are preaching in a systematic way through books of the Bible, that we are therefore inevitably preaching Christ and Him crucified. That ought to be the case, but is not necessarily so. Sadly, one may preach in a consecutive way through the Bible without preaching in a truly Christocentric way. Indeed, paradoxically, one may have a passion for preaching the Bible without having a passion for preaching Christ and Him crucified.[52]

Ferguson is even more specific and insightful about the priority of preaching Christ in verse-by-verse exposition as he exhorts:

We need to return to a true preaching to the heart, rooted in the principle of grace and focused on the person of the Lord Jesus Christ. Then people will not say about our ministry merely, 'he is an expository preacher'; or 'that was practical,' nor even 'he cuts open our consciences'; but instead, 'he preached Christ to me, and his preaching was directed to my conscience.'[53]

Therefore, though the evangelistic objective will be achieved in every sermon preached, there will be another objective to be achieved for every sermon preached which may be related to one of the other five of Brown, Clinard, and Northcutt's categories for major objectives.

Additionally, in regards to the specific objective statement, the expositor must express a purpose statement reflecting the necessary response of God's people to His Word rather than 'the response the pastor desires for the congregation'. We would hope that the pastor's desired response for the congregation would be the natural and actual response to the expounded portion of God's Word which God has intended for that portion of His Word. I think it is best not to assume such equality between the pastor's desire and God's intention. Therefore, the specific purpose statement must be the God-intended purpose of the passage rather than the desire of the pastor for the congregation. After all, the pastor is not preaching his sermon but God's Word if he is involved in expository preaching. It is only fitting that God's purpose for His Word would be intentionally declared to God's people as God's ambassador attempts to explain God's Word to them. However, the authors are entirely correct as they assert that the purpose statement of the sermon must be written out just as carefully as the statement of the sermon proposition.[54]

General Purposes

General purposes for a sermon may include the supplying of insight not commonly known or discovered by the hearers at this time; increasing of interest in, commitment to truth that is commonly known and has been known by many for a long time; strengthening convictions based upon partial or imprecise foundations. However, specific purposes will always be directed to acting upon the truth which they now possess with greater insight, interest, commitment, and conviction.

Using the Apostle Paul as his model, Craig Skinner deduces four general purposes in the preaching of the apostles:

1. To inform or enlighten. A sharing of information for the hearer's understanding. It suggests a witness's declaration of the truth.

2. To inspire or comfort. This is application, and is one step above enlightenment. It carries a devotional quality of comfort that uplifts the meaning of the truth declared into specific relevance for the hearer concerned. As the relation between the information and the personal need of the hearer is declared, there is a rise of faith and interest. Such preaching inspires and comforts by means of its personal relevance.

3. To motivate or appeal. The continuity of the witness to the truth, and its specific significance to the hearer concerned, is taken further with the assurance that this practical relevance can be real through a commitment to it. From beginning to end in Scripture, the truth of God is revealed, related to need, and then used to structure the appeal to the will for moral action.

4. To edify or develop. To build up or bring to completion through a progression of stages, so that individual believers are brought further to maturity as their character is fashioned more and more to the image of Christ.[55]

Each of these four general purposes should be accomplished in every sermon. These general purposes for preaching deal with basic needs which are universal to all men. As Warren Wiersbe writes, 'When we're preaching about universal needs, we're also ministering to people personally and touching them where they hurt.'[56]

In order to be the kind of pastor that ministers to people through his preaching he must be a real pastor, one who knows their needs and can make the connection between biblical truth and its ability to affect the lives of those who hear him preach. In essence, a truly good pastor is an effective preacher – a preacher whose preaching impacts the daily living of his hearers as he enlightens their minds to the understanding of a biblical text. In like fashion, a truly good preacher is an effective pastor as he has fed, shepherded, and tended his sheep through the purposeful preaching of God's Word. Phillips Brooks was very insightful as his counsel in this regard. He writes,

> The preacher needs to be a pastor, that he may preach to real men. The pastor must be a preacher, that he may keep the dignity of his work alive. The preacher, who is not a pastor, grows remote. The pastor, who is not a preacher, grows petty. Never be content to let men truthfully say of you, 'He is a preacher, but no pastor;' or, 'He is a pastor, but no preacher.' Be both; for you cannot really be one unless you are the other.[57]

Unless the preacher truly has a shepherd's heart he may be concerned only with the content of the sermon to the exclusion of the intent of the sermon.

It is both wise and practical for the pastor to understand that the most basic difference between a lecturer and a preacher is that a lecturer is greatly concerned with elucidating a subject through his lecture, while a preacher is greatly concerned with achieving an objective through his preaching.[58] An honest objective in preaching can only be achieved through the faithful exposition of Scripture – the very thing that distinguishes a good shepherd who is a faithful expositor. Therefore, good content in a sermon – content that accurately explains the meaning of a biblical text – is a nonnegotiable, but it is negligible if it is not offered in an attempt to obtain the God-intended purpose for that content in the lives of the congregation.

Knowledge of the Bible then must be coupled with knowledge of human nature (which is known most accurately from the revelation of mankind in Scripture) so that biblical truth can be proclaimed with the greatest intention possible – to change the lives of the hearers. One author stated that, 'A man may know the Bible from Genesis to Revelation, he may know every theological treatise from the day of Augustine ... and if he does not know human nature, he is not fit to preach.'[59]

A purpose statement, made in the sermon introduction, unifies and clarifies for all who will hear the sermon both the content and the intent of the sermon. When the sermon is preached to its conclusion, the ultimate unifier of the sermon's content is the purpose that the preacher proposed in the introduction and has now been achieved in the process of preaching. Therefore, when the sermon is over, all who heard the message should have a clear understanding of why the preacher preached what he preached. Not only was the preacher's content understood but the preacher's intent for preaching the content was discerned. This assures the utmost meaning for the preaching enterprise – when precepts are marshaled for a purpose.

Every faithful preacher of the Word of God seeks to see hearts and lives changed through his preaching. Charles Simeon asked three questions about each sermon he preached: 'Did it humble the sinner? Did it exalt the Savior? Did it promote holiness?'[60] It will be of tremendous encouragement to the expositor to be able to answer each of these questions in the affirmative, having preached the passage. He will know that his message has been, in no small way, generally purposeful.

Specific Purposes

It has been stated that the test of a preacher's worth is when his congregation goes away saying, not, 'What a beautiful sermon' but 'I will do something.'[61] The 'something' that the hearer will do identifies the specific purpose the preacher had for preaching the message.

A specific purpose statement is an accurate expression of our intended achievement within an individual sermon and it must always relate to personal commitment. Skinner suggests a four-fold criterion which any specific purpose statement should conform. It should be brief enough to remember, clear enough to be written down, specific enough to be measured so that its achievement may be recognized, and related enough to the everyday life of the listener to be of value.[62]

The very intention of being practical in our preaching, even to the extent that one would dare articulate his purpose for preaching in the sermon introduction, is supported by Warren Wiersbe when he writes:

> If you doubt the authority of God's Word, then you won't apply it and perhaps shouldn't even be preaching it. If you worry about pleasing people in a pluralistic society and maintaining a politically correct stance, then by all means stay away from personal applications of the Scripture. If your sermons are religious essays on current affairs, then there won't be much to apply. But if you preach the Word, depend on the Holy Spirit, love Jesus Christ and your people, and realize that your time of ministry is short, you will want to make the truth of God personal and practical to the listeners.[63]

How very true! But the question is, will it be obvious that you are such a man not only in the application of the truth brought out in the body of the sermon, but will it be soundly sensed in the sermon introduction that you have a specific purpose in preaching this sermon that is to directly change all who will hear the message?

The ministry of the Apostle Paul is a faithful model and needed reminder that the preaching ministry of a true shepherd of God's people will seek continued change in their lives through the preaching of God's Word. This means that he will always preach so that there will be, in effect, a summons to live 'a life worthy of God'.[64] But moreover, each message must detail a more specific way such a worthy life and worthy walk before God is to be achieved.

The specific aspect of how the text to be treated makes a direct or indirect impact on the worthy life becomes the thrust for the sermon's purpose. Likewise, much of Paul's ministry was devoted to the cause of 'strengthening the Churches'[65] as he made returned visits and wrote letters to them. Certainly, every pastor seeks to see individual members of a congregation and the corporate body of the Church strengthened through his preaching. Yet, the means for this general purpose to become a reality will be indicated through a much more specific purpose statement that is announced in the sermon introduction and should be, therefore, discernable to all who hear the sermon.

The purpose statement of a sermon concentrates on the change to be accomplished in the lives of the hearers. The change is according to what the text requires people to believe, feel, or do.[66] Ultimately, what the hearers are to do is the chief objective of the sermon. The beliefs and feelings of the hearers are not insignificant. The Word of God will and should impact our beliefs and feelings. In fact, change in beliefs and feelings must occur if one's will is changed leading to a change in behavior. Grant and Reed offer this portion of wise counsel:

> When you think of application you may think first of appealing to the will, telling people what to do and how to do it. But the

will is only truly engaged if the heart and mind join hands. Aim first for the heart. Then, when you tell them what to do, people will understand how to fulfill the desire of their heart. You will release them to joyful obedience rather than burdening them with obligations.[67]

A changed life results from a changed heart. The heart then, is the ultimate object to be impacted by the preaching of the Word and the preacher dare not lose sight of this ultimate objective. If he does, he does so to the diminishment of his preaching. It is reported of Spurgeon that he would sometimes digress from his theme to tell a story or relate an anecdote to get the attention of an indifferent person in his audience, or to get attention after some distraction, and he would be criticized for not sticking to his subject. Spurgeon, however, replied to the charge that he 'stuck to his object' anyway.[68]

The purpose of a sermon is directed toward personal transformation of the hearers by means of 'behavioral objectives'[69] that should be achieved by the hearers if they are willing to comply with the truth of the passage. Preaching with a purpose does more than inform the hearers but also seeks to transform them through what they hear explained and applied. Presenting the claims of Christ to the hearers for personal change in their lives is required in order that the preacher can truly be a man of God.

> The dilemma, then, is not how the preacher can present the claims of Christ. He has no alternative but to present them as Jesus did – absolute, uncompromising necessities. To do otherwise is to water down the gospel, strip away its power to transform, and prostitute the glory of the high calling. The dilemma is man's. How does he hear and respond to the call of the gospel and the claims of Christ upon him? What does he do about these almost impossible claims of Christ? Whenever the claim and demand for ethical purity is made lovingly, passionately, and realistically, the preacher has then fulfilled his task as a man of God.[70]

Stating the Purpose: An Indication of a Significant Sermon

A preacher fulfills his calling to preach the Word not only as he is faithful to explain the God-intended meaning of the text from which he preaches. In addition to this he must be determined to see lives changed as hearts are affected by some specific purpose accomplished through the preaching of God's Word.

A Challenge to be Purposeful in Preaching

To preach purposefully is not easy and purposeful preaching is not all that common. It is greatly beneficial when it is done. It is unfortunate when it is not done, for the hearers as well as the preacher. One preacher and homiletician writes:

> I have listened to sermons that without aim did 'go round in an eddy of purposeless dust, effort unending and vain.' And I have preached them, too. The technique is not difficult. Like an Englishman at his bath, you plunge right in and splash around a bit. Having nothing to say which has seemed to you of sufficient importance to compel a clear analysis, you fill in the necessary time with a few remarks. You aim at nothing in particular and hit it squarely in the middle. The only sane question a hearer can ask when it is over is, What on earth was it all about? And the only sane answer anyone can give is, About everything. Or, nothing. You are to have a framework – and let it show.[71]

How can we ward off such a lamentable situation? Is it possible to preach with purpose every time we preach? Is there any way we can assure that when we preach we will have a clearly discernable statement of purpose in the sermon introduction?

I believe there is a way to assure that when we preach we are preaching with a clearly discernable, specific objective. A check and balance system would be to complete the following statement – 'My purpose in preaching this sermon is_____' – and then complete the statement with what you have understood to be the very purpose God has established for the text of Scripture in the lives of His people. This is as straightforward as one may be. This statement can be rendered from sermon to sermon in a variety of ways so that the word 'purpose' is not stated every time but it will be just as apparent as if it were used. For example, other statements could be used such as: 'Having heard this message today, you should be able to _____' or 'We will see, with the help of this passage, that you must _____ if you are to _____' or 'I trust that this morning you will be willing to _____.'

It might be refreshing to hear a preacher, before he preaches an obviously purposeless sermon, say in his introduction: My purpose in preaching this message is 'to stay employed as your pastor,' or 'to preach because you expect me to preach and I don't want to disappoint you,' or 'to continue to make progress in the exposition of Matthew's Gospel,' or 'to make sure I'm finished preaching this sermon before you're finished listening to me preach it!' Such a disclosure would be shocking, but it would only be shocking because he would be saying the very thing you would come to conclude having heard the sermon, that is, he had no purpose for preaching it.

Let's look at some perspective purpose statements, variously stated, dealing with various subject-matter.

* My purpose in preaching this passage is for you to commit yourself to spend time every day in prayer and reading of the Bible.

* When we have completed our examination of this passage of Scripture I want you to leave this place experiencing the forgiveness of sins that only God can provide as you confess your sins, all your sins, to Him.

* This morning I want you to respond to this precious portion of God's will for every believer – to embrace suffering for the cause of Christ in a godless society as the approval of God on your life.

* As we look at this text of Scripture you will discover the true test of humility, and I want you to pass the test

from this day forward, so that every day you live you will glorify God through Christ-like humility.

* We will discover from this text that we have an assignment from God; here it is – we are to love our enemies regardless of their hateful actions and attitudes toward us.

* As a believer you must worship God each Lord's Day through joyous, sacrificial giving which you have determined previously and intend only to do for God's pleasure.

* Today you must determine before God that you will never live another day without troubling yourself to serve others by intentionally discovering and meeting their needs according to your ability to do so.

* In response to this passage you must stop thinking that sharing Christ with the lost is the responsibility of others and start sharing Christ with unbelievers as you fulfill your role as an ambassador of the Living Lord.

* Having heard this message today, your response must be that you will submit fully to those who have a place of God-given authority in your life.

* I trust that you will continually thank God for each trial you face as you trust Him to mature your faith and purify your life.

To preach intentionally, with a purpose that is clear and credible is do-able, advisable, and a necessary part of a sermon introduction preached by a man who has something to say and wants what will be said to make a real difference in the lives of his hearers. I want to challenge you to never preach another sermon that does not have a hearer-directed purpose statement that is justified by the Scriptures to be expounded for every sermon you preach!

Needs, Values and Persuasion

How can purpose statements, like those listed above, be used in the lives of people to persuade them to act differently? Such statements give people something to attend to, they provide a degree of perceptibility, and they sound somewhat credible even before there is any exposition of a passage of Scripture. Though attention, perception, and credibility are necessary ingredients of the persuasion process, action will not ensue necessarily from attended statements that are properly perceived and considered credible. Such statements must be related to those wants and needs of the audience that are at the moment urgent to them or can be shown to be urgent by the preacher.[72]

An indifferent man does nothing because he wants nothing, and he will remain indifferent until desire is born within him. Therefore, a man can assent to propositional truth without acting upon it. A believed proposition, to produce action, must be regarded as expressing something necessary to the attainment of an immediate, urgent want and to be consistent with one's scheme of values.[73] Herein lies the great opportunity for the expositor to be a very persuasive preacher. Through the text to be scrutinized, a hearer's values and wants may suffer profound correction as a clear contrast is understood between truth as it must be, a correct understanding of the biblical text, and that truth as it is being attended to partially or incorrectly, or not being attended to at all, in the life of a hearer.

Each individual chooses or rejects goals based upon their ability to satisfy one's needs. One regulates the means by which one hopes to attain these goals by using measuring sticks known as values. A value is a concept of acceptable behavior by which an individual chooses from available means and ends of action.[74] Obviously then, for anyone hearing a sermon, persuasion will take place only as one comes to a different understanding of the goals, needs, and values of one's life.

Let's look at one purpose statement listed above – 'As a believer you must worship God each Lord's Day through joyous, sacrificial giving which you have determined previously and intend only to do for God's pleasure.' For the sake of clarity and brevity I will not consistently reference the possibility of giving off the cuff, with no prayerful and careful consideration or the possibility of giving out of a corrupt motive – to bring recognition to oneself in the act of giving. If one is going to be persuaded to change from one who gives inconsistently, nominally, and with little or no joy to one who gives consistently, joyfully, and sacrificially, much change must take place in the needs, goals, and values of the hearer.

The hearer must understand that the worship of God is a need one possesses. The hearer must understand that giving of one's financial resources is a legitimate way to worship God so it, therefore, becomes a goal to be achieved since it accomplishes one's need to worship God. The hearer must understand that to give, but to do so occasionally, joylessly, and miserly will not be acceptable to God – it will not qualify as act of acceptable worship. Joyful, sacrificial giving each Lord's Day, having been determined beforehand, and given without calling any attention to the giving of the offering, become the values or the measuring sticks by which the worship of God through one's giving is measured. With these values being understood from Scripture, a potential worshipper must either decide that acceptable worship of God will not be a reality, or one understands that his worship of God has been lacking or inadequate but this will no longer be the case. The hearer determines to change in how he gives as an act of worshiping God so that he will comply with the instruction of God's Word on the matter.

The change in becoming one who gives/worships God unacceptably to one who gives/worships God acceptably can only take place with integrity as the Word of God is expounded and the entirety of one's understanding is revolutionized. In other words, the hearer's needs, goals, and values now coincide cognitively and volitionally with the insight and insistence of God's Word. To state the same thing by using previous terminology, there is a changed behavior in the matter of giving because there has been a changed heart about it.

Persuasion Possibilities Regarding the Hearer's Needs
There are three basic connections between a preacher's proposals and the wants and needs of his hearers. First, a preacher may argue that his proposal will satisfy a given need which is not now satisfied, or will remove an obstacle that prevents the satisfaction of the need. Second, a preacher may argue that his proposal will satisfy a need better or more thoroughly than it is now being satisfied. Third, a preacher may argue that his proposal will assure the continued satisfaction of a need, and that under other circumstances they may be deprived of something important to them.[75] One of these connections between a proposal and the hearer's wants and needs should be incorporated in every sermon.

In dealing with acceptable worship through one's giving, all three may be incorporated. Any believer who thinks that they can worship God and not give from their financial resources will certainly have to conclude that their disobedience to God's Word in this area is a stumbling block that will prevent them from meeting their need to worship God acceptably. Others who attempt to worship God through their giving, yet their giving is not in line with the instruction from God's Word, may be persuaded to change how they give because of the expositor's ability to convince them from Scripture that their efforts, though well-intended, are not consistent with that which must happen for their worship of God to be more meaningful and more pleasing to God. As long as they continue to follow this pattern of consistent, joyful, sacrificial giving their worship of God through their offerings will continue to be pleasing to Him.

Persuasion Possibilities Regarding the Hearer's Values

Similarly, there are four basic connections between a preacher's proposals and the values of his hearers. First, a preacher may argue that his proposal is wholly consistent with the values of those who are redeemed. Second, a preacher may argue that his proposal violates fewer or less worthy values than other proposals for solving a problem. Third, a preacher may argue that his proposal is in urgent need of adoption, even though it violates commonly accepted values. Fourth, a preacher may argue that his proposal violates known values but these values are unsound and must be either modified or replaced with different values.[76] Again, the proposal for consistent, joyful, sacrificial giving as worship may combine several connections to the values of the hearers. The first and third connection would both be incorporated to persuade believers to change their pattern of giving as worship. If a believer is to change how he gives, he must understand that this new pattern is only consistent with what a believer should do and therefore this must be adopted even if others commonly refuse to do so.

The Emotional Effect of Persuasion on the Hearers

The primary means of exciting emotion in a message is to relate one's propositions to the needs and values of the hearers. To allege that an urgent need can soon be gratified produces joy or elation. To allege that an urgent need will ultimately be gratified produces hope. To allege that an urgent need has been satisfied or is about to be satisfied because of the activities of another person or others produces gratitude and affection. To allege that urgent needs have been attained by one's own effort, or one's own efforts have satisfied the needs of others, or that one has maintained one's values, or one has done these things better than others, or that one has done them in the face of difficulties or obstacles, produces pride.[77]

To allege that we have unwittingly or deliberately violated our own values or frustrated others in the satisfaction of their needs produces shame or remorse. To allege that others enjoy satisfactions which are rightfully ours, or are equally deserved by us, but which we do not have produces envy and anger. To allege that something instrumental to the satisfaction of our needs has been destroyed produces sorrow or grief. To allege that the satisfaction of one urgent need will make the satisfaction of another urgent need unlikely or impossible produces anxiety. To allege that something or someone has deprived us or intends to deprive us of the satisfaction of our needs produces anger or hate. To allege that something or someone has deprived us or intends to deprive us of the satisfaction of our needs and there is nothing to be done to prevent it produces fear in addition to anger or hate. To allege that the above situations exist, not for us but for others, produces sympathy or pity.[78]

Though one may use assertion, arguments, statistics, testimony, and other common means of support to excite the emotions, the most common approach is the use of vivid description and narration to depict actual emotion producing situations.[79] The intensity of the emotion he evokes will necessarily vary, therefore, with the degree of reality attained by his verbal reconstruction of events. A skilled preacher describing a situation might move his hearers while an unskilled preacher might leave his hearers cold and indifferent.[80]

Emotion tends to focus attention on the communication and prevents the mind from wandering. Intense emotion causes inattentiveness to parts of the communication.

Moderate to strong excitation of the emotions not only causes the best comprehension of material but also facilitates an intelligent behavioral response. Intense excitation of the emotions causes hearers to respond on the basis of emotion alone without any regard to the intellect.[81]

Achievement of the Purpose Statement for the Sermon
In order for the purpose statement to be achieved, or to facilitate achievement by the end of the sermon, some corollary

Stating the Purpose: An Indication of a Significant Sermon

questions need to be raised in the sermon introduction and answered in the body of the sermon or in the conclusion. Though the effort of this book is on the sermon introduction rather than the conclusion, it is worthwhile to note these questions because they can be asked in the introduction of the sermon and then answered in the sermon body or conclusion. The following questions help to clarify and facilitate the actualization of the purpose of the sermon in the lives of the hearers. Not every one of these questions need to be raised in the introduction or attended to in the sermon body or conclusion. Obviously, any one of them raised in the introduction must be dealt with in the sermon and any of these that will be dealt with in the sermon may be raised in the sermon introduction.

* What attitude is necessary in order for this to become a reality?
* What sacrifices will have to be made in order for this to become a reality?
* What things must be avoided in order for this to become a reality?
* What things are prerequisite in order for this to become a reality?
* What are the false perceptions associated with this as a reality in one's life?
* What will cause this to be done minimally when this is actualized?
* What will cause this to be done incorrectly in my life, or in a displeasing way to God?

Consider the Following Questions

1. What was Luther's response to the timorous disposition of Erasmus regarding his preference to not make assertions from difficult doctrines?

2. Since the Word of God is the source of authority in preaching, what is it that those who desire forceful exposition are looking for in the expositor?

3. What role does the preacher have regarding the perceptibility of authority and how is this caused?

4. What must an expository preacher provide for his hearers in order for him to be shamelessly bold and exceedingly purposeful in his preaching? If he fails to do this, what is the substance and the result of his preaching?

5. As the King's messenger, what is it that the preacher cannot protect his hearers from? What is it that he cannot produce in his hearers? What is it that his role as a messenger provides to his preaching?

6. How must a preacher consider himself if he is to be a faithful messenger of the King? What is it he is sure to have happen in his preaching? What must never become a concern for him as long as he is a messenger? What must his hallmark be?

7. What are the factors that make a sermon a message marked with integrity?

8. What are the two analogies characteristic of an expositor, in his study and in his pulpit, at which he must be equally good?

9. How does the sermon proposition compare and contrast to the purpose of the sermon?

10. What are the three-fold criteria for purposeful preaching?

Stating the Purpose: An Indication of a Significant Sermon

11. What is meant by the germinal and terminal laws in preaching, which is more important, and what is the status of the preacher until both of these are understood thoroughly?

12. What are the four general purposes that should be accomplished in every sermon?

13. What is the most basic difference between a lecturer and a preacher?

14. What are the three questions Charles Simeon would ask himself in evaluation of each message he preached and what benefit might these questions have for every preacher in his preaching?

15. What are the four-fold criteria to which every specific purpose statement of a sermon should conform?

16. What must transpire in order for an indifferent person to act upon propositional truth?

17. What has happened in the life of one who has been persuaded to change one's behavior to conform to the teaching of Scripture?

18. What are the three persuasion possibilities regarding a hearer's needs?

19. What are the four persuasion possibilities regarding a hearer's values?

20. Which serves better to cause hearers to comprehend and comply with truth – moderate to strong excitation of the emotions, or intense excitation of the emotions? Why is this so?

Words to Live and Preach by

The Faithful Messenger of God

Proverbs 11:2 – When pride comes, then comes dishonor, but with the humble is wisdom.

Proverbs 12:17 – He who speaks truth tells what is right, but a false witness, deceit.

Proverbs 12:19 – Truthful lips will be established forever, but a lying tongue is only for a moment.

Proverbs 12:26 – The righteous is a guide to his neighbor, but the way of the wicked leads them astray.

Proverbs 13:2 – From the fruit of a man's mouth he enjoys good, but the desire of the treacherous is violence.

Proverbs 13:17 – A wicked messenger falls into adversity, but a faithful envoy brings healing.

Proverbs 14:5 – A faithful witness will not lie, but a false witness speaks lies.

Proverbs 14:25 – A truthful witness saves lives, but he who speaks lies is treacherous.

Proverbs 15:2 – The tongue of the wise makes knowledge acceptable, but the mouth of fools spouts folly.

Proverbs 25:13 – Like the cold of snow in the time of harvest is a faithful messenger to those who send him, for he refreshes the soul of his masters.

Chapter Eight

Setting the Context:
The Earliest Indication of an Expository Sermon

Most preachers would probably view the idea of establishing the background of the passage and reviewing context of the passage as unnecessary and obtrusive elements that would only serve to make a sermon introduction boring and needlessly lengthy. Undoubtedly, the inclusion of such material will add to the time needed to introduce a sermon. For example, expository preacher John MacArthur writes: 'My introductions tend to be somewhat lengthy, because I have to set the historical and cultural background of a text and review the context.'[1] MacArthur is correct. His sermon introductions are somewhat lengthy, on average about fifteen and a half minutes in length,[2] but are commonly more substantial than the typical sermon one might hear on the Lord's Day. For the cause of excellence in expository preaching, the inclusion of such material, though adding to the time requirement for preaching, is not only necessary but will be a much-needed addition to that which is commonly absent from the typical sermon introduction.

In this chapter, four introductions from John MacArthur are included to exemplify that which is so infrequently done and yet that which is so significant for truly excellent expository preaching – setting the context. The four introductions of MacArthur are of the following lengths of time: 19:06, 10:31, 14:13, and 13:56. Admittedly, many would be aghast at such time commitments to an introduction for a sermon. And unfortunately, many would find these times to be more appropriate time allotments for the preaching of entire sermons rather than the times used in the introductions of sermons. Such thinking is not only adhered to by many who are found in the pews but also the majority of those who preach from our pulpits as well as those who teach preaching in the classrooms of theological seminaries.

The Components of Contextualization
In establishing the context in sermon introductions for expository preaching we must understand and incorporate three components: orientation, summarization, and connection. *Orientation* involves establishing cultural and historical data as well as scriptural cross references in order to provide contextualization for the subject-matter that will be preached in the sermon. *Summarization* involves a synopsis of the development of the book as it has been established by the texts that already have been preached. *Connection* involves the reviewing of the last sermon preached, that is, reminding the hearers about the last sermon's proposition, main structure, and the textual terrain corresponding to the main structure.

These three contextualization components of a sermon introduction may be likened to the landing of an airplane. There is the initial decent of the airplane from its cruising altitude (the background material), the approach to the runway and the touch down of the airplane on the runway (the summary of the divisions of the book), and the taxiing of the airplane to the gate at the terminal (the connection of the immediately preceding context). Just as in air travel it is necessary to get the passengers from where they were, the cruising altitude, to where they want to be, the airport terminal, so it is in taking the hearers from where they have been in the biblical book in past sermons to where they will be in the book in the present sermon.

Austin Phelps, in his book *The Theory of Preaching*, asserts that an introduction which makes a connection with the preceding discourse is one of many varieties in which a preacher may approach the task of sermon introduction. Specifically Phelps writes: 'An eighth variety of approach is the introduction connective with the preceding discourse. This will often, not always, be the most natural exordium in serial preaching.'[3] However, when preaching through a biblical book an introduction that does not make a connection with preceding sermons is not only an unnatural and abrupt intrusion to the development of the book but it will minimize the ability of the hearers to accrue a comprehensive understanding of the book as it is preached.

The question must be raised about the rationale for establishing the context in the introduction of a sermon – why do this? There are two reasons why this should be done. First, establishing the context through orientation, summarization, and connection will help to provide a better understanding of the sermon to be preached. Second, establishing the context through orientation, summarization, and connection will help to provide a better understanding of a biblical book as each sermon is preached throughout the study of that book.

Another question or two must be raised regarding the effectiveness of establishing the context in a sermon introduction – does it really promote better understanding and if it does, how does it do so? A seven-fold reinforcement is provided by establishing contextualization in a sermon introduction. These seven factors include: accuracy, thoroughness, relatedness, completion, perspective, retention, and volition. We will see that the seven-fold reinforcement for the effectiveness of orientation, summarization, and connection are corroborated from the fields of learning theory and hermeneutics.

Though the contextualization components of orientation, summarization, and connection are not commonly advocated by homileticians, nor incorporated by preachers in sermon introductions, they have not been omitted from homiletical instruction altogether. They have been treated in a pedestrian fashion, as something that will occur naturally with little or no intention or forethought, or in an optional approach, something that may be done. In the theory of homiletician Austin Phelps, for example, making a connection with previous sermons is advocated as an approach that may be incorporated into an introduction. Nathaniel Van Cleave also suggests that making a connection with the preceding sermon is important when preaching a series of sermons. He writes, 'Sermons in a course or series can often be best introduced by a brief synopsis or summary of the preceding sermon of the week before.'[4] Unfortunately, the connection to the previous message is limited to only one of nine possible ways to introduce a sermon.[5]

Expository preaching is certainly serial preaching. In fact, expository preaching is typically understood as a series of sermons that seek to expound consecutive texts of a biblical book from its first to last verse. Therefore, rather than seeing the synopsis of the previous sermon and the summary of preceding textual terrain as one of many ways to introduce a sermon, it is better to understand these as one element, among other elements, that is to be incorporated into a sermon introduction. Lloyd-Jones writes:

> When you continue the same subject in a subsequent sermon you must in a few sentences at the beginning sum up what you have already said, and then develop it. But again you must make sure that this sermon also is an entity and a whole, and is complete in and of itself.... There may be people present who were not there on the previous Sunday, and they will feel that because they were not present then that they cannot grasp what you are saying now.[6]

Lloyd-Jones is correct. When we are preaching through a book of the Bible, we must help those who were not present the week or weeks before this sermon to understand what they have missed, namely the flow and development of the book up to the text to be preached. Additionally, for those who have heard the previous message and messages, the summarization will serve as a needed reminder to recover what they have heard.

As Lloyd-Jones rightly insisted, every sermon must be complete in itself, a free standing sermon. This is especially true when you are preaching a series. However, when preaching through a book of Scripture each sermon is both a free standing sermon yet a sermon that makes a valuable contribution to a series of sermons being preached. Therefore, each sermon must successfully accomplish both roles – to make a significant individual contribution and at the same time make a valuable collective contribution to the series being preached.

The only way to ensure that any sermon accomplishes both roles of being free standing and contributing to the series is to take time in the introduction of the sermon to give a brief summary of the development of what you have been saying previously, review the last sermon, and orient the hearers to the subject-matter of the sermon they are about to hear. Not to do this is a very real snare to the preacher who would desire to do excellent work in expository preaching. Though there is a possibility to be too long in giving a synopsis of the previous sermon and the developmental flow of the book, a summary is nevertheless essential for the people if they are to understand the sermon most clearly and understand the contribution that the text being expounded makes in developing the flow of the biblical book.

The possibility that summarization could be done ineffectively, however, does not constitute grounds for not incorporating this material nor does it diminish the valuable contribution this material makes to an excellent introduction when it is done well. As Lloyd-Jones put it, the summary of the previous progress made in the exposition of the book 'will help all of them, even those who attend regularly; and for strangers who may attend, it is essential. So you must show the context of this particular sermon in the series, and its relationship to the whole, and perhaps throw out a hint of what is going to follow. But it must be an entity in itself – that is most important.'[7]

Seven Benefits of Contextualization

Let's consider briefly the seven factors that reinforce the value of contextualization through orientation, summarization, and connection. These seven factors originate from the fields of learning theory and hermeneutics. Our purpose here is to establish the validity of contextualization in a sermon introduction through the means of a few basic principles of the learning process and the process of biblical interpretation. Having briefly considered these seven factors, we will examine four introductions of expository preacher, John MacArthur. In examining these introductions, the contextualization components of orientation, summarization, and connection will be pointed out. Additionally, the seven factors of accuracy, thoroughness, relatedness, completion, perspective, retention, and volition, should be perceptible as the introductions are read.

1. Accuracy

The principle of context is widely considered the most important element for a correct interpretation of a biblical passage. When the context of a passage is not understood there is the greatest possibility of a mishandling of the text. Consideration of the context is extremely important for three reasons. First, words, phrases, and clauses may have multiple meanings, and examining how they are used in a given context can help determine which of several meanings is more likely. Second, thoughts are usually expressed by a series of words or sentences, that is, in association, not isolation. Third, false interpretations often arise from ignoring the context.[8]

Though the causes for misinterpretation are many, the most common and most certain way to get into an aberrant understanding of a text is the failure to regard the context. Walter Kaiser and Moises Silva affirm that 'contextual interpretation is one of the most basic principles to keep in mind when we seek to understand what people say and write.'[9] Even more significantly for preaching through a book of the Bible, Kaiser and Silva assert: 'If we read and understand the book as a whole document, not only will we be able to appreciate the total message of the book but we will also be in a much better position to solve any specific interpretive problems that we may come across.'[10]

Expounding texts sequentially through a book of the Bible provides the preacher with a distinct advantage in handling appropriately each passage he will attempt to expound. As an expositor reminds his hearers of the texts that have already been explained to them he provides a meaningful foundation for how the preaching portion is to be understood in light of its context as well as continuing to develop an overall understanding of the entire book as it is preached week after week.

Contextualization in a sermon introduction deals, primarily, with reviewing the texts that have been preached already rather than looking ahead to passages that will be preached in the future. However, just as the principle of context in hermeneutics deals with the passages that precede and succeed the text, so also the contextualization of the sermon introduction may review material preached already as well as referencing subsequent texts that will be preached in the weeks to come. The material before the passage serves as a radar which guides our approaching of the passage, and the material following the passage serves as a radar which guides our leaving of the passage. If we can track the material approaching and leaving the particular passage, we have the framework in which the passage is to be understood.[11] More often than not, it is important to prioritize the material already covered rather than that which will be covered in the weeks ahead.

As a Bible expositor, in the introduction of his sermon, reviews the material of the preceding contexts, he is prevented from *isolating* from its context the text from which he will be preaching. Isolationism is not only a problem in interpreting Scripture but it is also a barrier to the hearers in their ability to grasp the flow and development of a biblical book as it is preached to them throughout many weeks. Isolationism occurs when we fail to interpret a single Scripture text in light of its context or when we isolate the Scripture from its immediate literary surroundings.[12] When we try to interpret a text isolated from its context misinterpretation will result. Furthermore, as Francois Fenelon suggests:

> Detached passages, without their context being known, are robbed of their beauty for everything is consecutive in the Scripture and this consecutiveness is its grandest and most astonishing feature. In failing to understand the context: one takes passages in the wrong sense; one makes them say whatever one wishes; and one satisfies himself with ingenious interpretations which, being arbitrary, have no power to persuade men and change their habits. I want preachers not to be satisfied with pasting together similar passages. I would want them to explain the principles and the interconnections of the doctrine of the Scripture. I would want them to capture its spirit, its style, its figures, that all the discourses might serve to convey the understanding and the flavor of it. They need nothing more to be eloquent; for only to do thus would be to imitate the most perfect model of eloquence.[13]

When we try to introduce a sermon isolated from its context a failure to comprehend and appreciate the biblical book will result.

Even if the summarization is incorporated into the sermon introduction, its presence does not assure that the hearers will comprehend and appreciate this material. In other words, though reviews are crucial to true expository preaching, not just any attempt to incorporate review matter will be serviceable.

An inadequate review may be the product of a hurried and impatient preacher who is more concerned with getting into the preaching text for this sermon to the point where he will not spend sufficient time to re-address the previous texts which are the immediately preceding verses of the preaching text. Additionally, an inadequate review may be made because of a lifeless and colorless effort on behalf of a preacher.[14] Therefore, an inadequate review may result from an insufficient quantity of material incorporated in the review, or a qualitatively inept manner of treatment for the reviewed material.

Providing that the review material is neither qualitatively inept nor quantitatively insufficient, establishing the preaching text's context is a crucial element for the hearers to discern the accuracy of treatment that the expositor provides for the passage he is treating. When the context has been established the hearers can determine with a greater degree of certainty whether the text is being accurately interpreted in light of its previous verses.

2. Thoroughness

Thoroughness in preaching cannot be achieved in preaching without the context of the preaching passage being considered. One of the most common and egregious errors in non-serial preaching is to preach a text without seriously addressing the context of the passage. No matter how long the preacher preaches and no matter how detailed the examination of the text may be, he cannot truly be thorough in handling his passage if he does not establish the context of the passage. For the most part, the context of the passage includes an immediate and remote connection to the preaching portion. Milton S. Terry is helpful in understanding this as he writes:

> The word *context*, as the etymology intimates (Latin, *con*, together, and *textus*, woven), denotes something that is woven together, and, applied to a written document, it means the connexion of thought supposed to run through every passage

which constitutes by itself a whole. By some writers it is called the connexion. The immediate context is that which immediately precedes or follows a given word or sentence. The remote context is that which is less closely connected, and may embrace a whole paragraph or section.[15]

A preacher will not be handling his text thoroughly without establishing how the preaching passage is an outgrowth of the immediately preceding verses that incorporate the paragraphs and section of the book in which it is a part.

Learning theory would have us know that it is only as material is understood well that understanding can be advanced by subsequent material. Here then is the demand for thoroughness in preaching. Everything that can be comprehended should be understood as fully as possible. Thoroughness of this sort is the essential condition of true teaching. Imperfect understanding impedes the rate at which ample knowledge of a subject may be attained.[16]

The field of hermeneutics would be in agreement with the insistence that understanding of biblical texts must proceed from the known to the unknown. That which is uncertain in a text can be understood only by means of that which is known and that which can be understood clearly in the text in order to comprehend the more difficult portions of the passage. But comprehension must be the result of proceeding in the direction from the known to the unknown.

Since expository preaching moves sequentially through the biblical texts from one sermon to the subsequent sermon, there is a built-in advantage of coming to each new text having already become familiar with the context of each subsequent passage to be preached. And just as this increasing familiarity of the context helps the expositor interpret each text he comes to in his study of the biblical book from which he preaches, so also the establishing of the context in the introduction of each sermon he expounds will be a clarifying force for those who hear him preach.

Therefore, there is little excuse for ignorance or neglect regarding context and language of the texts preceding the preaching passage each time one introduces the next text to be expounded. 'To disregard contextual or linguistic factors suggests ignorance, carelessness, or an intentional omission of unwelcome data.'[17] Furthermore, a preacher who fails to inform or remind the congregation of the context when introducing a sermon deprives the hearers of the key hermeneutical principle that served as a great advantage to himself when he was in his study trying to understand the passage – understanding the unknown in light of the known, that is, the previous context of the passage. If a preacher is only interested that his hearers listen to him as he preaches his sermon, then establishing the context of the passage is of no significance to him in this preacher-centered pursuit. However, if he truly is interested in expounding Scripture so that they may understand God's Word, then why would an expositor ever consider omitting contextualization in the introduction of his sermon? A Word-centered, people-centered pursuit cannot afford such an omission since he would be violating basic necessities for learning new information and understanding biblical truth in a thorough and accurate manner.

3. Relatedness

As the context of the preaching passage is established, the hearers are afforded a sense of relatedness, or an appreciation of the passage being preached, because the preaching portion supplies the hearers with an updated understanding of the biblical book being expounded. Each additional sermon then provides not only specific but a more general understanding of biblical truth. It is the expository preacher who can truly be about establishing the knowledge of Scripture in his preaching. Learning theory suggests that knowledge is predicated on the ability to relate one concept to another. Therefore, the act of knowing is in part an act of comparing and judging, that is, relating new material to past understanding.[18] Explanation uses facts and principles already understood to make clear new data.[19]

We have addressed the importance of understanding the context in order to deal with the content of the preaching passage. This has been a deep-seated conviction and practice for preaching as of the Protestant Reformation. Ulrich Zwingli, the Reformation leader in Zurich who emphasized the importance of interpreting Bible passages in light of their contexts, believed that pulling a passage from its context 'is like breaking off a flower from its roots'.[20] However, sometimes the obvious is forgotten simply because it is so self-evident. One cannot properly handle context until he has a good grasp of biblical content. The interpreter must know the content of the book from which the particular passage he is interpreting comes. In other words, biblical content is essential for the much-needed grasp of context.[21] Content informs the context and context interprets the content. Relatedness is the byproduct of preaching through consecutive passages of a biblical book. The content of each successive passage is understood better as the context is expanded. The clear or unclear treatment of a passage will not remain an isolated commodity. It has been stated that, 'a cloud left upon the lesson of yesterday casts its shadow over the lesson of today. On the other hand, the thoroughly mastered lesson throws great light on succeeding ones.'[22] The relatedness of a biblical text to the subsequent text is maximized through the contextualization components of summarization and connection.

4. Completion
The completion of any type of instruction must be made by review and application. The review is necessary to perfect knowledge, to confirm knowledge, and to render this knowledge ready and useful. John Milton Gregory writes:

> It would be difficult to overstate the value and importance of this law of review. No time in teaching is spent more profitably

than that spent in reviewing. Other things being equal, the ablest and most successful teacher is the one who secures . . . the most frequent, thorough, and interesting reviews.[23]

As we have already indicated, disregarding the context is one of the greatest problems in Bible interpretation. By disregarding the 'total surroundings' of a Bible verse, we may completely misunderstand the verse. We need to take into consideration the sentences and paragraphs that precede and follow the verse and also to take into consideration the cultural setting in which the passage and even the entire book is written.[24] Therefore, a review is more than a repetition. A machine may repeat a process, but only an intelligent agent can review it. The repetition done by a machine is a second movement precisely like the first; a repetition by the mind is the rethinking of a thought. A review involves fresh conceptions and new associations, and brings an increase of facility and power of a hearer's comprehension. The review provides a hearer to occupy, in fuller force, the ground of which the first study was only a reconnaissance.[25]

Learning theory suggests that a review is not an added excellence which may be dispensed with if time is lacking; it is one of the essential conditions of all true teaching. Not to review is to leave the work half done.[26] The profit of a review is not dependent upon a prodigious recalling of what was treated previously. A review may be partial recalling selective facts or principles, or recalling an event, or some difficult clarification of question. Even a complete review may be a cursory reviewing of the whole field by raising and answering a few general questions, or it may be a full and final reconsideration of the whole ground.[27] The application of a review for expository preaching is the provision of the contextualization components of summarization and connection. The summarization component provides a more general review of the development of the remote previous texts while the connection component provides a more specific review of the immediately preceding text preached the week before.

5. Perspective
Reviews made from one week to another are helpful since the lapse of time changes the point of view of the hearers, so that they may appreciate more fully later what they might have only marginally appreciated initially. At every review we survey the lesson from a new standpoint. Its facts rise in a new order and are seen in new relations. Truths that were overshadowed in the previous study are now brought out into light.[28]

6. Retention
The human mind does not achieve its victories by a single effort. There is a sort of a mental incubation as a result of which some splendid discovery may spring forth.[29] Each review establishes new associations, while at the same time it familiarizes and strengthens the old. The instruction that is presented only once is likely to be forgotten. That which is thoroughly and repeatedly reviewed is woven into the very fabric of our thoughts, and becomes part of the equipment of our knowledge. In preaching through a biblical book, the hearers will understand the book only as they have the opportunity to retain what they have been exposed to through the many texts that have been explained only as they receive summarizations of the ground that has been covered.

7. Volition
The measure of one's achievement in preaching is found by what our hearers can remember permanently and, having remembered, can use that instruction in daily living. Frequent and thorough reviews can alone give firm hold and free

handling of the truth. The plastic power of truth in shaping conduct and molding character belongs only to the truths which have become familiar to an individual. Familiarity comes, most often, by repetition. If we would have any great truth sustain and control us, we must return to it so often that it will rise up in the mind as a dictate of conscience, and pour its steady light upon every act and purpose with which it is concerned.[30]

The most comprehensive sway on one's volition comes from the most comprehensive knowledge of Scripture. As valuable as the knowledge of a few choice verses from a biblical book may be, a command of the flow and development of a book of the Bible on one's volition is far better. A Scriptural truth may be reviewed by a new application to the heart and conscience or to the judgment of the duties and events of the life. I don't know if the point can be made better than how John Milton Gregory put it when he wrote, 'In the Bible, more than any other book, are reviews needful and valuable. Not only does the Bible most require and most repay repeated study, but most of all ought Bible knowledge be familiar to us. Its words and precepts should rest clear and precise in the thought as the dictates of duty.'[31]

Contextualization Components in Sermon Introductions

The components of orientation, summarization, and connection are priceless in the introductions for expository preaching. We need to see how they make a valuable contribution.

Let's examine four sermon introductions by John MacArthur paying particular attention to how he establishes the context of the passage in the introduction, in order to clarify the exposition of the text he will be preaching. For the purpose of clear reference each paragraph will be designated with a P and a number: P1 being paragraph one, P2 being paragraph two, etc.

Introduction One – Romans 4:18-25

Text

P1 We look forward to tonight as we go back in the book of Romans and return to the fourth chapter. So take your Bible, handy there, if you will and open it to Romans chapter four. We're trying to work our way through this great chapter of twenty-five verses on the faith of Abraham, a very classic chapter presenting the great illustration of salvation by grace through faith.

P2 Now in this fourth chapter of Romans, as you know if you've been with us, the Apostle Paul presents Abraham, the Father of the nation of Israel, as the model, the prototype, the supreme example, of salvation by faith. The Bible teaches that a man is made right with God by faith. That is, it's not something we do, it's something we believe. And in believing, righteousness is given to us and we are made right with God. And the great illustration of that is Abraham. And he begins with that illustration in the very first verse of the fourth chapter.

P3 Now keep in mind also, that the book of Romans basically presents the gospel of God. In fact, that wonderfully rich phrase, the gospel of God, appears in Romans in the very first verse of the first chapter. It is the good news from God. And the good news is that men can be saved by faith, not through their own works. And Abraham is the great illustration.

P4 Romans, you will remember, begins with a penetrating and deep, and, at the same time, a comprehensive and wide look at the sinfulness of man – chapter one verse eighteen through three verse twenty. That whole section shows the sinfulness of man. That's the bad news. And then the solution to that is found in chapter three, verse twenty-one through chapter five, verse twenty-one. And there you have the Good News, that in spite of the sin of man God has provided salvation and righteousness and redemption through the Lord Jesus Christ. Now, we're right in the middle of that section. We've looked at chapter three, we will look at chapter five, and we are in chapter four.

P5 Chapter three verses twenty-one to thirty-one states the teaching of salvation by faith. Chapter four illustrates it and chapter five demonstrates it, shows its results. So, the statement of the doctrine in chapter three, the illustration in chapter four, and the result in chapter five.

P6 Now, the Great illustration of this is Abraham and his unique faith. In order to really understand all that Paul is saying in the fourth chapter, you have to understand the story of Abraham. Now I have been, through this chapter, feeding you little bits and pieces of the story and I hope its beginning to fill up so that you understand the fullness of it.

P7 The man's name originally was Abram – A, B, R, A, M, no H, A in the middle – Abram. And it meant father of many. And nobody was more inappropriately named than he was. He was the father of nobody – nobody at all. And yet he was named Abram, the father of many.

P8 Now, at the age of sixty, after that much life of barrenness, God came to him and God called him out of idolatry in the city of Ur, said 'I want you to get out of this place.' It was the sovereign call of God, very much like the call of the Apostle Paul. It seems as though Abram had little to do with it all, initially. God calls him out, he obeys God, leaves, at least in part, dragging along a lot of his relatives as baggage. He wound up only going as far as Haran and staying there for fifteen years. Not quite making the full move that

God had intended. But at the end of the fifteen years, by now he has reached the age of seventy-five, he moves out of Haran and sets out for the land of promise which God had originally given to him. He leaves his home, his people, his land, his idols, the whole thing, takes his wife and moves on to an unknown destination. Now, it is essential to begin with to note that Abraham was chosen sovereignly by God. And he responds to the sovereign choice of God simply by believing God. God says, 'You go and I will bless you' and he believes it. He believes it and he goes. And that's basically the story of salvation – God sovereignly comes, calls a person, the person responds, and says, 'That's what You say, that's what I'm to do, I believe it, I accept it.' And in that simple term Abraham is defined to us as the father of our own kind of faith.

P9   Now when God called Abraham, He also told him that he would produce a seed, that he would have offspring. In fact, ultimately his offspring would number as the sand of the sea and the stars of the heaven. We shouldn't be so surprised at that comparison. Dr. James Genes, astronomer, some years ago said that it is very likely that the stars of the heavens equal the sand of all the seas. And so He told him that he was going to have a great number of those who would come to be his posterity. Now, the problem is, here is a man who is told he is going to produce multitudes of people and he is in fact the father of nobody. He's never produced anybody. He has no seed. All he has is a promise. He has no land. All he has is a promise. He's looking for a son and he's looking for a land. And he moves out in faith. Why? Because he believed God. You say, why did he believe God? I don't know because the Bible doesn't tell us that part. How did God convince him that he was to be believed? I don't know, the Bible doesn't tell us that. But somehow God convinced him. Now when God wants to do something He can do it, can't He, if He chooses? Of course. And all of us are redeemed not only because God called us, mark this, but because God produced in us the response. And so when God called Abraham, He also produced in Him the response. The call, in whatever form it came, was convincing enough to make Abraham believe when there really was no human reason to believe and all the odds were stacked against him. So we meet the man who was the father of nobody on the way to nowhere. And all he basically knows is that God has told him to do it and beyond that he knows nothing, except that God's going to fulfill His promise. And he believes that. For some reason he believes it. The only reason we can ascribe to it is that God planted within his heart that confidence.

P10 Now, once he finally leaves Haran at the age of seventy-five and makes his way into Canaan, which is the place to which God sent him, he is immediately faced with some very severe tests on his faith. First, a famine – Genesis chapter twelve. Then a Pharaoh, also Genesis chapter twelve. Then a fight with his brother – Genesis thirteen. Then fear – Genesis fifteen. Then foolishness – Genesis sixteen. And so he has to wade through all this stuff: a famine, a Pharaoh, a fight, fear, and foolishness. And if you think that was easy, you're wrong. And he was waiting for a fulfillment. But all through all of this difficulty he held on to God's promise. And this is supernatural. It doesn't make any sense, humanly. And it must not have been very easy. Dr. Barnhouse points out some of the difficulty of the situation in a very interesting paragraph in his commentary on Romans. He writes this:

'Now Abram was an Oriental. He was used to the palaver of the Orientals. Furthermore, he was strategically located athwart the roads of the camel caravans that carried the commerce of the ancient world between Egypt and the North and East. He owned the wells, and his flocks and herds were great. The Scripture says that "Abram was very rich in cattle, in silver, and in gold" – Genesis 13:2. When the caravans of the rich merchants came into the land, either from the north or from the south, they stopped at Abram's wells. The servants of Abram took good care of the needs of the camels and the servants of the traders. Food was sold to the travelers. And in the evening time the merchants would have come to Abram's tent to pay their respects. The questions would have followed a rather set pattern. Abram, how old are you? Well, who are you? Well, how long have you been here? Well, where did you come from? Well, what is your name? To which Abram would be forced to name himself: 'Abram,' father of many.

'It must have happened a hundred times and a thousand times, and each time it was more galling than the time before. 'Oh, father of many! Congratulations! And how many do you have?' And the answer was so humiliating to Abram: 'None.' And, many a time there must have been the half concealed snort of humor at the incongruity of the name and the fact that there were no children to back up that name. Abram must have steeled himself for the question and the reply, and hated the situation with great bitterness.'

And Barnhouse adds another word, he says:

'It was a world of cloth and goat skins, where all lived in tents, and where there was little privacy from the eyes and none in the realm of the ears. And there must have been many conversations on the subject – who was sterile, Abram or Sarah? Was he really a full man? Oh, he was the patriarch, his word was law. He had a multitude of cattle and the many servants but he had no children and his name was "father of many".'

So says Barnhouse, and I think gives us some insight on what it must have been like in that time for Abram.

P11 Well, the pressure applied to them caused Sarah to come up with a great idea. She decided that Abram needed to live up to his name. And so she offered him her servant-girl by the name of Hagar and said to him, 'You go into Hagar and let her conceive a son for you and this will save your face and demonstrate if, in fact, you are virile enough to produce.' And of course, the word must have spread through the thin tents very rapidly that Abram had, in such desperation, stooped to try to gain a seed through the union with a servant. And it worked. And Hagar became pregnant. And everybody knew that it was Sarah then who was the problem. And Sarah felt despised and oh did she hate Hagar. But Abram now had his heir. And the next caravan that came through, when they said, 'What is your name?' and he said 'Abram,' and they said, 'Oh father of many. How many?', at least he could say: 'One.'

P12 Finally, at the age of eighty-six, he had one. And I really believe that Abram wanted that one to be the fulfillment. Because in Genesis 17:18, listen to what Abram says to God: 'O that Ishmael might live before Thee.' O that Ishmael may be the one to whom You look, God, the one You receive. You see, he produced a son from his own natural powers. He produced a son from his own human virility.

P13 Thirteen years later, now he is ninety-nine. His son is thirteen years old. He's ninety-nine and God comes to him and God says, 'Abram, that wasn't the one. That was the son of your natural virility, not the son of my supernatural power.' Now mark that. 'That was the son of your flesh, not the son of divine energy. But I'm going to give you another son. This is the son of promise. This is the son you could never produce.' And then God says, 'From now on your name will be Abraham.' You know what that means? The father of multitudes. Now the year between that promise when his name was changed and its fulfillment must have been again a painful year. Because now he had to say, 'Father of multitudes.' Oh, how many? 'One.' So he's sort of working up to living up to his name, rather slowly. By the way, may I hasten to add that Abram took the name Abraham and used it and that was indicative of his faith, wasn't it? He happily called himself Abraham because he believed God. Ishmael, then, was the son of natural generation and Isaac was the son of supernatural generation, and a year later when he was one hundred years old he had a son, Isaac.

P14 Abram begot Ishmael in the human strength. Abram begot Isaac, mark it, in the power of God. That becomes very important. Look with me for a moment to Galatians chapter four – Galatians chapter four, verse twenty-one. One of the very most difficult portions of the New Testament, and we're not going to dig into it in great detail, you can listen to our teaching on that some other time, but I do want to point out the basic connection. Galatians 4:21 says:

'Tell me, you that desire to be under the Law, do you not hear the Law?' If you desire to live by the Law, in other words, if you try to accomplish God's goals by the flesh, if you desire to live that way then remember that the Law says "Abram had two sons, the one by a bondmaid the other by a free woman." That is one by Hagar the slave, the other by Sarah, the free woman. "But he who is of the bond woman," that's Ishmael, "was born after," what? "The flesh." That child was born of the natural power of Abraham. "But he of the free woman was born by promise."

P15 And there we find the divine connection. Ishmael illustrates then, mark it, Ishmael and Isaac are illustrations in Galatians four, Ishmael illustrates the principle of living by what? The flesh. Isaac illustrates the principle of what? Living by the promise of God. And that becomes the allegory, the only allegory by the way so stated in all of Scripture, of the fourth chapter of Galatians.

P16 Ishmael then is an illustration of a son born in the usual way and is a living representative of all those who believe they can accomplish God's will through their human effort. Did you get that? And Isaac is a son born of faith by a supernatural miracle and an illustration of all who receive spiritual birth, so that Isaac and Ishmael become living patterns and illustrations. The contrast, now go back to Romans four, the contrast is between human effort and divine power. God would never tolerate Ishmael as the son of His promise because that was the child produced by Abraham. He would only tolerate Isaac as the son of His promise because he was supernaturally conceived. Now Abraham believed that. Abraham accepted that and waited for the son, Isaac, to be born.

P17 We meet him then in Paul's picture after he has heard the promise and is waiting for the birth of Isaac. And we pick up the story in verse eighteen. And Paul says of Abraham, (Rom. 4:18-25 read aloud).

P18 Now Paul, then, closes the chapter on Abraham with this tremendous section, it's very clear as we go through what he is saying and I want you to follow it. Remember that the first eight verses of the chapter show that salvation comes by faith not works.

P19 Then, verses nine to seventeen show that salvation comes by grace not law. Now, these verses show that salvation is through divine power not human effort. And that is demonstrated in the life of Abraham, as all the others are as well.

P20 Now, as we look at Abraham's faith in the last section of verses eighteen to twenty-five, I want you to note three realities, three realities: the analysis of faith, the answer to faith, and the application of faith. The analysis of faith, the answer to faith, and the application of faith.[32]

Assessment

Several things must be noted regarding introduction one. First, nineteen minutes and six seconds were needed for this introduction. Second, the introduction is composed of material that established the context of the passage to be preached primarily through the component of orientation. However, this introduction strongly demonstrates all three components involved in contextualization, or establishing the context of a passage in the sermon introduction through orientation, summarization, and connection. This introduction exhibits much orientation by explaining the cultural background of the passage, some summarization through a concise summary of the chapters preceding the preaching text (Rom. 4:18-25), and a solid connection through an explanation of how the immediately preceding context (Romans 4:1-17) connects with the preaching portion.

In P2 there is a brief summarization for the entirety of the fourth chapter as dealing with Abraham, who serves as the prototype of salvation which is by grace, through faith.

P3 provides orientation through the assertion that the whole book of Romans is a presentation of the gospel of God.

Setting the Context

Summarization is given in P4, in that, Romans 1:18–3:20 is summarized as the bad news, whereas Romans 3:21–5:21 is summarized as the good news. P5 continues summarization of the good news specifically in that Romans 3:21-31 gives the teaching of salvation by faith, Romans 4 gives an illustration of salvation by faith, and Romans 5 gives the result of salvation by faith.

P6-17 supplies a wealth of orientation material through a historical account of the life of Abraham from his call from God to his waiting on God to supply the son of His promise. Specific cultural data is supplied to reinforce the dynamic of Abraham's faith as viewed through his personal situation and the manners and customs of his times.

P18 provides specific summarization in that Romans 4:1-8 illustrates that salvation comes by faith not works.

P19 provides specific connection to the previous sermon in which it was discovered that Romans 4:9-17 illustrates that salvation comes by grace not law. The message to be preached from Romans 4:18-25 illustrates that salvation comes by divine power not human effort.

P20 suggests the structure for the sermon to be preached as three realities of the faith of Abraham.

This introduction provides tremendous insight into the flow and development for the first four chapters of the book of Romans. A brief reference was provided for chapter five, summarizing that chapter as demonstrating the result of faith. This very brief preview of chapter five would take MacArthur five sermons to preach. One may quickly see how the excellent job of summarization, exemplified in this introduction, would furnish the hearers with a thorough knowledge of the book of Romans as such treatment is rendered throughout the preaching of the epistle. If it is truly a desire on behalf of the would-be-expositor for his hearers to have a working knowledge of the book when he has finished his exposition of that book from the first to the last verse, then the merit of such extensive contextualization is immediately obvious.

Introduction Two – Romans 5:1-2

Text

P1 Tonight, as I mentioned this morning, we embark on a wonderful study of the fifth chapter of Romans, Romans chapter five. And Romans is a book, believe me, that taxes your mind, taxes your soul as well. It is so profound, so deep, and so rich with the truth of God. And yet, because of the wonderful inspiration of the Holy Spirit, because of the fact that He is our resident truth teacher, as we saw this morning, its truths can be opened to our minds. And I trust that as we look at the first eleven verses, not just tonight but in tonight's message and then the next couple of weeks, that you are going to find yourself rejoicing in the tremendous security of your salvation. This is a great, great passage.

P2 I was reading a book this week that was given to me and it was a book that had many interesting statements in it. It was a theology book. One of them was this, and I quote, 'Some truly converted people have fallen from grace and the danger of doing so threatens every Christian.' Now, that is a very, very important statement, if it's true. If it is true that some Christians have lost their salvation and every Christian is in danger of doing that, that is indeed an important thing to know. For, if you can lose your salvation you had better find out fast how to hang on.

P3 Now, this is a subject that through the years has been very hotly debated in theology. There have always been those who have affirmed that you could lose your salvation and those who have affirmed that you could not, and the battle has gone on through the years. The issue of eternal security, or the perseverance of the

Setting the Context

saints, or as laymen sometimes call it, the 'once saved always saved' doctrine, and some in our time, today in many churches, some of you in your own background, some of you maybe even to this very day believe that a Christian can lose his or her salvation. Sometimes we hear about those who 'backslide' and fall away from the knowledge of Christ. Now, this particular doctrine that says you can lose your salvation, basically, makes salvation conditional. In other words, your salvation is only good, as long as you meet the conditions of maintenance. In other words, God has saved us and now if we continue to match up with the standard we can hold on to that salvation, if at any point we fail to live up to the standard we lose it.

P4 Now, it doesn't take much insight to realize that that is basically a works righteousness perspective. In other words, you are really saying that salvation is conditional in the sense that my works have to stay up to standard or I forfeit my salvation.

P5 Now this, I believe, is exactly the issue to which Paul speaks in Romans five. And it fascinates me that in many, many treatments of the subject of the security of the believer, Romans five isn't even discussed which amazes me. Or, sometimes it appears as a footnote when I think it may be, of all the passages in the New Testament, the most absolutely definitive text ever written on the security of our salvation.

P6 Now, let me see if I can tell you why it's here and why I say that. Paul is writing, basically, to affirm the gospel. And his thesis in chapters three and four is that salvation comes by grace through what? Faith. And that faith is all that is necessary to appropriate eternal salvation.

P7 Now this is quite revolutionary to a Jew, frankly, who has been reared on a works righteousness system of salvation. In other words, by doing certain works he gains the favor of God. And, frankly, that is exactly how all other world religions are built – on the goodness of man, man living up to some religious code, some ethical standard. And so, when Paul articulates in chapter three and chapter four that salvation is a free gift, that it is given by God's grace that is unearned and undeserved, and is appropriated by faith and faith alone and that is all, men find that very difficult to comprehend. Because men basically are into works, they're into human achievement, they're into self-righteousness, they're into lifting up themselves by their own bootstraps.

P8 Basically, the philosophy of men and the religions of the world is, 'I'm good, I'm religious, God would never send me to hell.' You've heard that myriads of times. 'I mean, I'm a good person, I'm religious, I do my best, I believe, and I'm sure God would never condemn me.' And it is very hard for people who have been reared and taught to understand that they get into God's Kingdom by being good or ethical or moral to hear that it only a matter of faith, particularly the Jew. And since Paul is arguing in Romans with an imaginary Jew from time to time, I don't doubt that that's in his mind right here. And he has just made this long treatise about Abraham being justified by faith as an illustration of the justification by faith in chapter three.

P9 Now, immediately a Jew is going to say this: 'Paul, you say that faith is all that is needed for salvation. You say that faith is enough. Are you sure it's enough? I mean, are you sure that you just get in by faith and that's all? I mean, once your in there, don't you have to keep some kind of standard up? Aren't you required to live at a certain level or you're going to lose it? Are you sure it's faith and faith alone by which we stand? It seems so oversimplified. Are you sure it will work? Can faith keep us saved? I mean, don't we have to live up to some level? Or, what about the future judgment, Paul? Is faith enough to assure us that we will escape the condemnation of God in the time of great judgment?' Or he might have questioned it this way, 'What maintains this salvation by faith? If we get in by faith what keeps us there, what maintains it?'

P10 And I believe that's why chapter five is here because Paul is speaking directly to that issue. Because the natural question they're going to have is that it is too easy. I mean, you just get in and you're in forever and it's all by grace and it's all by faith, and that's it.

P11 And you know, sometimes we have the same problem. In fact, if you go around espousing the doctrine of eternal security, that is, that you are saved forever, invariably if you run into someone who doesn't believe that they will ask you that very same question – 'You mean to tell me that you can be a Christian and just do anything you want?' That is inevitably the question they will ask. I've been asked that question a hundred times. 'You mean when you become a Christian there's no standard after that and you can just do whatever you want? Doesn't your salvation somewhat depend upon your obedience?' And so forth. That is precisely the issue to which Paul speaks in this passage.

P12 And he presents six great links in a chain that ties a true believer eternally to the Savior, six great links in the chain that ties a believer eternally to the Savior. And we're going to look at each of these six, maybe two tonight, two next week, and two the week after. And they are six great truths, believe me, six great realities. And the chain is so secure. I mean, after these three weeks you are going to go out of here knowing full well that if you have come to Jesus Christ you will belong to Him forever. That's a marvelous thing to know. I'd hate to live in eternal insecurity. Now, there are six links in the chain and we're going to see them as we flow through the text.

P13 Now, let me say another word. One of the things that Satan does in attacking a Christian is to attack him at the point of his assurance of salvation. Satan likes to make us doubt our redemption. That's why when you put on the armor, in Ephesians six it says to put on the helmet of salvation. And Paul writing to the Thessalonians further defines that by calling it the helmet of the hope of salvation. Why? Because Satan wants to deal devastating blows to your head in the area of doubt, to doubt that you are really saved, to doubt that you are really redeemed, to doubt that God is really holding you in the palm of His hand forever, to doubt that you really belong to God. He wants you to believe that, somehow, some way, you forfeited your redemption. And so he blasts away at you, making you feel insecure, intimidating you. And so you must have on the helmet of the hope or the confidence that you are really redeemed. And I want to help you get your helmet on and show you why you can know that you do belong to God forever.[33]

Assessment

The time spent in this introduction was ten minutes and thirty-one seconds. This introduction began a departure from the previous section from the book of Romans which ended in chapter four. The thrust of this introduction is to introduce the new treatment to be given to the subject of salvation – its security. There is no reference to the former treatment of the theme of salvation, its possession by grace through faith as demonstrated by Abraham. Because of the importance of the security of the believer, effort is given to establish this new direction for the treatment of salvation. Here, we find more disclosure for future sermons rather than the former. This emphasis is quite appropriate since this introduction introduces a short series which will require three sermons to complete. Obviously, then a forward direction intended to set up the series, rather than a focus upon a theme that has been completed, is in order.

P2 surfaces the crucial matter of falling from grace, which infers the possibility of a believer losing one's salvation. The series of three sermons will be directed to provide evidence why this cannot take place, and even more, to show how secure one's salvation is – to the degree that it is not possible for a believer to be saved and subsequently lose one's salvation. In other words, the effort of contextualization in P2 is that of orientation. P3 and P4 continue to establish the significance of this subject, the security of the believer.

P5 and P6 provide summarization as chapters three and four are briefly readdressed. P7-P9 proceed to orient the hearers regarding the historical difficulty of mankind to understand the enormous concept that salvation is simply accomplished by grace through faith. In these paragraphs, MacArthur argues how the Jew in the Apostle Paul's day would be estranged to such a concept. Then, P10 provides a quick summarization for the placement of the content of chapter five at precisely this point in the epistle since in this chapter it will be discovered that salvation is maintained just as it began, by grace through faith.

P11 continues the thrust of orientation as MacArthur argues that our present day and culture is no less prone to understand and accept salvation as by grace through faith. Therefore, P12 provides the connection to the study of the subject of the security of salvation through the exposition of Romans 5:1-11 which will present six great links in a chain that ties a true believer eternally to the Savior. The last paragraph of the introduction returns to the task of orientation as a cross reference is cited that helps the hearers understand the protection God affords the believer to withstand the attacks of the Adversary which will be unleashed on the believer in an effort to doubt the security of one's faith.

Introduction Three – Romans 5:2-5

Text

- P1 We are looking at a great, great chapter, it's a chapter I confess to you that is beyond me in many ways, its riches are so profound, but how thrilling has been our limited, cursory, look at the first verse and a half which we looked at last week.

- P2 Basically, the message of the first eleven verses of Romans five is very simple. And I'm not going to pull any punches or keep any secrets, the message is you can't lose your salvation. Your salvation is forever. It is eternal. It is everlasting. It is unchanging.

- P3 Peter says in I Peter 1:5 'We are kept by the power of God.' What a great statement. We are kept by the power of God. And without question, the most comforting, the most assuring, the most confidence building, the most joy producing of all Christian truth is that our salvation is forever. That is a tremendously exciting reality. The believer's joy and the believer's comfort really depends upon the sense of security of salvation. And so Paul is affirming that in this great text of Romans five. It is the heart of the passage that our salvation, our justification by faith, is secure in the power of God.

- P4 Now, as we noted last time, and I don't want to take a long time in introduction because there's so much here, but last time we noted that this subject fits into the flow of Paul's thought in Romans. You remember that he begins, in the epistle to the Romans, by dealing with the wrath of God against sinful men. And then he offers an escape from the wrath of God. The wrath of God is unfolded in chapter one, chapter two, and the first half of chapter three. And then the escape is unfolded in chapter three, the second half, and chapter four. And he says if you believe in the person and work of the Lord Jesus Christ, simply believing, that is by true genuine saving faith, you are justified, made right with God. There's no works involved, there's no effort involved, there's no human enterprise involved, it's a matter of believing what God has done in Christ – justification by faith, being made right with God, by believing in Jesus Christ.

P5 Now that seems so incredibly simple to the Jew that it would be very difficult for him to handle that. Because, you see, he was basically reared in a works system. It would even seem incredible to a Gentile who was raised in a religion of human achievement, in which all false human religion is. And to hear that all you need to do is to believe in the Lord Jesus Christ and be made right with God forever is more than they could have hoped for. And so the natural question that follows is that you are going to say to yourself, 'Boy, this seems too simple, too clear, too easy, there's got to be more than just believing. And so you ask yourself, is this enough? If all I do is believe, is that enough to save me, can that keep me? Will that be enough in the day of judgment when I stand before a holy God and it's time to find out the real issue of eternity? Is my faith alone in Jesus Christ going to hold me there? Am I going to survive the judgment?

P6 And that is why, in chapter five, Paul speaks to this issue. Because anyone who is newly converted and comes to Christ through faith is going to naturally ask the question, How long is this good for? How do I keep it? Is there anything I do to lose it? Now that I've got it, is it mine forever? And that is the reason he approaches the subject in the way that he does. And we're not surprised by that.

P7 Look with me for a moment at Ephesians chapter one and I'll show you a parallel. In Ephesians, the apostle Paul begins to unfold the great realities of the gospel. And in verse thirteen of chapter one, he talks about 'the gospel of your salvation'. 'In whom also you believed, you were sealed with the Holy Spirit of promise.' So, here he's talking about your salvation and the gospel that saved you, and when you were saved you were given the Holy Spirit. Then he says when you were saved through believing and you've received Jesus Christ, you were given the Holy Spirit who sealed you, stamped you authentic, stamped you permanently the possession of God, and verse fourteen says the Holy Spirit became the *arabon*, the earnest, the engagement ring, or the down payment, or the guarantee that someday you would ultimately come to full glory. In other words, the giving of the Holy Spirit is in a sense the guarantee, a very important truth.

P8 Now watch this. He articulates the gospel of salvation in verse thirteen and fourteen, in its fullness – you believe, you receive Jesus Christ, you are given the Holy Spirit, and so forth. And immediately he says, I, after I heard of your faith in the Lord Jesus, I heard that you were converted and the demonstration of your love for the saints, I began continually to pray for you. And for what did he pray? I prayed that the God of our Lord Jesus Christ, the Father of glory, would give you something. What is it? What is it that a Christian needs most? What is it that you would want first of all to give to a new believer in Christ? What is it that would be your first prayer request? Here it is. I pray that the Father of glory would give to you the Spirit of wisdom and revelation in the knowledge of Him so that the eyes of your understanding would be enlightened and you would know what is the hope of His calling and the riches of the glory of His inheritance in the saints. In other words, I want you to be able to comprehend what is yours in having Christ. I want you to have the hope of His calling. In other words, what He has begun in your life ultimately He will fulfill, that's what hope is, and the riches of the coming glory of the inheritance promised to the saints. So Paul says, now that I know that you are saved I'm praying for you and my first request is that you'll understand that your salvation is forever, and that you have a hope, and that you have an inheritance, and that you have a coming glory.

P9 So we are not surprised then, going back to Romans five, when Paul in Romans essentially does the same thing. He speaks to the matter of the gospel of salvation in chapters three and four and in chapter five he really affirms the fact that this salvation is forever.

P10 Now, the apostle gives us six great links in the security of the believer, six links in the chain that ties us to the Savior forever, six great realities. He says here that we have peace with God, we have standing in grace, we have hope of glory, we have possession of love, we have certainty of deliverance, and we have joy in God. And each of those acts, as I see it, is a link in the chain that eternally secures us to Christ. And so when the enemy hits you with doubt and you begin to wonder whether you are really saved, you begin to question that, you can retreat to the promised realities of this particular passage.

P11 Now, remember the first two that we looked at last time. The first one is in verse one. Therefore, being justified by faith, that is, through the act of believing in Jesus Christ, that's all there is in salvation from the human side, we simply believe. Through that act we have, first of all, peace with God through our Lord Jesus Christ. And we pointed out last time, as Psalm 7:11 says, that God is angry with the wicked every day. God is at war with men whether men are consciously at war with Him or not. Some people say, Well I don't know how I could make peace with God, I've never been mad at Him, I've never been angry with Him, I've never been at war with Him. That's not the issue. He is at war with you because you are a sinner and you are an object of His wrath, and in fact, he calls such children of wrath in Ephesians 2:3. Christ comes into this, Christ bears the wrath of God on the cross, Christ is the substitute, He receives the punishment, He receives the fury and the anger and the vengeance of God against sin on our behalf, and so we have peace with God. And it says in Isaiah 32:17, the work of righteousness shall be peace and the effect of righteousness shall be quietness and assurance forever. So when Christ does His work of righteousness He brings peace with God. And that means we're at peace with God. And it's going to be that way forever because God has poured out all of His wrath already on the Lord Jesus Christ.

P12 Secondly, we saw that we have standing in grace, verse two, by whom also, that is through Jesus Christ, we have access by faith into this grace in which we stand. We talked about the word *access*. Christ has given us access to God. And as we open the door, which is our access, we step into the kingdom, standing in what? In grace. And grace is a place where all sin is forgiven. Grace is a place where all sin is forgotten because of what Christ has done on the cross and because He ever lives to make intercession for us. So Jesus opens the door to God and there we enter we find no condemnation, no judgment, no vengeance but only and incessantly do we find grace.

Setting the Context

P13 Now, at this point, and I need to interject that someone might bring up a passage of Scripture and say, 'Well, you know, you can be in grace but you can fall from grace.' And this is often the argument of the people who want to deny that our salvation is secure. They say you can fall from grace and they point out one Scripture, and I'd like for you to turn to it: Galatians 5:4, Galatians 5:4. And it says there, Christ has become of no effect unto you whosoever of you are justified by the law, ye are fallen from grace. And people say, 'See, right there proves that you can fall from grace.'

P14 That's right. It does say that, but would you notice to whom it says that. It says it to people who try to get saved by what? By law. You go back to verse two, 'behold, I Paul say unto you that if you be circumcised,' in other words, if you think you can be saved by surgery, if you believe you can be right with God by some kind of physical operation, then Christ means nothing to you, Christ is of no use to you. You don't need Him. He's profitless because you can be saved by your surgery. And then in verse four he says, Christ is also of no effect to you if you are justified by the law. In other words, if you think you can be made right with God by your law keeping and your self-righteousness and your own religious works then, equally, Christ is useless to you. And these are the kinds of people who are fallen from grace. What does it mean? It means that you are fallen from the way of the grace principle of salvation. It really isn't defining Christians in terms of salvation, it's defining non-Christians, people who come to God, as it were, or attempt to come to God some other way than through grace. You are fallen, as it were, from the grace principle. The true principle that saves is grace. It is not teaching us that a Christian standing in grace can fall out of grace. The context would be utterly foreign to that concept. We who are saved through the Spirit, verse five, we wait for the hope of righteousness by faith, not by law. So it is simply falling from the principle of grace as a way of salvation.

P15 Now, Christ's death then provides for us these two things – peace with God, and standing in grace. Now I want to show you the third link, and I don't know if we'll get past this, I had intended to do two each time but this is so rich, the third link, verse two again. We have access by faith in the grace in which we stand and we rejoice or we exalt, or actually we boast, we make our boast in hope of the glory of God. The third link in our security is hope of glory.

P16 We are secure because we have peace with God, we are secure because we stand in grace, and we are secure because we have been given the hope of glory. In other words, to put it another way, God has promised us future glory.[34]

Assessment
The time spent in introducing this sermon was fourteen minutes and thirteen seconds. This introduction demonstrates a strong connection with the previous sermon. This would be expected since the last sermon introduction served as a transition to redirect the theme of salvation from its reception to its retention. Therefore, the need to return to the thrust of the last message is apparent, especially since this sermon will be a continuation of that which was begun in the last sermon.

P2 immediately establishes summarization in presenting Romans 5:1-11 as proofs for a believer's eternal security. This brief paragraph not only looks back but forward to advance the concept of the security of the believer which began in the previous message.

P3 provides orientation by affiliating the security of the believer because of the power of God which keeps us saved, as I Peter 1:5 is referenced.

P4 provides summarization in prototypical fashion as the development of the book is revisited from chapter one to chapter five. P5 and P6 continue summarization by reintroducing the difficulty both Jews and Gentiles would have in regards to being saved simply by grace through faith.

P7 through P9 return to orientation by referring to Ephesians chapter one, where the believer's sealing by the Holy Spirit is discussed, thus reorienting the hearers to the theme of the eternal security of the believer.

Summarization is given in P10 by restating the theme of six great links in the chain that ties the believer eternally to the Savior. All six links of the chain are delineated.

P11 and P12 make a connection to the text to be preached as the twofold sermon structure from the previous sermon are restated and reviewed.

P13 and P14 return to orientation material. At this juncture, an objection that some hearers may have is raised which stems from a passage of Scripture some view as grounds for a believer's loss of salvation. The objection is refuted through the explanation of the text of Galatians 5:4.

P15 provides connection as the previous two links of the chain are restated and the third link of the chain in named. P16 summarizes the progress made with the theme of the believer's eternal security because of the two previous links and the inclusion of the third link of the chain to be discussed in this sermon.

Introduction Four – Romans 5:5-11

Text

P1 Let's look together at Romans chapter five, Romans chapter five. And we're going to looking again at the first eleven verses, this monumental passage of the Word of God dealing with the security of salvation.

P2 Now, let me introduce our thinking tonight along this line. We live in a day of unfaithfulness. Men cannot be trusted, basically. We have learned, if we have learned anything about men, that you can't trust them. They don't keep their promises, they don't keep their word, whether you're talking about individuals or whether you're talking about nations, it's the same thing. People can't be trusted. They are not worth what they say they are in terms of their integrity. Husbands are unfaithful to their wives, to the vows they've made. Wives are unfaithful to their husbands. Children are unfaithful very often to live according to the principles their parents have taught them. And parents are very often unfaithful to give to their children that which they should. People are unfaithful to promises they make to employers and people with whom they work, and so on. Employers are often unfaithful to fulfill their obligations and responsibility to those who are in their employ. And I suppose we would have to acknowledge that Christians are frequently unfaithful to God, though God is never unfaithful to them. No one of us can claim immunity from this terrible sin of being unfaithful, the sin of being untrustworthy, the sin of not living up to your promise, the sin of not keeping your word. The only one in all of the universe that is always faithful and always keeps every promise in full is God. And that, my friends, is a very important truth because it is upon the faithfulness of God that everything we believe in stands. God must be able to be trusted or our eternal destiny is at stake, everything we do is at stake. And it is indeed refreshing by contrast, it is indeed blessed, to be able to lift our eyes above the scene of unfaithfulness to the beloved God who is always faithful.

P3 Back in the Pentateuch, that first set of books, which we read about God, what He is like, we read this, Know therefore that the Lord thy God, He is God, the faithful God. And the Apostle Paul said, in 2 Timothy 2:13, that He remains faithful, He cannot deny Himself. And what he meant by that was it is His nature to be true to His word, so He will be. And I love the phrase of Isaiah. Isaiah said faithfulness is the belt around God's waist. It's that which encompasses Him and holds everything else together. His faithfulness is the belt that holds all other attributes in place. The Psalmist, in Psalm 36:5, says: 'Thy mercy, O Lord, is in the heavens and Thy faithfulness is unto the clouds.' And Jeremiah echoed a similar thought when he said, 'Great is Thy faithfulness.' And I guess you're kind of stuck with that concept – great is Thy faithfulness or Thy faithfulness reaches unto the clouds, because we really have no way in human language to describe the infinite faithfulness of God. In Hebrews 10:23 the writer says, 'He is faithful that promised,' in other words, if God makes a promise He is faithful to fulfill it.

P4 Now, those are samples of a Scripture filled with comments about the faithfulness of God. And one area where His faithfulness stands out is in the area of preserving His people unto glory, preserving His people unto glory. He stands out in the area of keeping us, of securing us in our salvation. He is faithful to do that. In I Corinthians 1:9, it tells us that God is faithful by whom you are called to the fellowship of His Son. And the verse before that says, God will confirm you unto the end, that you may be blameless unto the day of our Lord Jesus Christ. Paul is saying, if you are saved, God is going to confirm you to the end and the basis, on which you can know that, is that God is faithful by whom you are called.

P5 If God promises you eternal life, what will He give you? Eternal life. God is not like men. God is faithful. And that's why I Peter 4:19 says this, that believers can have confidence to do this, now listen to what the verse says, commit their souls to His keeping, who is a faithful Creator. In other words, when we give our soul to God by faith in Jesus Christ, we can know that God will be faithful to keep it until the end and bring His children to glory. That's His promise. God is faithful, then, to preserve His people to glory.

P6 Now, this comes again and again in the New Testament. Not only do we see the faithfulness of God in the Old but as well in the New. And just a couple of passages that sort of reinforce it in my mind: 1 Thessalonians 5:23 says, the very God of peace sanctify you wholly and I pray God, listen to this, your whole spirit and soul and body be preserved blameless until the coming of our Lord Jesus Christ. Now just listen to that. The Apostle Paul says, I pray that your whole spirit and soul and body will be preserved blameless until the coming of the Lord Jesus Christ. Now, that is a prayer for security, isn't it? That you're going to be blameless throughout time until you face Jesus Christ. The next verse says, and faithful is He who called you, who also will do it. One of the greatest passages in all the Bible for the security of the believer, I Thessalonians 5:23-4. This is what I hope for you, that God will preserve you and He will preserve you. Faithful is He that called you, who also will do it – great statement of confidence.

P7 In 2 Thessalonians chapter three and verse three, the Lord is faithful who shall establish you and keep you from evil. And we have this confidence in the Lord concerning you that you both do, and will do, the things which we command and the Lord direct your hearts into the love of God and the patient waiting for Christ. He says we have this confidence about you that you are going to walk in obedience and you're going to live the way you ought to live because God is faithful and He will keep you. And we said last time that God keeps you from His side, and from our side He energizes us to walk in obedience so we persevere. From the divine side, God keeps us. From the human side, we remain faithful. But it is only possible to remain faithful because God keeps us and infuses us with His power. And that is what Paul means in 2 Thessalonians chapter three. Philippians 1:6, I remind you of, we quoted it two weeks ago, being confident of this very thing that He who began a good work in you will perform it until the day of Jesus Christ.

P8 Now, all of these Scriptures are telling us the same thing. And whenever I hear the debate about eternal security or the perseverance of the saints, somebody said to me, in fact, my own daughter said to me the other day as she was talking to another young person about whether you are secure in your salvation and this other person didn't believe you were, can you give me one verse, Dad, that will prove that you are secure in your salvation? Just one. And I was sort of dumbfounded at the moment because I could immediately think of about fifty. It's not something that is a thin argument based on some obscure statement somewhere. It is replete throughout Scripture that God is faithful to those He calls to bring them to glory. And we've been looking at that concept for the last two weeks.

P9 Now, let's go back to Romans five. With that as an introduction we want to say this, the whole idea of the security of the believer, then, is premised on the attribute of God that we call faithfulness. And all these other Scriptures that we read, including Romans five, simply describe to us, listen carefully, they simply describe to us how God implements His faithfulness. We are kept by His faithfulness. And we learn in Romans five, and elsewhere, how He implements that keeping faithfulness.

P10 Now, there are six links in an unbreakable chain that unite us to the Savior. And we've been looking at that in verse one and all the way down to verse eleven. And we suggested these six links: first, peace with God; second, standing in grace; third, hope of glory; fourth, possession of love; fifth, certainty of deliverance; and sixthly, joy in God. Now, we're going to go into those, hopefully we're going to be able to finish them tonight.

P11 Now, remember that the first link that ties us to the Savior is peace with God, verse one: 'Therefore, being justified by faith we have peace with God through our Lord Jesus Christ.' In other words, from now on God is on our side. We've made our peace. And it isn't so much that we were hostile against God as it was that God was hostile toward us. Remember? God was angry about our sin. The Bible says, God is angry with the wicked every single day, Psalm 7:11. So, we are secure because we are at peace with God. His anger is satisfied, His wrath is satisfied, in the death of Jesus Christ.

P12 Secondly, we are secure because we stand in grace, verse two. 'By whom also we have access by faith into this grace in which we stand.' Now, grace operates where there is sin. If you don't have any sin, then you don't need any grace. Right? So, grace operates where there is sin. Now, if we stand in grace, then when we sin, what happens? Grace operates. And what does grace do? Forgives our sin because of Christ. And so, we are secure then, not only because we've made peace with God and His wrath has been spent on Christ, but because we stand in grace. And grace is God's undeserved favor to sinners.

P13 Thirdly, we are linked eternally to the Lord through the hope of glory, the end of verse two. We rejoice in hope because of the glory of God. And remember, the last time I told you, and I think this is such a tremendous point, that we are secure because God saved us to bring us to glory. There are three tenses to salvation – past, present, future. We have been saved. We are being saved. We shall be yet saved. We wait for the full salvation, the redemption of our bodies, the full and ultimate glorification. And we looked at Romans eight and it said, whom the Lord justifies, He also what? Glorifies. So He has saved us to bring us to glory. Salvation wouldn't even be salvation, you couldn't even call it that, if you could lose it. You can't even define it that way, because salvation can only be defined as three parts, that is – past, that is, we have been saved from the sins of the past. Present, we are being saved. Future, we shall yet be saved in full glory. And so the hope of glory links us to Christ.

P14 And then we noticed, verse three. Not only that, but we also rejoice at the result of our tribulations because we know that tribulation, not only does it not take away our salvation, not only does it not weaken us, but rather it produces endurance, and endurance produces proven character, and proven character has a greater hope. So, Paul is saying we are anchored to the Savior by the promise of ultimate glory, and even when we go through trials, that just increases our hope of glory because trials produce proven character, and the more spiritual character you have the more spiritually mature you are, the more confident you are in the hope of ultimate salvation. And that's why verse five says, hope does not disappoint us, it is not something we are ashamed of, because we know God will bring to pass what He has promised.

P15 So, the security of our salvation is based on peace with God, standing in grace, and hope of glory.

P16 Now, let's go to the fourth link, and one with which we are so wonderfully familiar, as we look at verse five. And hope makes not ashamed, or does not disappoint, because the love of God is shed abroad in our hearts by the Holy Spirit who is given to us. Now, stop there for the time. Here we find the fourth link and we'll call it the possession of love.³⁵

Assessment
Thirteen minutes and fifty-six seconds were needed in this introduction. This introduction exhibits substantial summarization and connection components. Again, this would be natural since this is the final introduction for the three sermon series presenting the eternal security of the believer. Since most of the development of the theme has already been accomplished and this message will continue and bring closure to the series, strong summarization and connection are necessary.

P2 through P8 provide orientation through the contrast of man's faithlessness contrasted to the perfect faithfulness of God.

P9 through P11 provide summarization for the three sermon series regarding the evidences for why a believer's salvation is secure for eternity. P9 states all six links in the chain that ties a believer eternally to the Savior. P10 reviews the first link while P11 summarizes the second link, both being the content for the sermon preached two weeks previously. P12 and P13 make connection by summarizing the content of the last sermon which dealt with the third link in the chain. P14 provides summarization by updating the progress made to this point – links one, two, and three.

P15 makes the final connection by introducing the fourth link in the chain.

The strengths of MacArthur's introductions are in extreme contrast to the typical sermon introduction one may hear on any given occasion from any pulpit. His introductions demonstrate a great deal of orientation, summarization, and connection material. Orientation material may well be expected in any introduction since the necessity to orient the hearers to the subject matter to be preached in a sermon is so very basic. In fact, if this is not done well, the sermon introduction has failed to accomplish a most basic requirement and it, therefore, cannot be effective. That which is immediately obvious about MacArthur's introductions is the amount of orientation material that is incorporated.

Furthermore, the distinctiveness of his typical introduction is his commitment to provide summarization material and to provide a connection with the last sermon preached. In listening to MacArthur preach through a book of the Bible, he provides an opportunity to understand and appreciate the content of the book, how it is divided, and how the book is laid out in a logical progression.

In listening to books of the Bible expounded by other expositors who were excellent in conveying the meaning of the text they were preaching but failed to incorporate contextualization components in their introductions as MacArthur does, I found the cumulative difference to be profound. The difference being that, sermon by sermon, the text was made clear but, through the weeks taken to preach through the book, there was the inability to know the message of the book, what the various themes of the book are, and how they are developed and divided throughout the book. This resulted because it was never the purpose of the expositor to have the hearers acquire such knowledge, which was obvious because such content was not provided week after week throughout the preaching of the book.

I remember hearing one man preach through I Peter for about 24-26 sermons. When he was finished I was so frustrated because, having listened to many excellent sermons, all from I Peter, I didn't understand the flow, development, the message, the themes, the divisions of I Peter more than I did before the series began. This is a poor return on an investment for anyone who hears a biblical book expounded from the pulpit. Yet, such a result is all too common in the exposition of biblical books.

The expositional excellence of most expository preachers would be increased immediately and significantly simply by learning to incorporate the contextualization components of orientation, summarization, and connection in their sermon introductions. In all probability, you may need help in developing the knack for contextualization in your sermon introductions. Let me give you a challenge if this is the case. If you can find an expositor who does a better job than John MacArthur in the task of contextualization in his sermon introductions, then hear him. If you, like me, are unable to find anyone who even begins to rival MacArthur in contextualization, then by all means why don't you make it a priority to learn from this master expositor and hear him! By no means will the benefit derived from listening to MacArthur be limited to how to contextualize a sermon introduction well, but this may be the most unique benefit you will derive from listening to him.

Consider the Following Questions

1. What are the components of contextualization and how do they function within a sermon introduction?

2. Why does it make sense to understand reviewing the previous sermon as a responsibility of every introduction rather than an approach to introducing a sermon especially if one is preaching through a book of the Bible?

3. What is the two-fold rationale for providing contextualization in a sermon introduction?

4. How do the contextualization components of summarization and connection help those hearers who heard the sermon last week?

5. How do orientation, summarization, and connection make a contribution to the sermon being free standing yet a sermon that makes a valuable contribution to the series of which it is a part?

6. Which of the sevenfold reinforcements of contextualization do you find most significant for yourself when hearing a sermon introduction, and what is your reason for this?

7. In reference to the sevenfold reinforcements resulting from contextualization, which one do you believe to be of greatest importance for the hearers and which do you believe would hold the least benefit to the hearers? Explain your reasoning for these answers.

8. Which of the seven reinforcements do you think is most accomplished in each of MacArthur's four introductions? Explain your answers.

9. Which introduction most effectively reinforces accuracy?

10. Which introduction most effectively reinforces thoroughness?

11. Which introduction most effectively reinforces relatedness?

12. Which introduction most effectively reinforces completion?

13. Which introduction most effectively reinforces perspective?

14. Which introduction most effectively reinforces retention?

15. Which introduction most effectively reinforces volition?

16. Which of the four introductions did you find to be the most effective introduction and does this answer correspond to the answers you provided for questions 6-15?

Words to Live and Preach by

Wisdom—The Superlative Excellence

Proverbs 1:20, 30-33 – Wisdom shouts in the street, she lifts her voice in the square; "They would not accept my counsel, they spurned all my reproof. So they shall eat of the fruit of their own way and be satiated with their own devices. For the waywardness of the naïve will kill them, and the complacency of fools will destroy them. But he who listens to me shall live securely and will be at ease from the dread of evil."

Proverbs 2:1-8 – My son, if you will receive my sayings, and treasure my commandments within you, make your ear attentive to wisdom, incline your heart to understanding; for if you cry for discernment, lift your voice for understanding; if you seek her as silver, and search for her as for hidden treasures; then you will discern the fear of the Lord, and discover the knowledge of God. For the Lord gives wisdom; from His mouth come knowledge and understanding. He stores up sound wisdom for the upright; He is a shield to those who walk in integrity, guarding the paths of justice, and He preserves the way of His godly ones.

Proverbs 3:13-18 – How blessed is the man who finds wisdom and the man who gains understanding. For her profit is better than the profit of silver and her gain better than fine gold. She is more precious than jewels; and nothing you desire compares with her. Long life is in her right hand; in her left hand are riches and honor. Her ways are pleasant ways and all her paths are peace. She is a tree of life to those who take hold of her, and happy are all who hold her fast.

Proverbs 4:7-9 – The beginning of wisdom is: Acquire wisdom; and with all your acquiring get understanding. Prize her, and she will exalt you; she will honor you if you embrace her. She will place on your head a garland of grace; she will present you with a crown of beauty.

Chapter Nine

The Sermon Proposition: The Cornerstone of a Sermon

Organization and Preaching

In all preaching, including expository preaching and all such preaching that would never be confused as an attempt to explain a passage of Scripture, this much is certain: the preacher must know what he will be talking about in the sermon and what he will be saying about whatever he will be talking about in the sermon – this is his most basic responsibility of cognition. Additionally, he must be able to help those who will hear him preach discern what he will be talking about and what he will be saying about that subject-matter – this is his most basic responsibility of communication. 'The hearer does not cling to a speaker who, undertaking to guide him, seems to be ignorant whither he is going.'[1] It is through the means of a sermon proposition and the structure of the sermon that these matters are achieved effectively. The most basic conception for a well-designed sermon is the 'embodiment and extension of an important idea, of which the first element is a clearly defined subject and the second element is structural assertions concerning the subject.'[2]

Clarity regarding the subject-matter of the sermon as well as the treatment of the subject-matter must be communicated in the sermon introduction. The sermon introduction is the necessary place for the hearers to understand the subject-matter of the sermon and the treatment the subject will receive by the preacher on this preaching occasion.

In the introduction of the sermon the preacher states and repeats, at least once, the sermon proposition. Through a clearly articulated statement of the sermon proposition the congregation will know what the preacher will be preaching on and, in a general way, what he will say about the subject. Only in the body of the sermon will the hearers understand fully and specifically what the preacher is saying about the subject-matter of the text as he expounds the text with the help of the sermon structure derived from the passage to be preached. The old adage of 'tell them what you are going to tell them, tell them, and then tell them what you told them' cannot be set aside in preaching without sacrificing clarity.

One of many things to be done in a sermon introduction is to clearly communicate to the hearers what you will be saying in the sermon they are about to hear. In other words, the sermon introduction is the place in the sermon where the preacher tells the hearers what he will be talking about in the sermon. In the body of the sermon he will tell them the meaning of the passage. And among other responsibilities the preacher has in the sermon conclusion is to tell them what he has told them in the sermon. The expositor of Scripture owes it to his hearers to inform them, as of the sermon introduction, what he will be addressing in his sermon. If the hearers of a sermon cannot discern what the preacher will be talking about before he begins to preach the body of the sermon he has failed them because he simply has not afforded them the basic information they need in order to follow a sermon with understanding.

Notice, for example, G. Campbell Morgan's clear indication of how his text of Matthew 16:21 will be treated as he preached his sermon *The Pathway Of The Passion*. In Morgan's final two paragraphs of his sermon introduction he said:

As I have said, Matthew summarizes all the teaching from Caesarea Philippi to Calvary in these words: 'He must go unto Jerusalem, and suffer many things of the elders and chief priests and scribes, and be killed, and the third day be raised up.'

In that summary there are three matters which demand our attention. The first is that of the *compulsion*: 'He *must* go unto Jerusalem.' The second is that of the *course* marked out: 'suffer... and be killed.' The third is that of the *consummation*: 'and the third day be raised up.'[3]

It would have been easy for Morgan's hearers to discern how the reputable expositor was going to treat the pathway of Christ's passion by the three matters of the compulsion, the course, and the consummation of His journey to Jerusalem. Although this portion of the introduction could have attained greater clarity through a more thoroughly synthesized sermon proposition and structure, Morgan's three matters of Christ's compulsion, course, and consummation provide some indication as to the subject-matter of the sermon.

Unfortunately, however, such clarity commonly is neither advocated nor practiced in preaching today. For example, consider the sermon introduction of Fred Craddock's *expository*[4] sermon from Acts 2:2-21, entitled *On Being Pentecostal*. The intended treatment of the passage and clarity for what the sermon would be about was indicated by one vapid, vacuous sentence – 'And that's what I'd like for us to do; think again about Acts 2 and Pentecost.'[5] In reality, Acts 2 was not dealt with at all except to say that a very large crowd was present, being made up of Jews from every nation under heaven, along with converts to Judaism and other visitors. So this proposition, at best, indicates that Acts 2 will receive treatment that is so uncertain that it can only be indicated by the phrase 'think again about Acts 2 and Pentecost.' There is no clarity conveyed about the meaning of the text of Acts 2:2-21, that is, how it would be divided and how each division would be developed. Even though it may be understood that the sermon is to be about Pentecost, there is no indication as to what will be said about Pentecost.

The sermon proposition is an entity of the sermon introduction. The development of the proposition, the sermon structure, is the conceptual framework of the body of the sermon, and therefore guides the exposition of the text. Though the sermon structure works with the sermon proposition, only the sermon proposition will be considered in this chapter. However, it is of little or no value to have a clearly stated proposition in the introduction if there is not a tight, logical, and obvious connection between the sermon structure in the body of the sermon that corresponds to the sermon proposition. After all, the sermon structure is simply the sermon proposition unfolded in a point by point manner. Therefore, much attention will be given to the goal of producing sermon outlines for the sermon body that will be helpful to the preacher and the congregation in a subsequent book, *How Effective Sermons Advance*: the sermon structure. Our specific goal in this chapter is to understand how to develop a clear proposition that will be helpful to the preacher and the congregation in the introduction of the sermon.

Clarity of the Sermon Proposition
Clarity is a chief component for both the sermon structure and the sermon proposition. Since 1912, through J.H. Jowett's oft-quoted statement insisting upon clarity in the sermon's proposition, propositional clarity has been a cornerstone element of homiletical instruction. Specifically, Jowett wrote:

> I have a conviction that no sermon is ready for preaching, not ready for writing out, until we can express its theme in a short, pregnant sentence as clear as a crystal. I find the getting of that sentence is the hardest, the most exacting, and the most fruitful labour in my study. To compel oneself to fashion that sentence, to dismiss every word that is vague, ragged, ambiguous, to think oneself through to a form of words which defines the theme with scrupulous exactness, – this is surely one of the

most vital and essential factors in the making of a sermon: and I do not think any sermon ought to be preached or even written, until that sentence has emerged, clear and lucid as a cloudless moon. Do not confuse obscurity with profundity, and do not imagine that lucidity is necessarily shallow. Let the preacher bond himself to the pursuit of clear conceptions, and let him aid his pursuit by demanding that every sermon he preaches shall express its theme and purpose in a sentence as lucid as his powers can command.[6]

A more appropriate and definitive call for clarity for a sermon proposition has never been written to date.

Clarity regarding the sermon proposition is not just a good idea and something to be attained, if possible. It is truly essential. Donald L. Hamilton has stated the case well: 'A sermon without a clear proposition is like a ship without a rudder or an automobile without a steering wheel. Keeping it on course will be very difficult, if not impossible!'[7] The result of a sermon without a clear proposition will be an unclear purpose, an unclear direction, and an unclear argument. The audience may feel a sense of frustration since effective communication has been hindered by a lack of preciseness. The preacher himself may also be frustrated as he is unable to present clearly that which he desires to present.

The Arduous Task of Constructing Clear Sermon Propositions

The starting point for a clear, effective sermon proposition and its related outline is very diligent work. Halford Luccock expressed the reality of this very well as he insisted that the preacher must 'toil like a miner under a landslide'. This expression enlarges on two axiomatic realities of preaching – firstly, the preaching ministry must rest on a life of study and, secondly, that 'real study and the creative work coming from it and running along with it are painfully hard.'[8] Don McDougall comments upon the hard work necessary to craft the sermon proposition and structure specifically, as well as being a good expositor of the Bible in general.

Good expositors of the Bible have disciplined themselves to work hard and long. Nowhere is that discipline and hard work more demanding and rewarding than in determining the central idea (the sermon proposition) and structure of the passage.[9] ... Undoubtedly, there are some great natural athletes. When it comes to the field of expositors, however, probably no such thing as a great natural expositor exists. To be a true and acknowledged expositor of the Word requires discipline. It takes hard work and thorough preparation for which there are no substitutes. A lot of time and effort must be spent establishing the central idea and determining the outline of a passage.[10]

A clear, effective sermon proposition, like everything else that is a part of good preaching, will not be easy to achieve; yet it must be achieved. If a preacher cannot achieve clarity at this juncture he can never be clear in his preaching; and a lack of clarity exacts a costly price to be paid in the process of preaching. As Augustine wrote, 'Who does not realize that a person who is not understood cannot be listened to either with pleasure or with obedience?'[11]

However, even if one fully subscribes to this most beneficial counsel, it seems to me that a very important question needs to be raised and answered regarding propositional clarity. The question is simply this – how is clarity achieved in writing a sermon proposition? Is it simply working diligently to craft a carefully articulated statement that is to be uttered from the pulpit in such a way that the congregation will not miss it nor misunderstand it?

Surely the careful construction and forceful declaration of the sermon proposition must be a starting point for propositional clarity. William G. T. Shedd comments on both of these factors. He contends that the proposition should be stated in the most concise manner possible. It is, or should be, the condensation and epitome of the whole discourse, and should, therefore, be characterized by the utmost density of meaning. Additionally, the proposition should be stated in the boldest manner possible. Every teaching, or tenet, of revelation, ought to be laid down with a strong confidence of its absolute truthfulness. When the proposition of a sermon is a legitimate derivative from a passage of Scripture, it ought to be expressed in such a manner as to preclude all hesitation, doubt, or timidity, in the phraseology. A weighty conciseness, and a righteous boldness, ought to characterize the terms and form of the proposition.[12]

Even as these general assertions are understood and applied to the development and delivery of a sermon proposition, I suggest that the very character of the propositional statement is significant if it is to engender clarity and integrity between the propositional statement announced in the introduction and the sermon structure or outline of the message to be articulated in the body of the sermon. Constructing the propositional statement that is clear and appropriate for the passage is seldom an easy assignment.

All propositional statements, even when finely crafted, are not created equal. Not all clear propositions wield the same ability to supply the needed coherence to the outline of the sermon body. The plural noun proposition distinguishes itself in its inherent ability to be easily identified in the introduction as well as relating to the outline in the sermon body in a tight, logical way.

Plural Noun Propositions
In his book *Design for Preaching*, Grady Davis argues for a necessary understanding on behalf of a congregation as they hear one preach – an understanding that is sufficient only as two 'structural questions' are effectively answered by the data supplied to them by the preacher. These questions are: What is the man talking about? and, What is he saying about it?[13] These two questions are the framework for congregational understanding in the context of preaching. The preacher can be clear about these matters in the pulpit only if he has gained personal clarity about these matters in his study. A sound sermon must be the embodiment of an organic relatedness

of thought that establishes one subject and elaborates upon that subject in an identifiable way. The simple necessity of such sermonic cohesiveness, however, does not guarantee its presence in a message. Davis' lament for the absence of such organic soundness in preaching, as well as his insistence upon it, is justified:

> It may seem childishly simple to say that every sermon consists of only two things: what is talked about, and what is said about it, a subject with one or several predicates. To say it is indeed simple; to act on it must be very difficult, judging by the evidence. A man who has been to college and seminary, a man who has preached for years, can speak as if he never heard of this primary fact.... No overlay of brilliant or witty talk, apt quotations, choice anecdotes, can hide a misshapen body of thought. There is no way to correct these elemental faults of design except to keep pressing the question, 'What am I to talk about? What must be said about it?'
>
> To learn to preach, a man must develop his sense of form, his feeling for the shape and organic structure of a thought. This is the first step in learning. To feel the shape and structure of his idea is also the first and chief task in preparing any given sermon, down to the last one a man will preach before he dies. No man ever graduates from this, or gets above it.[14]

In the proclamation of a sermon that is truly sound, any listener should be able to report accurately the pastor's sermon – this is what he was talking about and this is what he said about it.

In general terms, this minimally constitutes clarity in preaching – the ability of a hearer to articulate what the preacher was talking about and what he said about it. But the question must be raised, is minimal clarity sufficient for preaching? I strongly affirm that minimal clarity is inadequate! Instead of listeners being able to state in general terms what the preacher was talking about and what he said about it, they should be able to recite with some degree of specificity what he actually said regarding the subject-matter. Is it possible for a listener to recover both the general thrust of the sermon as well as the more important specific statements the preacher made pertaining to the subject-matter of the sermon? I believe it is not only possible but it is essential for listeners to be able to do this, having heard a sermon. However, this will be possible only if the listener is allowed to discern a specific statement of the general thrust of the sermon, to discern how many specific statements will be incorporated to clarify the general thrust of the sermon, and to discern the specific clarifying statements of the general thrust of the sermon. These conditions are fulfilled best through the usage of a plural noun proposition.

Benefits of a Plural Noun Proposition

Many authors and professors of preaching agree that a sermon proposition bearing a plural noun or keyword has a distinct advantage to produce a strong sermonic structure by unlocking the divisions most notable for an exposition of a particular text and sermon.[15] In his book, *Power in Expository Preaching*, Faris D. Whitesell enumerates seven benefits of using the plural noun propositional approach in expository preaching. He lists these benefits as follows:

> 1) to classify, label, or catalogue the main points, keeping them all in one category; 2) to point the direction you intend to follow with your thesis; 3) to give unity to the sermon; 4) to aid in parallel construction of main points; 5) to test the main points proving whether or not they fit the outline; 6) to link the main points together, tying them into a neat bundle; 7) to make the sermon easier to memorize and easier for the hearers to remember.[16]

A former professor of mine, Craig Skinner, presents a strong advocacy for plural noun propositions as he writes: 'I have examined many hundreds of volumes, including many in the general preaching and secular fields, for this study and found nothing of any quality in terms of valid sermon structure other than this thesis-interrogative-keyword approach.' He contends that the thesis-interrogative-keyword approach, or the plural noun proposition approach, is the finest developed for expository preaching and is in full accord with the best ideas in contemporary speech theory and educational psychology. He deemed it appropriate to insist that any sermon without a thesis, expressed or implied, cannot be a sermon, as it advocates no basic truth. Additionally, Skinner insists that most good sermons, on analysis, will be found to have affinity with the (thesis-interrogative-keyword) structure.[17]

Without the use of a keyword, or plural noun, a sermon proposition degenerates into a factual yet simple statement rather than a worthwhile sermon proposition which causes people to want to know more about the subject-matter contained in the propositional statement.[18]

The Basis of a Plural Noun Proposition
The basic presupposition of the plural noun propositional approach in preaching is that the proposition will be expanded by dealing with more specific truths derived from the text. In other words, there will be structure in the message, that is, the proposition will be unfolded by two or more points in the sermon.

Since there will be more than one line of advancement of the subject-matter of the proposition, there must then be a plural noun in the proposition. The plural noun will correspond to the divisions of thought in the sermon structure.

In order to understand sermon propositions, we must understand that a sermon will always have a plurality of points. In preaching, a preacher will always be saying various things (the points of the sermon structure) about the one thing he is preaching about (the sermon proposition). To truly say one thing about something will either be no sermon at all, or a sermon that is incredibly brief. On the other hand, however, if one does more than say one thing about something, he will be advancing thought. Shedd made the case for the necessity

The Sermon Proposition

of plural sermon points by arguing that there are two things in rhetoric – the statement of a thing and the development of the thing stated. The statement of a sermon proposition cannot be the development or amplification of the proposition. The development or amplification of the proposition is the main points of the sermon. Likewise, the statement of a main point of a sermon is not the development or amplification of the main point. The development or amplification of the main point is the substructure. Every sermon must contain subordinate points which flow out of each other and yet are distinct from each other. If this is not the case, then there is no development, no progress or none of the elements of oratory.[19]

Advancement of thought can take place in two very distinct ways. A preacher can advance thought in a rambling, disorderly way that is hard to establish the precise advancement being made of the proposition. Or, he can advance the subject-matter in a clear, orderly fashion so that the development of the proposition can be clarified by the more specific thoughts upon the subject-matter.

To argue for a one point sermon is to misunderstand the difference between a sermon proposition and a sermon point. One author, in the attempt to advocate 'one-point communication', effectively establishes the necessity for multi-point communication. He writes:

> The older three-point sermon style should be abandoned in this hard-hitting day of single-emphasis communication. This is not to say, however, that the sermon outline might not have several piers that support the argument. It's just that these points of supporting logic should not be allowed to develop separate themes. They should all contribute to building a single emphasis, which the sermon develops from the lone theme it champions.[20]

The author is quite right in his assertion that 'the lone theme,' or the proposition, should be championed by the 'several piers that support the argument,' or sermon points. Again, his assertion that 'these points of supporting logic should not be allowed to develop separate themes' only underscores the very purpose of a sermon outline regarding a sermon proposition – to develop it, not to distract from it. Sermon points that do not develop the proposition constitute an ineffective, flawed structure. The solution to poor structure is not an attempt to have no structure at all.

Examples of Plural Noun Propositions

Perhaps some examples of non-plural noun propositional statements versus plural noun propositional statements will help to distinguish and compare the two approaches. For reference purposes, the following four examples will be referred to as couplet 1, couplet 2, couplet 3, and couplet 4, with the non-plural noun propositional statement occurring first in each.

Couplet 1

'Parents should be pleasing to God in the raising of their children.'

'In this chapter we discover three qualities of parents who are pleasing to God in the raising of their children.'

Couplet 2

'Those who suffer persecution are blessed by God.'

'In His Sermon on the Mount, Jesus affirms that those who suffer persecution are doubly blessed as persecution brings to them two benefits.'

Couplet 3

'It is important to correct a faulty understanding of sin.'

'In our passage this morning we will find three correctives for the most common misunderstandings regarding sin.'

Couplet 4
'The Christian life is often not as fulfilling as it could be.'
'Joyful, responsible living as a child of God is conditioned upon compliance to the three requirements we shall see in this text.'

Assessment of Plural Noun Propositions
Several observations are immediate. The non-plural noun propositions are briefer. The non-plural noun propositions do not suggest the intended treatment the subject-matter will be given in the sermon. There is no number used in the non-plural noun propositional statement which informs the hearers how many points will be discussed in the sermon regarding the subject-matter. Obviously, the plural noun propositions tend to be longer than a non-plural noun attempt to say the same thing. However, the longer statement of the plural noun proposition is certainly worthwhile as it conveys much in the few additional words.

It is important to understand that the non-plural noun statements are a significant start in the formulation of a sermon proposition, specifically, a plural noun proposition. These significant starter-statements possess an inherent weakness in that they do not and cannot shoulder the load necessary to make a more definitive declaration regarding the subject-matter, treatment, and structure of the sermon to be delivered.

I couldn't agree more with the thoughts of a popular and powerful preacher of the early to mid-nineteenth century who noted that, 'the turning of certain leading thoughts, as they arise, into propositions, marks the rate of progress, indicates direction, and blazes one's way through the forest.' He continued, 'We never have the full use of language, as an instrument of thought, unless we cause our thoughts to fall into assertory shape.'[21] Even though the previous thoughts were not made with plural noun propositions as a frame of reference, they are uniquely relevant to them.

How then does one construct a plural-noun proposition? In order to facilitate the understanding and implementation of plural noun propositions, I will provide a step-by-step process for making plural noun propositions out of non-plural noun statements for all four of the couplets mentioned above.

Crafting a Plural Noun Proposition
In the previous examples of non-plural noun propositions, the basic statements found in them are what may be called the thesis, theme, or central idea of the biblical passage and, therefore, the sermon. I will use the term 'thesis' to refer to these non-plural noun statements.

The process of crafting a plural noun proposition includes eight steps. These steps do not formulate a rigid sequence of events that must be followed. For example, the amount of major assertions can be identified (step three) and the development of each of the main points can be charted (step seven) before the plural noun is clearly discerned (step five) or the statements of the main points are fashioned (step four). In this case, step seven occurs before steps five and four are completed. Additionally, step five has been accomplished before step four is finalized. Synthesis must be done but there is no invariable step by step occurrence in its achievement. One should only be satisfied with the fact of its occurrence and not the sequence of occurrence. The eight steps are enumerated as such only as an attempt to typify a common sequence of events.

The first step for establishing a plural noun proposition for a sermon is to synthesize a basic understanding of a passage, the thesis. This is critical, remembering that this statement supplies the answer to the question, 'What is this passage about?'

With the thesis of the passage in mind, the second step is to understand how the thesis is developed and treated in the passage. In other words, the development of the thesis will be the answer to one of the following interrogatives: who, what, when, where, why, or how? Deciding which interrogative,

The Sermon Proposition

when supplied to the thesis, best reflects the truths of the text as answers to the interrogative supplied to the thesis. The determination of this interrogative, which is to be supplied to the proposition and is indicative of the passage, is the completion of the second step.

The third step is to identify how many components are unified by the plural noun thus establishing how many main points the sermon will contain. Having diagrammed the passage the major assertions of the text can be identified with relative ease.

The crafting of the sermon points of the passage is the fourth step. Having decided which interrogative best describes the treatment of the thesis, one can craft the actual statements of the main components of the text, which become the main points of the sermon, so that these main point statements both answer the interrogative and reflect the understanding of the passage.

The fifth step is to discern the plural noun that most accurately unifies the points of the sermon, each of which answer the interrogative supplied to the basic thesis statement of the passage. The answering of the interrogative supplied to the basic thesis and the reflection of the passage, that is, the unifying concept of each of the statements of theological principle or sermon points, must be accomplished by the plural noun.

The sixth step is to be certain that there is an actual and accurate correlation between the basic proposition of the sermon, the supplied interrogative, the statements of the sermon points, the amount of main points contained in the passage, and the plural noun of the sermon proposition.

The seventh step is to discover the development of the main points of the sermon by content of the passage and reflect the development of the main points by establishing subpoints for the main points of the passage.

The eighth step is to modify, revise, or correct the statements of the plural noun proposition, the main points, and the substructure through the best exegesis and most thorough study of the passage one can accomplish.

Now let's apply these steps to the thesis statements of the four couplets given above. For example, in couplet three, the non-plural noun propositional statement 'It is important to correct a faulty understanding of sin' is an excellent thesis statement for the biblical passage, Matthew 5:21-26. Having established this as a thesis statement for the passage, the thesis is interrogated by determining which of the interrogatives best describe the treatment the Lord provides for the subject-matter.

According to what the Lord says in this passage it seems appropriate to understand His instruction as a response to the implied interrogative 'how.' With the interrogative 'how' supplied to the thesis 'It is important to correct a faulty understanding of sin' one gets the resulting thesis question – 'How does one correct a faulty view of sin?' This question is critical since Jesus depicts three common misperceptions regarding sin and supplies the needed understanding to correct these misperceptions. Thus, the Lord is supplying 'correctives' to the prevalent problem of a faulty view of sin. Specifically, He supplies three of these correctives as He indicates three common misperceptions regarding sin. Therefore, the resulting plural noun proposition would be something like, 'In our passage this morning we will find three correctives for the most common misunderstandings regarding sin.'

This plural noun proposition suggests the following: the sermon to be preached will have three points, each sermon point will infer a misconception of sin commonly held by Jesus' disciples and the multitude who heard Him preach, and each sermon point will be a corrective to a common misperception of sin. The sermon structure correlating to this plural noun proposition would be:

* To have a correct understanding of sin you must identify sin as an internal disposition.

The Sermon Proposition

* To have a correct understanding of sin you must equate sin against man as sin against God.

* To have a correct understanding of sin you must act to minimize the consequences of your sins.

In regard to the first couplet, 'Parents should be pleasing to God in the raising of their children' is a good thesis statement for the passage, I Samuel 1. This chapter deals with the birth and lineage of Samuel through his godly parents Elkanah and Hannah. However, an important clarifying comment must be offered regarding using the aforementioned thesis for preaching from I Samuel 1. The primary intent of the chapter is to reveal the particular circumstances of the birth of this one who would be used by God greatly in the life of the nation Israel. It is only through the details of Samuel's birth and lineage that insight regarding the godliness of his parents is apparent. The fact of his birth and lineage, how God miraculously controlled them, is primary. The condition of his parents' godliness, though factual, is secondary. I am not arguing that the secondary significance of Samuel's parents would be inappropriate treatment of the passage as long as the orientation material of the sermon introduction brings out the primary focus of a sovereign, omnipotent, covenant-keeping God miraculously effecting the birth of this prophet of the Lord.

In reading this chapter, three things are apparent about Samuel's parents, especially his mother: although imperfect, they are devoted to God; to accomplish their purpose in life they are dependent upon God; and in the raising of their child they are dedicated to God. Elkanah and Hannah serve as a good model for parents who wish to be pleasing to God in the raising of their children. What was true for them should be true for all parents who know the Lord, that is, they should be pleasing to Him in their task of raising their children. But the question is, 'what' does it take to be parents who are pleasing to the Lord? What qualities constitute parents who please God? What are the hallmarks or qualities that epitomize the lives of parents with whom God is well-pleased?

The interrogative 'what' will be crucial for establishing a plural noun proposition that will accurately depict the thesis of this passage as well as the observable qualities of Samuel's parents. With the interrogative 'what' supplied to the thesis 'Parents should be pleasing to God in the raising of their children,' one may derive the thesis question – 'What is necessary to be parents who are pleasing to God in the raising of their children?' The three qualities that can be observed regarding Elkanah and Hannah help to construct the plural noun proposition – 'In this chapter we discover three qualities of parents who are pleasing to God in the raising of their children.' This plural noun proposition obviously portends of three sermon points, each one being a quality of Samuel's parents and all parents who would be pleasing to God in the raising of their children.

* God is pleased with parents who are devoted to Him in spite of their imperfections.

* God is pleased with parents who are dependent upon Him to accomplish their purpose in life.

* God is pleased with parents who are dedicated to Him in the training of their children.

In the second couplet we find a statement that will be a thesis for a plural noun proposition. The statement, 'Those who suffer persecution are blessed by God' is a thesis for a message preached from Matthew 5:10-12. Jesus makes two statements regarding the blessedness of those who suffer persecution. Even though persecution and blessedness have a definite spiritual connection they do not pose an initial logical connection. The significant interrogative in this passage is 'why.'

When the interrogative 'why' is supplied to the thesis – 'Those who suffer persecution are blessed by God' the interrogative question is – 'Why is it that those who suffer persecution are blessed by God?' In general, the answer is because persecution is indeed a beneficial reality. More specifically, the answer is given by the plural noun proposition, 'In His Sermon on the Mount, Jesus affirms that those who suffer persecution are doubly blessed as persecution brings to them two benefits.' The following two sermon points would attend this propositional statement:

* Believers are benefited when persecuted because persecution bears a proof of citizenship in the kingdom of heaven.

* Believers are benefited when persecuted because persecution brings a promise of reward in the kingdom of heaven.

As to the fourth couplet, 'The Christian life is often not as fulfilling as it could be' is a thesis statement that will serve as the crux of a plural noun proposition – 'Joyful, responsible living as a child of God is conditioned upon compliance to the three requirements we shall see in this text.' Either the interrogative 'when' or 'who' could be applied to the thesis statement, each of them providing a slight distinction in the phraseology of the sermon points. If the interrogative 'when' is used, then the sermon structure would be as follows:

* Joyful, responsible living results when you pray persistently for the unique necessities of your life.

* Joyful, responsible living results when you trust unquestionably in the perfect faithfulness of your God.

* Joyful, responsible living results when you strive exclusively for the equitable treatment of your neighbor.

If the interrogative 'who' is applied then a slight emphasis may be discerned in the following structure:

* Joyful, responsible living is experienced by those who pray persistently for the unique necessities of their lives.

* Joyful, responsible living is experienced by those who trust unquestionably in the perfect faithfulness of their God.

* Joyful, responsible living is experienced by those who strive exclusively for the equitable treatment of their neighbor.

Though different interrogatives may be supplied to the thesis, the main points will be altered in a marginal way. Actually, the different interrogatives make emphatic what would be understood clearly by the structure that would unfold from the thesis if controlled by the other interrogative.

In the main points that unfold from the thesis controlled by the interrogative 'when,' what is emphatic is the resulting reality that occurs as certain conditions are met by an individual. In the main points that unfold from the thesis controlled by the interrogative 'who,' what is emphatic is a description of the kind of individual who experiences the reality.

Unacceptable Words to be Used as Plural Nouns
In the formulation of a plural noun proposition it is never acceptable to use the word 'things' as a plural noun. Warren Wiersbe warns that the word 'things,' when used as a key word in a sermon proposition, is 'too broad' and it 'isn't likely to attract much interest'.[22] This is certainly true but,

beyond that, it must be recognized that the word simply is not declarative. It says nothing.

Moreover, when the word 'things' is used as a plural noun it strongly suggests that the preacher really has not been able to synthesize the passage well enough so that he can articulate productively what he would like to talk about. No preacher would want to advertise that. In fact, if he is going to talk about 'things', to what degree can the listener be certain as to what the preacher will be saying about his subject-matter? The answer is zero degree of certainty about the treatment of the subject-matter outside of the obvious fact that four 'things' indicates that the sermon will have four points.

The number accompanying the plural noun indicates to the listeners how many points will be contained in the sermon. If 'things' is used to convey to the listeners how many points will be contained in the message, then the word is worthless since it essentially means 'points' and that is understood already by the number used in the propositional statement. The word 'points' is just as useless as a plural noun since it is equivalent to 'things' and either word can, at best, only relate to the sermon outline and not the sermon proposition.

A plural noun proposition is not beneficial if it is used simply to indicate that a preacher has a number of 'things' to say or a number of 'points' to make about the subject-matter of a biblical text. Therefore, the words 'things' and 'points' must never be used as the plural noun in a plural noun proposition.

Unadvisable Words to be Used as Plural Nouns

Additionally, two other words, 'aspects' and 'truths,' must be severely curtailed in usage. Anything can be an aspect of something. An aspect of something asserts as fact that there is a relationship but a relationship that cannot be described in more definitive terms. When using the word 'truths' as the plural noun for a sermon proposition, the extent of disclosure being made to the congregation is that what is being communicated is not falsehood. In other words, the preacher is saying first and foremost about the subject-matter he will be preaching upon is, 'I will not be lying to you about this issue.' It goes without saying that a preacher will not be fabricating falsehood about the subject-matter of the sermon. Therefore, 'truths' declared about any subject-matter is no great disclosure. Truths should be declared about every subject of every sermon. We, then, could preach 'truths' for every subject of every sermon we will ever preach.

'Truths' and 'aspects' must see extremely limited duty in plural noun propositions. Granted, they may be used, but they must be sparingly used. Using these two terms is like playing for a tie in a football game. If that is the best you can do then you do it, but you can't feel very good about it – although you did not lose, you clearly did not win. So it is when we preach about truths and aspects of something.

The Hearer's Perception of Sermonic Integrity
A more objective, as well as practical, way to help assure that there is a comprehensible integrity between the sermon proposition and the sermon structure is to make certain the congregation has identified the preacher's proposition when it is stated in the introduction of the sermon. The preacher must state the proposition clearly. Yet again, what is stated clearly and what is stated unclearly incorporates some subjectivity.

Clarity as perceived by the preacher is a different matter than clarity as perceived by the congregation. Because of the hard work done by the preacher, having discovered and written out a propositional statement in his study, then clearly announcing this statement in the pulpit as he introduces the sermon, the preacher may assume, quite incorrectly, that he has made himself clear on the matter. Such an assumption will inevitably lead the preacher astray.

The truth is, no matter how intentional the preacher is, no matter how clear he desires to be, no matter how well he

The Sermon Proposition

articulates the propositional statement, not everyone will get it! The stated proposition will not be grasped by all the first time it is communicated, regardless of how clearly it was communicated! Therefore, the preacher must repeat the propositional statement at least once.[23] He is well advised to repeat his proposition several times in the introduction of the sermon.

Repetition of Plural Noun Proposition

When I preach, I strive to provide in every sermon introduction at least three statements of the sermon proposition. Having stated the proposition the first time, I will state it again immediately without any other material intervening and I will state it exactly as I did the first time. Later on in the introduction I will state the proposition for the third time, perhaps with a little diversity of statement to avoid redundancy while attempting to secure comprehension. Repetition is the first crucial factor for a clear propositional statement.

Placement of the statement is the second crucial factor for clarity in a sermon proposition statement. The last statement of the sermon introduction is significant. It must accomplish two tasks: it must conclude the sermon introduction and it must signal the transition to the sermon body. Only the sermon proposition contains the means by which both tasks can be accomplished with conceptual and functional clarity. Therefore, the very last sentence of the sermon introduction will be final statement of the sermon proposition, whether it is the second time or the fifth time the proposition is declared.

It is virtually impossible for one to be too clear, but it is incredibly easy to not be as clear as one must be in informing the congregation as to what the sermon will be about. Repeated statements of the sermon proposition and placement of the final repetition of the sermon proposition are two crucial factors for clarity in a sermon proposition.

However, repetition and placement cannot determine clarity, unconditionally. No matter how many times a verbose, hazy, uncertain concept is stated, it will not be perceived as being clear to those who hear it. In order to make compact, definitive statements about a subject, one must master the subject. That is, he must understand his subject thoroughly. Therefore, the third crucial factor for sermon proposition clarity is a thorough understanding of what the sermon will be about as reflected in a descriptive, definitive, distinguishable statement. A descriptive, definitive, distinguishable statement which is repeated in the sermon introduction and ends the introduction provides the three factors by which a preacher helps his hearers apprehend with clarity his sermon proposition.

Sermon Proposition Quality
What is it that constitutes a proposition and structure that may fairly be described as 'good'? A good proposition and structure, which works the same for the preacher as well as his listeners, is qualified as 'good' if it is 'specific enough to get their hands on it, interesting enough for them to want to stay with it, and so full of life and anticipation that they can't let go of it.'[24]

A Three-fold Threat to Sermon Proposition Quality
Warren Wiersbe is insightful as he surfaces three possible problems regarding sermon propositions which militate against the prospect that a proposition will be a good one. Wiesbe cautions against the problems of predictability, departure from the biblical text or an inaccurate guide to the biblical text, and irrelevance toward the hearers.

The first area of caution lies in the fact that, although a sermon proposition helps to forge out a clear outline, yet there may be an attending predictability and sameness of treatment for texts because of a sermon preparation that has grown mechanical. He points out that through the proposition, timeless truths will be supplied for the sermon but these may vary in character from one sermon to the next taking on the form of affirmation, or question, or exclamation, or exhortation.[25]

Second, care must be taken in the construction of the sermon proposition so that the statement is directed toward the understanding and treatment the text will receive by means of the sermon structure. He rightly insists that the proposition 'unifies the *content* of the sermon, so it discourages the preacher from covering too much territory or wandering of into foreign lands.'[26] Additionally, he suggests that 'The development of the message grows out of the union of the text and the proposition' and 'If the proposition is what it ought to be, it will contain the 'homiletical DNA' that will determine how the message develops.'[27]

Third, the propositional statement will be directed toward life because 'an outline isn't a message any more than a recipe is a meal or a blueprint is a house.'[28] If the proposition and the structure flowing from it is as it should be, then they will be statements 'about God and human life' touching 'people where they live' and making 'people see, think, feel, and want to obey' the text expounded to them.[29]

A Three-fold Task for Sermon Proposition Quality

A good proposition must communicate the biblical writer's message. Therefore, while it must be discovered by the preacher in diligent study of the passage, it must not be created by the preacher. According to Don McDougall, a preacher must comply with a three-fold task in order to have a good sermon proposition. He must: (1) find the author's central theme; (2) build a message around that theme; and (3) make that theme the central part of all he has to say.[30]

A Three-fold Test for Sermon Proposition Quality

The quality of the sermon proposition can be tested by asking the following three questions.

Does the sermon proposition depict the central idea of the text? Since it is the responsibility of the preacher to discover the central idea of the passage, which will become his sermon proposition, how does one go about discovering the central idea of the text? McDougall suggests three ways the central idea of the passage can be discovered. The central idea of the passage can be found from a single statement in the passage, from the larger context of the passage, and from recurring ideas in the passage.[31]

* Does the sermon proposition reflect the attributes or the qualities sought for in a plural noun proposition such as accuracy, specificity, conciseness, interest, and relevance?

* Does the sermon proposition provide actual insight as to what the sermon will be about?

The sermon proposition fills a significant part in a sermon. It must be a reliable guide to the hearers informing them of the direction, scope, and content of the sermon. Therefore, the desire and ability to do good work in constructing the sermon proposition statement is invaluable. The inability to do good work in constructing a good sermon proposition will be costly for the one who preaches as well as the ones who hear him preach. When a sermon is preached and no one knows, with a great deal of certainty, what the sermon was about, it will inevitably be the situation that the preacher's sermon proposition and structure were poorly crafted and communicated. On the contrary, good work in crafting the sermon proposition not only accurately portrays what the message will be about but such work becomes the cornerstone for clear communication, the foundation for qualitative sermon structure.

Consider the Following Questions

1. What is the preacher's most basic responsibility of cognition? What is his most basic responsibility of communication?

2. What is the most basic conception of a well-designed sermon?

3. What is the old adage for preaching that cannot be set aside without sacrificing clarity?

4. What are the two axiomatic realities of preaching suggested by Halford Luccock and the expression he used to represent these realities?

5. What areas of preaching, according to Don McDougall, require an expositor's most demanding discipline as well as a lot of time and effort in order to establish?

6. How do hearers respond to a preacher who lacks clarity in his preaching, in the view of Augustine?

7. What did William G. T. Shedd say in reference to the expression and characteristics of a sermon proposition that is a legitimate derivative from Scripture?

8. What are Grady Davis' two structural questions which form the framework for understanding in the context of preaching?

9. How does the use of a plural noun proposition and the structure unfolding from it make a contribution to constitute more than the minimal clarity sufficient for preaching?

10. What are the seven benefits for using a plural noun proposition, according to Faris D. Whitesell?

11. What is the basic presupposition that a plural noun proposition makes regarding the sermon structure?

12. How do Shedd's 'two things in rhetoric' necessitate a plurality of sermon points?

13. How is the sermon proposition discussed most profitably?

14. In what way does sermon structure contribute to the discussion of the text?

15. What is important to understand about non-plural noun propositional statements, how are they referred to, and what is their inherent weakness?

16. What are the eight steps involved in crafting a plural noun proposition?

17. What word is unacceptable, what words are unadvisable for usage as a plural noun, and why are they so?

18. What constitutes the difference between the preacher and his hearers regarding perceived clarity of the sermon proposition?

19. What are the three factors by which a preacher helps his hearers apprehend the sermon proposition with clarity?

20. What constitutes a 'good' sermon proposition and structure?

21. What is the three-fold threat to sermon proposition quality?

22. What is the three-fold task for sermon proposition quality?

23. What is the three-fold test for sermon proposition quality?

Conclusion

I've tried to make a case for the need of more effective and substantial sermon introductions. In order to be more effective, the typical sermon introduction will have to become more substantial. How much more substantial? The introduction must be substantial enough to get the attention of the hearers. The introduction must be substantial enough that the preacher can provide sufficient evidence that the sermon to be preached will be a life-changing message and, therefore, cause the hearers to develop a vital interest in hearing the sermon. The introduction must be substantial enough that the hearers perceive that the sermon is intended to change their lives in some specific way. The introduction must be substantial enough that the hearers understand how the message to be preached will relate to the previous messages and texts which have been preached previously, thus providing a heightened understanding of the Bible book being expounded. The introduction must be substantial enough that the hearers know what the sermon will be about and what will be said about this subject. The introduction must be substantial enough to transition clearly out of the introduction into the body of the sermon and the exposition of the biblical text to be expounded that day. In other words, the introduction must be substantial enough that they know what to expect from the sermon and they are in an expectant state when the introduction is completed. Upon completion of the sermon introduction, the hearers are convinced that the sermon about to be preached to them is a 'must hear' matter!

When the hearers are convinced that the sermon will be a 'must hear' matter, it will not only be because of the material of the sermon introduction but also because of the manner of the preacher introducing the sermon. The hearers will not fail to recognize that the message to be preached is obviously important in the preacher's perspective, apparently being a sermon that the preacher wants to preach and must preach for the benefit of his hearers. In the final analysis, a 'must hear' congregation only congregates before a 'must tell' preacher. His fire, his passion, and his excitement for the message kindles a fire in the hearts of the hearers to hear his message – to see the message burn through him in the preaching of the sermon and to see if the message may, perhaps, burn in them as well when the preaching is concluded.

The greatest problem with a less-than-effective sermon introduction is that it identifies the one who introduced it as a less-than-effective messenger on this occasion. The truth is, if one is not ready to introduce a sermon effectively he probably is not ready to preach effectively, or at least, preach in optimum effectiveness. Better preaching starts with better sermon introductions! More than this must be done for the sake of better preaching but there is no more important place to start than preaching better sermon introductions!

Finally, I agree with what Warren Wiersbe affirmed regarding the crucial issue of sermon introductions – It is a real challenge to prepare an effective introduction, but with the Lord's help, it can be done.

References

Foreword by Richard L. Mayhue
[1] John R.W. Stott, 'Christian Preaching in the Contemporary World,' *Bibliotheca Sacra* 145: 580 (October—December 1988): 370.

Introduction
[1] My conviction is that the role of a pastor is reserved for men only. Therefore, the preacher of the Word, as a pastor-teacher, is a role exclusively reserved for men. God does and will use gifted women to speak to other women. However, for the sake of simplicity, I will use the male gender in referring to the 'preacher'.

[2] In his chapter on introductions, illustrations, and conclusions wherein he labels these as 'the three undervalued components' of the sermon, Richard Mayhue dissuades against the underrating of the sermon introduction: 'If a preacher fails to gain his audience's attention with a captivating introduction, he has probably lost them for the rest of the message' (Richard L. Mayhue, 'Introductions, Illustrations, and Conclusions' in *Rediscovering Expository Preaching* [Dallas, Word, 1992], 243).

[3] William E. Sangster, *The Approach to Preaching* (Grand Rapids: Baker, reprinted, 1974), 35.

[4] Spurgeon, *Lectures to My Students* (Grand Rapids: Zondervan, new edition, 1954),127.

[5] Haddon W. Robinson, *Biblical Preaching: The Development and Delivery of Expository Messages* (Grand Rapids: Baker, 1980), 159.

Chapter One. 'Must Hear' Preaching: The Desire of a Preacher and the Delight of a Hearer.

[1]'Must hear' preaching is terminology I have derived from Haddon Robinson's statement on page 167 in his book *Biblical Preaching* where he writes: 'There are three types of preachers: those to whom you cannot listen; those to whom you can listen; and those to whom you must listen.'

[2]David R. Breed, *Preparing to Preach* (New York: George H. Doran Company, 1911), 85.

[3]George E. Sweazey, *Preaching the Good News* (Englewood Cliffs, N. J.: Prentice-Hall, 1976), 95.

[4]M. Rue, *Homiletics: A Manual of the Theory and Practice of Preaching* (Chicago: Wartburg Publishing House, 1922), 489.

[5]Samuel McComb, *Preaching in Theory and Practice* (New York: Oxford University Press, 1926), 59.

[6]C. H. Spurgeon, *Lectures to My Students* (Grand Rapids: Zondervan, new edition, 1954), 133.

[7]C. H. Spurgeon, *An All-round Ministry* (Carlisle, Pennsylvania: The Banner of Truth Trust, reprinted 1986), 174.

[8]Spurgeon, 175.

[9]Breed, 86.

[10]J. W. Alexander, *Thoughts on Preaching* (Carlisle, Pennsylvania: The Banner of Truth Trust, reprinted 1988), 6.

[11]Alexander, 6.

[12]Alfred E. Garvie, *A Guide to Preachers* (London: Hodder and Stoughton, 1911), 186-7.

[13]Taylor, 134.

[14]Taylor, 132.

[15]C. J. Ellicott, *Homiletical and Pastoral Lectures* (New York: A. C. Armstrong & Son, 1880), 54.

[16]T. Harwood Pattison, *The Making of the Sermon* (Valley Forge: Judson Press, 1941), 146.

[17]Ellicott, 83.

[18]Charles Bridges, *The Christian Ministry* (Carlisle, Pennsylvania: The Banner of Truth Trust, reprinted, 1991), 281.

[19]Craig Skinner, *The Teaching Ministry of the Pulpit* (Grand Rapids: Baker, second printing, 1981), 172.

[20]Ellicott, 82.

[21]Ellicott, 81.

[22]Claude A. Guild, *Training Men to Preach and Serve* (Fort Worth: The Manny Company, 1968), 79.

[23]Ellicott, 82.

[24]James S. Stewart, *Heralds of God* (Grand Rapids: Baker, reprinted, 1972), 112.

References

[25] Stewart, *Heralds*, 113.
[26] Stewart, *Heralds*, 114.
[27] Austin Phelps, *The Theory of Preaching: Lectures on Homiletics* (New York: Charles Scribner's Sons, 1882), 274.
[28] Alexander Vinet, *Homiletics; or the Theory of Preaching*, translated and edited by Thomas H. Skinner, (New York: Ivison, Blakeman, Taylor & Co., 1880), 299.
[29] Vinet, 306-7.

Chapter Two. Introducing the Sermon: A Necessity or Nuisance.

[1] James M. Hoppin, *Homiletics* (New York: Funk & Wagnalls, 1883), 352.
[2] John A. Broadus, *A Treatise on the Preparation and Delivery of Sermons* (New York: A. C. Armstrong and Son, twentieth ed., 1893), 250.
[3] Broadus, 248.
[4] Broadus, 250.
[5] Woodrow Kroll, *Prescription for Preaching* (Grand Rapids: Baker, 1980), 160.
[6] Arthur S. Hoyt, *The Work of Preaching* (New York: The Macmillan Company, 1936), 176.
[7] Vinet, 304.
[8] Alfred Gibbs, *The Preacher and His Preaching* (Kansas City, Kansas: Walterick Publishers, 1939), 189-90.
[9] Daniel Kidder, *A Treatise on Homiletics, Designed to Illustrate the True Theory and Practice of Preaching the Gospel* (London: Dickinson & Higham, 1873), 147.
[10] Robert L. Dabney, *Sacred Rhetoric* (Chatham, Great Britain: W & J Mackay Limited, 1870. Reprint edition, Carlisle, Pennsylvania: The Banner of Truth Trust, 1979), 141.
[11] Vinet, 297.
[12] Vinet, 297.
[13] Vinet, 298.
[14] Vinet, 298.
[15] According to the instruction contained in Continued Witness Training, an evangelism training manual of the Southern Baptist Convention, for example, the FIRE acrostic represents the preliminary content of Family, Interests, Religious background, and Exploratory questions. It is suggested that this material be discussed with a lost person before sharing the gospel. This material constitutes the introduction to the gospel.
[16] Kerr, 54.
[17] Cited by Don DeWelt, *If You Want to Preach* (Grand Rapids: Baker Book House, 1957), 115.
[18] Robinson, 167.

[19] Matthew Simpson, *Lectures on Preaching* (New York: Nelson and Phillips, 1879), 140.
[20] William M. Taylor, *The Ministry of the Word* (Grand Rapids: Baker, reprinted, 1975), 126.
[21] Charles Reynolds Brown, *The Art of Preaching* (New York: The Macmillan Company, 1932), 97.
[22] George Jennings Davies, *Papers on Preaching* (London: George Bell and Sons, third edition, 1883), 238.
[23] William G. T. Shedd, *Homiletics and Pastoral Theology* (New York: Scribner, Armstrong & Co., eighth ed., 1876), 182.
[24] G. Ray Jordan, *You Can Preach!: Building and Delivering the Sermon* (New York: Fleming H. Revell Company, 1951), 116.
[25] Vinet, 304.
[26] Breed, 94-95.
[27] Taylor, 128.
[28] Broadus, 256.
[29] Robinson, 165.
[30] Robinson, 9. 165.
[31] Faris D. Whitesell and Lloyd M. Perry, *Variety in Your Preaching* (Old Tappen, N.J.: Fleming H. Revell Company, 1954), 155.
[32] John W. Etter, *The Preacher and His Sermon: a Treatise on Homiletics* (Dayton, Ohio: United Brethren Publishing House, 1885), 318.
[33] Gibbs, 195.
[34] Lloyd John Ogilvie in *Handbook of Contemporary Preaching*, edited by Michael Duduit, (Nashville: Broadman, 1992), 176.
[35] Pattison, 149-50.
[36] David Buttrick, *Homiletic Moves and Structures* (Philadelphia: Fortress Press, paperback edition – second printing, 1988), 86.
[37] Charles Reynolds Brown, *The Art of Preaching* (New York: The MacMillan Company, 1926), 96-7
[38] Hugh F. Pyle, *What Every Preacher Should Know!* (Murfreesboro, Tennessee: Sword of the Lord Publishers, 1981), 140.
[39] Donald E. Demaray, *An introduction to Homiletics* (Grand Rapids: Baker, 1974), 76.
[40] R. Ames Montgomery, *Preparing Preachers to Preach* (Grand Rapids: Zondervan, 1939), 80.
[41] Ilion T. Jones, *Principles and Practice of Preaching* (New York: Abingdon Press, 1956), 159.
[42] Jerry Vines, *A Guide to Effective Sermon Delivery* (Chicago, Moody Press, 1986), 110.
[43] Alex Montoya, *Preaching With Passion* (Grand Rapids: Kregel, 2000), 121.
[44] Charles W. Koller, *Expository Preaching without Notes* (Grand Rapids: Baker, 1962), 34.

References

⁴⁵John E. Baird, *Preparing for Platform and Pulpit* (Nashville, Abingdon Press, 1968), 27.

⁴⁶Baird, 97.

⁴⁷Ken Davis, *Secrets of Dynamic Communication* (Grand Rapids, Zondervan Publishing House, 1991), 139.

⁴⁸Davis, 135.

⁴⁹Stephen F. Olford with David L. Olford, *Anointed Expository Preaching* (Nashville: Broadman & Holman Publishers, 1998), 181.

⁵⁰Warren W. Wiersbe, *Preaching and Teaching with Imagination* (Wheaton, Illinois: Victor Books, 1994), 22-23.

⁵¹Warren Wiersbe & David Wiersbe, *The Elements of Preaching* (Wheaton, Illinois: Tyndale House Publishers Inc., 1986), 41.

⁵²Jerry Vines, *A Guide to Effective Sermon Delivery* (Chicago, Moody Press, 1986), 131.

⁵³Dewitt Holland, *Preaching in American History* (Nashville: Abingdon Press, 1969), 102.

⁵⁴Montoya, 123.

⁵⁵Ralph L. Lewis, *Persausive Preaching Today* (Ann Arbor: LithoCrafters, Inc., 1979), 235.

⁵⁶Jay Adams, *Pulpit Speech* (Grand Rapids, Baker, 1971), p.113.

⁵⁷John Hall, *God's Word Through Preaching* (Grand Rapids: Baker, reprinted, 1979), 123-24.

⁵⁸Lloyd-Jones, 214.

⁵⁹Fenelon, 108.

⁶⁰Jerry Vines, 74-75.

⁶¹Thomas J. Potter, *Sacred Eloquence: or the Theory and Practice of Preaching* (New York: Fr. Pustet, & Co., fifth edition, 1903), 131.

⁶²Alexander Vinet, *Homiletics; or the Theory of Preaching*, translated and edited by Thomas H. Skinner, (New York: Ivison, Blakeman, Taylor & Co., 1880), 297.

Chapter Three. Getting Attention: Good But Not Good Enough.

¹Alexander Vinet, *Homiletics; or the Theory of Preaching*, translated and edited by Thomas H. Skinner, (New York: Ivison, Blakeman, Taylor & Co., 1880), 298.

²Vinet, 300.

³Gardiner Spring, *The Power of the Pulpit* (Carlisle, Pennsylvania: The Banner of Truth Trust, third ed.,1986), 36-7.

⁴John R. W. Stott, *Between Two Worlds* (Grand Rapids: Eerdmans Publishing Company, 1982), 75-6.

⁵Spurgeon, Lectures, 128.

⁶G. Campbell Morgan, *Preaching* (Grand Rapids: Baker, 1974), 84.

⁷Gregory, 32.

⁸C. H. Spurgeon, *Lectures to My Students* (Grand Rapids: Zondervan, new edition, 1954), 130-1.
⁹Chapell, 229.
¹⁰Warren W. Wiersbe, *The Dynamics of Preaching* (Grand Rapids: Baker, 1999), 65.
¹¹Spurgeon, Lectures, 127.
¹²Haddon W. Robinson, *Biblical Preaching: The Development and Delivery of Expository Messages* (Grand Rapids: Baker, 1980), 160.
¹³Richard L. Mayhue, 'Introductions, Illustrations, and Conclusions' in *Rediscovering Expository Preaching* (Dallas, Word, 1992), 243.
¹⁴Robinson, 160-1.
¹⁵Jay Adams, *Pulpit Speech* (Grand Rapids: Baker, 1971), 54.
¹⁶Spurgeon, Lectures, 138.
¹⁷Robinson, 160-1.
¹⁸Wiersbe, Dynamics, 66.
¹⁹Leslie J. Tizard, *Preaching: The Art of Communication* (New York: Oxford University Press, 1959), 58-9.
²⁰Tizard, 61-2.
²¹John Milton Gregory, *The Seven Laws of Teaching* (Grand Rapids: Baker Book House, reprinted in 1954, fifth printing in 1959), 25.
²²Gregory, 26-7.
²³Gregory, 27.
²⁴Morgan, 86.
²⁵R. Bruce Bickel, *Light and Heat: The Puritan View of the Pulpit* (Morgan, PA: Soli Deo Gloria Publications, 1999), 24.
²⁶Jay Adams, Pulpit Speech, 54.
²⁷Jerry Vines and Jim Shaddix, *Power in the Pulpit* (Chicago: Moody Press, 1999), 219.
²⁸Haddon W. Robinson, *Biblical Preaching: The Development and Delivery of Expository Messages* (Grand Rapids: Baker, 1980), 160.
²⁹James M. Hoppin, *Homiletics* (New York: Funk & Wagnalls, 1883), 340.
³⁰Gregory, 33.

Chapter Four. Securing Interest: The Major Work of an Introduction
¹Batsell Barrett Baxter, *Speaking for the Master* (Grand Rapids, Baker, 1954), 111.
²Don DeWelt, 115.
³Jerry Vines and Jim Shaddix, *Power in the Pulpit* (Chicago: Moody Press, 1999), 221.
⁴James Earl Massey, *Designing the Sermon: Order and Movement in Preaching*, edited by William D. Thompson (Nashville: Abingdon Press, 1980), 50.

References

[5] Massey, 23.
[6] Lloyd-Jones, 92.
[7] McDill, 102.
[8] John Wood, 14.
[9] William Evans, *How to Prepare Sermons and Gospel Addresses* (Chicago: The Moody Press, 1913), 78.
[10] Haddon W. Robinson, *Biblical Preaching: The Development and Delivery of Expository Messages* (Grand Rapids: Baker, 1980), 167.
[11] James D. Berkley, *Preaching to Convince* (Dallas: Word Books, 1986), 65.
[12] Hendricks, 139.
[13] Roy H. Short, *Evangelistic Preaching* (Nashville: Tidings, 1946), 15-6.
[14] Leavell, 12-3.
[15] Demaray, 24.
[16] Demaray, 25.
[17] Joseph R. Sizoo, *Preaching Unashamed* (New York: Abingdon-Cokesbury Press, 1949), 49.
[18] D. Martyn Lloyd-Jones, *Preaching and Preachers* (Grand Rapids: Zondervan Publishing House, 1972), 13.
[19] Lloyd-Jones, 13-4.
[20] Lloyd-Jones, 15-6.
[21] Lloyd-Jones, 19.
[22] Cited from *Grace to You* radio broadcast, 'John MacArthur takes the Hot Seat,' aired on 2/13/04, an interview with Phil Johnson.
[23] Joseph Fort Newton, *The New Preaching* (Nashville: Cokesbury Press, 1930), 24.
[24] Newton, 116.
[25] Jay Adams, *Pulpit Speech* (Grand Rapids: Baker, 1971), 55.
[26] John MacArthur, Jr., "Frequently Asked Questions about Expository Preaching" in *Rediscovering Expository Preaching* (Dallas, Word, 1992), 348.
[27] Gregory, 24.
[28] Tizard, 62.
[29] Tizard, 62.
[30] Robinson, 163.
[31] Robinson, 164.
[32] Leslie J. Tizard, *Preaching: The Art of Communication* (New York: Oxford University Press, 1959), 59.
[33] Atkins, 225.
[34] Morgan Phelps Noyes, *Preaching the Word of God* (New York: Charles Scribner's Sons, 1943), 105.
[35] Howard G. Hendricks, *Teaching to Change Lives* (Portland, OR: Multnomah Press, 1987), 102.
[36] Hendricks, 156.

[37]Dale Carnegie, *How to Win Friends and Influence People* (New York: Pocket Books, 1977), 43.
[38]Carnegie, 41.
[39]Carnegie, 42.
[40]Carnegie, 50.
[41]Faris D. Whitesell, *Power in Expository Preaching* (n.p., Fleming H. Revell Company, 1963), 91.
[42]As quoted in "The Word of God for Every Man" by Morgan Phelps Noyes, *Preaching the Word of God* (New York: Charles Scribner's Sons, 1943), 107.
[43]Gregory, 33.
[44]Gregory, 32.
[45]Gregory, 36.
[46]Gregory, 36.
[47]Em Griffin, *The Mind Changers* (Wheaton, Illinois: Tyndale House Publishers, Inc., 1976), 136-38.
[48]Em Griffin, 138.
[49]James M. Hoppin, *Homiletics* (New York: Funk & Wagnalls, 1883), 342-43.

Chapter Five. Securing Interest: How Interest is Secured in an Introduction.

[1]Chapell, 229.
[2]Paul E. Scherer, *For We Have This Treasure* (Grand Rapids: Baker, 1944; paperback edition, 1976), 143.
[3]James Armstrong, 30.
[4]Roland Q. Leavell, *Prophetic Preaching: then and now* (Grand Rapids: Baker, 1963), 7.
[5]As cited in W. Robertson Nicoll's 'An Appreciation' of Dr. Alexander McLaren, 5 of the index of vol. 17 in Dr. Maclaren's *Expositions of Holy Scripture*, reprinted by Baker Book House.
[6]James Armstrong, 33.
[7]James Armstrong, 43.
[8]Cited by John Wood, *The Preacher's Workshop*, 12.
[9]Whitesell, 92.
[10]Demaray, 29.
[11]Wayne McDill, *The 12 Essential Skills for Great Preaching* (Nashville: Broadman & Holman), 169.
[12]McDill, 105.
[13]Gregory, 30.
[14]Gregory, 31.
[15]Gregory, 35.
[16]McDill, 106.

References

17. Bryan Chapell, *Christ-centered Preaching* (Grand Rapids: Baker, 1994), 229-30.
18. Gregory, 90.
19. Gregory, 90.
20. Gregory, 93.
21. John Milton Gregory, *The Seven Laws of Teaching* (Grand Rapids: Baker Book House, reprinted in 1954, fifth printing in 1959), 9.
22. Gregory, 11.
23. Gregory, 14.
24. Baab, 69-70.
25. Baab, 70-1.
26. Howard G. Hendricks, *Teaching to Change Lives* (Portland, OR: Multnomah Press, 1987), 100.
27. Gregory, 86.
28. Hendricks, Teaching, 104
29. Gregory, 15.
30. Gregory, 15.
31. Gregory, 16.
32. Gregory, 18.
33. Gregory, 59.
34. Gregory, 75.
35. Gregory, 79.
36. Gregory, 100.
37. Gregory, 101.
38. Howard G. Hendricks, *Teaching to Change Lives* (Portland, OR: Multnomah Press, 1987), 77.
39. Lloyd-Jones, 305.
40. Lloyd-Jones, 304.
41. Lloyd-Jones, 304.
42. Demaray, 30.
43. Leavell, 8.
44. Howard G. Hendricks, *Say it with Love* (Wheaton, IL: Victor Books, 1973), 27.
45. Stapleton, 46.
46. Fenelon, 76.
47. Lloyd-Jones, 95.
48. Lloyd-Jones, 97.
49. Gaius Glenn Atkins, *Preaching and the Mind of Today* (New York: Round Table Press, Inc., 1934), 31.
50. Lloyd-Jones, 83.
51. Donald E. Demaray, *Proclaiming the Truth* (Grand Rapids: Baker Book House Co., 1979), 21.
52. Fenelon, 87.

[53] Short, 28-9.
[54] Lloyd-Jones, 306.
[55] Glenn H. Asquith, *Renewed Power in Preaching* (Valley Forge, PA: Judson Press, 1983), 31.
[56] Atkins, 221.
[57] John Wood, 23.
[58] Lloyd-Jones, 91.
[59] John Mason Stapleton, *Preaching in Demonstration of the Spirit and Power* (Philadelphia: Fortress Press, 1988), 42.
[60] Stapleton, 42.
[61] Fenelon, 99.
[62] Short, 67.
[63] Lloyd-Jones, 91-2.
[64] Fenelon, 92.
[65] Fenelon, 95.
[66] Asquith, 42.
[67] Lloyd-Jones, 87-88.
[68] Scherer, 165.
[69] Short, 42.
[70] Short, 55-6.
[71] Otto J. Baab, *Prophetic Preaching: A New Approach* (New York: Abingdon Press, 1958), 124.
[72] Van Cleave, 40.
[73] Howard G. Hendricks, *Teaching to Change Lives* (Portland, OR: Multnomah Press, 1987), 125.
[74] Carnegie, 136.
[75] Carnegie, 145.
[76] Carnegie, 148.
[77] Carnegie, 172.
[78] Lewis, 111.
[79] Ralph L. Lewis, *Persausive Preaching Today* (Ann Arbor, Michigan: LithoCrafters, 1979), 108.
[80] Lewis, 110.
[81] Lewis, 110-11.
[82] Tizard, 89-90.
[83] Fenelon, 125.
[84] Lewis, 114.
[85] Lewis, 117.
[86] Lewis, 119.
[87] Lewis, 122.
[88] Lewis, 130.
[89] Lloyd-Jones, 53.
[90] Lloyd-Jones, 56.

References

[91] J. I. Packer, 'Why Preach?' in *The Preacher and Preaching*, edited by Samuel T. Logan, Jr. (Phillipsburg, New Jersey: Presbyterian and Reformed, 1986), 9.

[92] Newton, 139.

[93] Newton, 140.

[94] Jack D. Sanford, *Make Your Preaching Relevant* (Nashville: Broadman Press, 1963), 53.

[95] Atkins, 220.

[96] Atkins, 223.

Chapter Six. Stating the Purpose: An Indication of a Passionate Preacher.

[1] Howard G. Hendricks, *Teaching to Change Lives* (Portland, OR: Multnomah Press, 1987), 60.

[2] J. H. Jowett, *The Preacher: His Life and Work* (New York and London: Harper & Brothers, 1912), 147-49.

[3] Quote from Charles Spurgeon, cited by John Wood, *The Preacher's Workshop*, 43.

[4] Nichols, 123.

[5] Stephen F. Olford with David L. Olford, *Anointed Expository Preaching* (Nashville: Broadman & Holman Publishers, 1998), 161.

[6] Olford and Olford, *Anointed*, 161.

[7] John Hall, *God's Word Through Preaching* (Grand Rapids: Baker, reprinted, 1979), 115.

[8] Pierson, 23-4.

[9] G. Campbell Morgan, *Preaching* (Grand Rapids: Baker, 1974), 85.

[10] Skinner, 161.

[11] John Wood, 32.

[12] R. C. H. Lenski, *The Sermon:Its Homiletical Construction* (Grand Rapids: Baker, reprint, 1968), 79.

[13] William G. T. Shedd, *Homiletics and Pastoral Theology* (New York: Scribner, Armstrong & Co., eighth ed., 1876), 126.

[14] C. H. Spurgeon, *An All-Round Ministry* (Carlisle, Pennsylvania: The Banner of Truth Trust, reprint, 1986), 116.

[15] Gardiner Spring, *The Power of the Pulpit* (Carlisle, Pennsylvania: The Banner of Truth Trust, third ed.,1986), 133.

[16] James Armstrong, *Telling Truth: The Foolishness of Preaching in a Real World* (Waco, TX: Word Books, 1977), 22.

[17] James Armstrong, 24.

[18] Pierson, 22.

[19] Skinner, 171.

[20] Jay Adams, *A Consumer's Guide to Preaching* (Wheaton: Victor Books, 1991), 42.

[21]Jay Adams, Preaching with Purpose (Phillipsburg, New Jersey: Presbyterian and Reformed Publishing Company, 1982), 19.
[22]Bert Decker and Hershael W. York, *Speaking with Bold Assurance* (Nashville: Broadman & Holman Publishers, 2001), 153.
[23]Andrew W. Blackwood, *Expository Preaching for Today* (Grand Rapids: Baker, paperback edition, third printing, 1980), 79.
[24]Blackwood, Expository, 77.
[25]James B. Chapman, *The Preaching Ministry* (Kansas City: Beacon Hill Press, 1947), 59.
[26]James B. Chapman, 57.
[27]Mark Galli and Craig Brian Larson, *Preaching that Connects* (Grand Rapids: Zondervan Publishing House, 1994), 49.
[28]Alfred E. Garvie, *A Guide to Preachers* (London: Hodder and Stoughton, 1911), 108.
[29]Walter Liefeld, *New Testament Exposition* (Grand Rapids: Zondervan Publishing House, 1984), 97.
[30]Liefeld, 107.
[31]Liefeld, 112.
[32]J. Randall Nichols, *Building the Word* (San Francisco: Harper & Row Publishers, 1980), 121.
[33]Dale, 224.
[34]Dale, 226.
[35]Dale, 245-46.
[36]Jack D. Sanford, *Make Your Preaching Relevant* (Nashville: Broadman Press, 1963), 57.
[37]Hugh F. Pyle, *What Every Preacher Should Know!* (Murfreesboro, Tennessee: Sword of the Lord Publishers, 1981), 145.
[38]John Oman, *Concerning the Ministry* (New York: Harper & Bothers, 1937), 93.
[39]Oman, 148.
[40]Robert T. Oliver, *Persuasive Speaking* (New York: Longmans, Green and Co., 1950), 30.
[41]St. Francis de Sales, *On the Preacher and Preaching*, translated by John K. Ryan (np: Henry Regnery Company, 1964), 32. St. Francis de Sales took exception to the idea that a preacher must instruct, delight, and persuade – the common conception of a preacher's duty in preaching. He believed that delight was a certain result when a hearer is enabled by a preacher to be enlightened to the truth and moved by the truth. He believed that the attempt of the preacher to delight his hearers was a 'sort of tickling of ears, which derives from a certain secular, worldly, and profane elegance.' The preacher must delight the hearers, but this was not distinct from teaching and moving the hearers but was dependent on them. Any delight which was brought to the hearers apart from teaching

and moving them very often prevents them from being taught and moved (pp. 32-33).

[42]Oliver, 30-1.

[43]Thomas J. Potter, *Sacred Eloquence: or the Theory and Practice of Preaching* (New York: Fr. Pustet, & Co., fifth edition, 1903), 264-65.

[44]Potter, 266-67.

[45]Potter, 267.

[46]Potter, 268.

[47]Potter, 269.

[48]Potter, 269-70.

[49]Potter, 270-1.

[50]Potter, 273.

[51]Potter, 276.

[52]Potter, 278.

[53]Potter, 286.

[54]Potter, 286.

[55]Potter, 287.

[56]St. Francis de Sales, 63-64.

[57]Potter, p288-9.

[58]James Stalker, *The Preacher and His Models* (London: Hodder and Stoughton, 1891), 110.

[59]Stalker, 95.

[60]Potter, 291.

[61]Potter, 290.

[62]Broadus, 504.

[63]T. Forsyth, *Positive Preaching and the Modern Mind* (Grand Rapids: Eerdmans Publishing Company, 1966), 29- 30.

[64]Forsyth, 29.

[65]Howard G. Hendricks, *Teaching to Change Lives* (Portland, OR: Multnomah Press, 1987), 101.

[66]Forsyth, 28-9.

[67]Ralph L. Lewis, *Persuasive Preaching Today* (Ann Arbor, Michigan: LithoCrafters, 1979), 8.

[68]Lewis, 19.

[69]Lewis, 19.

[70]Lewis, 21.

[71]Lewis, 129.

[72]Raymond Calkins, *The Eloquence of Christian Experience* (New York: The Macmillan Company, 1927), 147.

[73]Charles S. Horne, *The Romance of Preaching* (New York: Fleming H. Revell Company, 1914), 254.

[74]Horne, 255.

[75]Calkins, 131-32.

⁷⁶Calkins, 134.
⁷⁷Calkins,135-36.

Chapter Seven. Stating the Purpose: An Indication of a Significant Sermon.
¹A. J. F. Behrends, *The Philosophy of Preaching* (New York: Charles Scribner's Sons, 1890), 110.
²R. Albert Mohler 'The Primacy of Preaching' in *Feed My Sheep* (Morgan, PA: Soli Deo Gloria Publications, 2002), 28.
³R. C. Sproul, 'The Teaching Preacher' in *Feed My Sheep* (Morgan, PA: Soli Deo Gloria Publications, 2002), 140.
⁴Hugh Thomson Kerr, *Preaching in the Early Church* (New York: Fleming H. Revell Company, 1942), 41-2.
⁵John Wood, *The Preacher's Workshop* (London: The Tyndale Press, 1965), 9.
⁶Calkins, 143-44.
⁷Don Kistler, 'Preaching with Authority' in *Feed My Sheep* (Morgan, PA: Soli Deo Gloria Publications, 2002), 224.
⁸John MacArthur, 'A Reminder to Shepherds' in *Feed My Sheep* (Morgan, PA: Soli Deo Gloria Publications, 2002), 283.
⁹Kistler, 226.
¹⁰Stalker, 98.
¹¹Calkins, 146.
¹²Calkins, 147.
¹³Robert L. Dabney, *Sacred Rhetoric* (Chatham, Great Britain: W & J Mackay Limited, 1870. Reprint edition, Carlisle, Pennsylvania: The Banner of Truth Trust, 1979), 126-28.
¹⁴Dabney, 128.
¹⁵Mohler, 10.
¹⁶Mohler, 12.
¹⁷Dabney, 110.
¹⁸The analogies of the star and lens were taken from Robert L. Dabney's imagery to explain the unity of a sermon's structure. Dabney, *Sacred Rhetoric*, 111.
¹⁹Dabney, 110.
²⁰Andrew W. Blackwood, *The Fine Art of Preaching* (Grand Rapids: Baker, 1976), 123.
²¹Em Griffin, *The Mind Changers* (Wheaton, Illinois: Tyndale House Publishers, Inc., 1976), 134.
²²Leslie J. Tizard, *Preaching: The Art of Communication* (New York: Oxford University Press, 1959), 26.
²³John A. Broadus, *A Treatise on the Preparation and Delivery of Sermons* (New York: A. C. Armstrong and Son, twentieth ed., 1893), 230.

References

[24] Broadus, 231.

[25] Bryan Chapell, *Christ-centered Preaching* (Grand Rapids: Baker, 1994), 40.

[26] Chapell, 41.

[27] Chapell, 42.

[28] Donald G. Miller, *The Way to Biblical Preaching* (New York: Abingdon Press, 1957), 126.

[29] Miller, 126.

[30] Sidney Greidanus, *The Modern Preacher and the Ancient Text* (Grand Rapids: Eerdmans Publishing Company, 1988.), 130.

[31] Miller, 141.

[32] James W. Cox, *Preaching* (San Francisco: Harper, 1985), 93.

[33] John MacArthur, Jr., "Delivering the Exposition" in *Rediscovering Expository Preaching* (Dallas, Word, 1992), 322-3.

[34] Cox, 99.

[35] Cox, 105.

[36] John R. W. Stott, *Between Two Worlds* (Grand Rapids: Eerdmans Publishing Company, 1982), 246.

[37] Nichols, 122.

[38] Miller, 113.

[39] Miller, 114-15.

[40] Miller, 118.

[41] R. W. Dale, *Nine Lectures on Preaching* (London: Hodder and Stoughton, 1890), 133-34.

[42] Arthur T. Pierson, *The Divine Art of Preaching* (London: Passmore And Alabaster, 1892), 21-22.

[43] Ken Davis, *Secrets of Dynamic Communication* (Grand Rapids: Zondervan Publishing House, 1991), 98.

[44] Craig Skinner, *The Teaching Ministry of the Pulpit* (Grand Rapids: Baker, 1973), 162.

[45] Skinner, 133.

[46] Skinner, 133.

[47] Miller, 119.

[48] H. C. Brown, Jr., H. Gordon Clinard, and Jesse J. Northcutt, *Steps to the Sermon* (Nashville: Broadman Press, 1963), 15.

[49] Brown, Clinard, and Northcutt, 16-17.

[50] Brown, Clinard, and Northcutt, 18.

[51] A. J. F. Behrends, *The Philosophy of Preaching* (New York: Charles Scribner's Sons, 1890), 12-13.

[52] Sinclair B. Ferguson, 'Preaching to the Heart' in *Feed My Sheep* (Morgan, PA: Soli Deo Gloria Publications, 2002), 213-14.

[53] Ferguson, 215.

[54] Brown, Clinard, and Northcutt, 45.

⁵⁵Skinner, 134-36.
⁵⁶Warren W. Wiersbe, *The Dynamics of Preaching* (Grand Rapids: Baker, 1999), 46.
⁵⁷Phillips Brooks, *On Preaching* (New York: The Seabury Press, reprint, 1964), 77.
⁵⁸Wiersbe, *Dynamics*, 48.
⁵⁹Ozora S. Davis, *Principles of Preaching* (Chicago: The University of Chicago Press, 1924), 234.
⁶⁰Wiersbe, *Dynamics*, 70.
⁶¹Wiersbe, *Dynamics*, 70.
⁶²Skinner, 138.
⁶³Wiersbe, *Dynamics*, 77-78.
⁶⁴James W. Thompson, *Preaching Like Paul* (Louisville, Kentucky: Westminster John Knox Press, 2001), 60.
⁶⁵Thompson, 57.
⁶⁶Reg Grant and John Reed, *The Power Sermon* (Grand Rapids: Baker, 1993), 47.
⁶⁷Grant and Reed, 47.
⁶⁸H. E. Knott, *How to Prepare a Sermon* (Cincinnati: The Standard Publishing Foundation, n.d.), 77-8.
⁶⁹Craig A. Loscalzo, *Preaching Sermons that Connect* (Downers Grove, Illinois: Intervarsity Press, 1992), 120.
⁷⁰Jack D. Sanford, *Make Your Preaching Relevant* (Nashville: Broadman Press, 1963), 61.
⁷¹Ralph L. Lewis, *Persausive Preaching Today* (Ann Arbor, Michigan: LithoCrafters, 1979), 178.
⁷²Wayne C. Minnick, *The Art of Persuasion* (Boston: Houghton Mifflin Company, 1957), 203.
⁷³Minnick, 204.
⁷⁴Minnick, 207.
⁷⁵Minnick, 214-15.
⁷⁶Minnick, 215-16.
⁷⁷Minnick, 226-17.
⁷⁸Minnick, 226-17.
⁷⁹Minnick, 228.
⁸⁰Minnick, 235.
⁸¹Minnick, 238.

Chapter Eight. Setting the Context: The Earliest Indication of an Expository Sermon.
¹John MacArthur, Jr., 'Moving from Exegesis to Exposition' in *Rediscovering Expository Preaching* (Dallas: Word, 1992), 296.
²Ben E. Awbrey, *A Critical Examination of the Theory and Practice of*

References

John F. MacArthur's Expository Preaching, Doctor of Theology Dissertation, New Orleans Baptist Theological Seminary, 1990, 152.

[3] Austin Phelps, 272.

[4] Nathaniel M. Van Cleave, *Handbook of Preaching* (San Dimas, CA: L.I.F.E. Bible College, 1983), 64.

[5] Van Cleave, 63-65.

[6] D. Martyn Lloyd-Jones, *Preaching and Preachers* (Grand Rapids: Zondervan Publishing House, 1972), 78.

[7] Lloyd-Jones, 198-99.

[8] Zuck, 106.

[9] Walter C. Kaiser, Jr., and Moises Silva, *An Introduction to Biblical Hermeneutics* (Grand Rapids: Zondervan Publishing House, 1994), 123.

[10] Kaiser, and Silva, 129.

[11] Bernard Ramm, *Protestant Biblical Interpretation* (Grand Rapids: Baker Book House, 1970), 139.

[12] Richard Mayhue, *How to Interpret the Bible for Yourself* (Winona Lake, Indiana: BMH, 1986), 80.

[13] Fenelon, 133.

[14] Gregory, 120.

[15] Milton S. Terry, *Biblical Hermeneutics* (Grand Rapids: Zondervan Publishing House, ninth printing of flexible edition, 1981), 210.

[16] Gregory, 60.

[17] Mickelsen, 351.

[18] Gregory, 61.

[19] Gregory, 62.

[20] Roy B. Zuck, *Basic Bible Interpretation* (n.p.: Victor Books, 1991), 47-48.

[21] A. Berkeley Mickelsen, *Interpreting the Bible* (Grand Rapids: Eerdmans Publishing Company), 100.

[22] Gregory, 65.

[23] Gregory, 108.

[24] Zuck, 76-7.

[25] Gregory, 108-09.

[26] Gregory, 114.

[27] Gregory, 109.

[28] Gregory, 111.

[29] Gregory, 112.

[30] Gregory, 113-14.

[31] Gregory, 115.

[32] Transcription of an introduction to a sermon preached by John MacArthur at the Grace Community Church, Panorama City, CA, 1982. 'Salvation By Divine Power—Not Human Effort' Romans 4:18-25, GC 45-39.

[33]Transcription of an introduction to a sermon preached by John MacArthur at the Grace Community Church, Panorama City, CA, 1982. 'The Security of Salvation' Part 1, Romans 5:1-2, GC 45-40.

[34]Transcription of an introduction to a sermon preached by John MacArthur at the Grace Community Church, Panorama City, CA, 1982. 'The Security of Salvation' Part 2, Romans 5:2-5, GC 45-41.

[35]Transcription of an introduction to a sermon preached by John MacArthur at the Grace Community Church, Panorama City, CA, 1982. 'The Security of Salvation' Part 3, Romans 5:5-11, GC 45-42.

Chapter Nine. The Sermon Proposition: The Cornerstone of a Sermon.

[1]George Jennings Davies, *Papers on Preaching* (London: George Bell and Sons, third edition, 1883), 233.

[2]Henry Grady Davis, *Design For Preaching* (Philadephia: Fortress Press, 1958), 29.

[3]G. Campbell Morgan, *The Westminster Pulpit, Volume VII*, (Grand Rapids: Baker, reprint, n.d.), 76-77.

[4]James W. Cox, editor, and Kenneth M. Cox, associate editor, *Best Sermons 1* (San Francisco: Harper & Row, 1988). In the preface of this book the editor and associate editor write: 'This book is the fruit of an attempt to bring together some of the best efforts of contemporary preachers to articulate their messages for congregations.' The book includes sermons categorized under the headings of evangelistic, expository, doctrinal/theological, ethical, pastoral, and devotional. This sermon was one of ten which were deemed 'expository' by the editor and associate editor.

[5]Cox and Cox, 67.

[6]J. H. Jowett, *The Preacher: His Life and Work* (New York and London: Harper & Brothers, 1912), 133-34.

[7]Donald L. Hamilton, *Homiletical Handbook* (Nashville: Broadman Press, 1992), 42.

[8]Halford E. Luccock, *In the Minister's Workshop* (New York: Abingdon-Cokesbury Press, 1944), 211.

[9]McDougall, 225-26.

[10]McDougall, 241.

[11]Saint Augustine, *On Christian Teaching*, translated by R. P. H. Green (New York: Oxford University Press Inc., 1997), 141.

[12]William G. T. Shedd, *Homiletics and Pastoral Theology* (New York: Scribner, Armstrong & Co., eighth ed., 1876), 183-84.

[13]Davis, 24.

[14]Davis, 26.

[15]See Craig Skinner, *The Teaching Ministry of the Pulpit* (Grand Rapids: Baker, 1973), 161-71; Lloyd M. Perry, *Biblical Sermon Guide* (Grand

References

Rapids: Baker, 1970), 27-36; Charles W. Koller, *Expository Preaching Without Notes* (Grand Rapids: Baker, 1962) 72-75.

[16] Faris D. Whitesell, *Power in Expository Preaching* (n.p., Fleming H. Revell Company, 1963), 61.

[17] Skinner, 169.

[18] Ken Davis, *Secrets of Dynamic Communication* (Grand Rapids: Zondervan, 1991), 42.

[19] Shedd, 193-94.

[20] Calvin Miller, *Marketplace Preaching* (Grand Rapids: Baker, 1995), 146.

[21] J. W. Alexander, *Thoughts on Preaching* (Carlisle, PA: Banner of Truth Trust, 1864), 95.

[22] Warren W. Wiersbe, *The Dynamics of Preaching* (Grand Rapids: Baker, 1999), 64.

[23] Hamilton, 64.

[24] Wiersbe, *Dynamics*, 61.

[25] Wiersbe, *Dynamics*, 65.

[26] Wiersbe, *Dynamics*, 60.

[27] Wiersbe, *Dynamics*, 62.

[28] Wiersbe, *Dynamics*, 62.

[29] Wiersbe, *Dynamics*, 61.

[30] Donald G. McDougall, 'Central Ideas, Outlines, and Titles' in *Rediscovering Expository Preaching* (Dallas, Word, 1992), 229.

[31] McDougall, 229-33.

Bibliography

Adam, Peter. *Speaking God's Word*. Downer's Grove, Illinois: InterVarsity Press, 1996.
Adams, Jay. *A Consumer's Guide to Preaching*. Wheaton: Victor Books, 1991.
Adams, Jay. *Preaching with Purpose*. Phillipsburg, New Jersey: Presbyterian and Reformed Publishing Company, 1982.
Adams, Jay. *Pulpit Speech*. Grand Rapids, Baker, 1971.
Alexander, J. W. *Thoughts on Preaching*. Carlisle, Pennsylvania: The Banner of Truth Trust, 1864, reprinted 1988.
Allen, Ronald J. and Bartholomew, Gilbert L. *Preaching Verse by Verse*. Louisville, Kentucky: Westminster John Knox Press, 2000.
Armstrong, James. *Telling Truth: The Foolishness of Preaching in a Real World*. Waco, TX: Word Books, 1977.
Asquith, Glenn H. *Renewed Power in Preaching*. Valley Forge, PA: Judson Press, 1983.
Atkins, Gaius Glenn. *Preaching and the Mind of Today*. New York: Round Table Press, Inc., 1934.
Augustine of Hippo, Saint. *On Christian Teaching*, translated by R. P. H. Green. New York: Oxford University Press Inc., 1997.
Awbrey, Ben E. *A Critical Examination of the Theory and Practice of John F. MacArthur's Expository Preaching*, Doctor of Theology Dissertation, New Orleans Baptist Theological Seminary, 1990.

Baab, Otto J. *Prophetic Preaching: A New Approach*. New York: Abingdon Press, 1958.

Baird, John E. *Preparing for Platform and Pulpit*. Nashville, Abingdon Press, 1968.

Baxter, Batsell Barrett. *Speaking for the Master*. Grand Rapids, Baker, 1954.

Baxter, Richard. *The Reformed Pastor*, ed. William Brown. 5th ed. 1656; reprinted Carlisle, PA: Banner of Truth, 1979.

Behrends, A. J. F. *The Philosophy of Preaching*. New York: Charles Scribner's Sons, 1890.

Berkley, James D. *Preaching to Convince*. Dallas: Word Books, 1986.

Bickel, R. Bruce. *Light and Heat: The Puritan View of the Pulpit*. Morgan, PA: Soli Deo Gloria Publications, 1999.

Blackwood, Andrew W. *Expository Preaching for Today*. Grand Rapids: Baker, paperback edition, third printing, 1980.

Blackwood, Andrew W. *The Fine Art of Preaching*. Grand Rapids: Baker, 1976.

Blackwood, A. W. *The Preparation of Sermons*. New York: Abingdon Press, 1948.

Brastow, Lewis O. *The Modern Pulpit: A Study of Homiletic Sources and Characteristics*. New York: Hodder & Stoughton, 1906.

Breed, David R. *Preparing to Preach*. New York: George H. Doran Company, 1911.

Bridges, Charles. *The Christian Ministry*. Carlisle, Pennsylvania: The Banner of Truth Trust, reprinted, 1991.

Broadus, John A. *A Treatise on the Preparation and Delivery of Sermons*. New York: A. C. Armstrong and Son, twentieth ed., 1893.

Brooks, Phillips. *On Preaching*. New York: The Seabury Press, reprint, 1964.

Brown, Charles Reynolds. *The Art of Preaching*. New York: The Macmillan Company, 1932.

Brown, Jr., H. C., Clinard, H. Gordon, and Northcutt, Jesse J. *Steps to the Sermon*. Nashville: Broadman Press, 1963.

Buttrick, David. *Homiletic Moves and Structures*. Philadelphia: Fortress Press, paperback edition—second printing, 1988.

Calkins, Raymond. *The Eloquence of Christian Experience*. New York: The Macmillan Company, 1927.

Bibliography

Carnegie, Dale. *How to Win Friends and Influence People*. New York: Pocket Books, 1977.

Carrick, John. *The Imperative of Preaching*. Carlisle, Pennsylvania: The Banner of Truth Trust, 2002.

Chapell, Bryan. *Christ-centered Preaching*. Grand Rapids: Baker, 1994.

Chapman, James B. *The Preaching Ministry*. Kansas City: Beacon Hill Press, 1947.

Clowney, Edmund P. *Preaching and Biblical Theology*. Phillipsburg, New Jersey, 1979.

Cox, James W. editor, and Cox, Kenneth M., associate editor. *Best Sermons 1*. San Francisco: Harper & Row, 1988.

Cox, James W. *Preaching*. San Francisco: Harper, 1985.

Craddock, Fred B. *Overhearing the Gospel*. Nashville: Abingdon, 1978.

Daane, James. *Preaching With Confidence*. Grand Rapids: Eerdmans Publishing Company, 1980.

Dabney, Robert L. *Sacred Rhetoric*. Chatham, Great Britain: W & J Mackay Limited, 1870. Reprint edition, Carlisle, Pennsylvania: The Banner of Truth Trust, 1979.

Dale, R. W. *Nine Lectures on Preaching*. London: Hodder and Stoughton, 1890.

Dargan, Edwin Charles. *The Art of Preaching in the Light of Its History*. Nashville: The Sunday School Board of the Southern Baptist Convention, 1922.

Davies, George Jennings. *Papers on Preaching*. London: George Bell and Sons, third edition, 1883.

Davis, Henry Grady. *Design For Preaching*. Philadelphia: Fortress Press, 1958.

Davis, Ken. *Secrets of Dynamic Communication*. Grand Rapids, Zondervan Publishing House, 1991.

Davis, Ozora S. *Principles of Preaching*. Chicago: The University of Chicago Press, 1924.

Decker, Bert and York, Hershael W. *Speaking with Bold Assurance*. Nashville: Broadman & Holman Publishers, 2001.

Demaray, Donald E. *An introduction to Homiletics*. Grand Rapids: Baker, 1974.

Demaray, Donald E. *Proclaiming the Truth*. Grand Rapids: Baker Book House Co., 1979.

DeWelt, Don. *If You Want to Preach*. Grand Rapids: Baker Book House, 1957.
Duduit, Michael, editor. *Handbook of Contemporary Preaching*. Nashville: Broadman, 1992.
Ellicott, C. J. *Homiletical and Pastoral Lectures*. New York: A. C. Armstrong & Son, 1880.
Elliott, Mark Barger. *Creative Styles of Pre*aching. Louisville, Kentucky: Westminster John Knox Press, 2000.
Emery, Donald W. *Sentence Analysis*. Chicago: Holt, Rinehart and Winston, Inc., 1961.
Etter, John W. *The Preacher and His Sermon: a Treatise on Homiletics*. Dayton, Ohio: United Brethren Publishing House, 1885.
Evans, William. *How to Prepare Sermons and Gospel Addresses*. Chicago: The Moody Press, 1913.
Exell, Joseph S., editor. *The Biblical Illustrator*, Vol. 22. Grand Rapids: Baker Book House, third printing, 1977.
Fant, Jr., Clyde E., Pinson, Jr., William M. *20 Centuries of Great Preaching*, Volume Two. Waco: Word Books, 1971.
Fenelon, Francois. *Dialogues on Eloquence*, translated by Wilbur Samuel Howell. Princeton, New Jersey: Princeton University Press, 1951.
Forsyth, P. T. *Positive Preaching and the Modern Mind*. Grand Rapids: Eerdmans Publishing Company, 1966.
Galli, Mark and Larson, Craig Brian. *Preaching that Connects*. Grand Rapids: Zondervan Publishing House, 1994.
Garvie, Alfred. *A Guide to Preachers*. London: Hodder and Stoughton, 1911.
Gibbs, Alfred P. *The Preacher and His Preaching*. Kansas City, Kansas: Walterick Publishers, 1939.
Grant, Reg and Reed, John. *The Power Sermon*. Grand Rapids: Baker, 1993.
Gregory, John Milton. *The Seven Laws of Teaching*. Grand Rapids: Baker Book House (rpt in 1954, 5th printing in 1959).
Greidanus, Sidney. *The Modern Preacher and the Ancient Text*. Grand Rapids: Eerdmans Publishing Company, 1988.
Griffin, E. *The Mind Changers*. Wheaton, Illinois: Tyndale House Publishers, Inc., 1976.
Guild, Claude A. *Training Men to Preach and Serve*. Fort Worth: The Manny Company, 1968.

Hall, E. Eugene and Heflin, James L. *Proclaim the Word*. Nashville: Broadman Press, 1985.

Hall, John. *God's Word Through Preaching*. Grand Rapids: Baker, reprinted, 1979.

Hamilton, Donald L. *Homiletical Handbook*. Nashville: Broadman Press, 1992.

Hendricks, Howard G. *Say it with Love*. Wheaton, IL: Victor Books, 1973.

Hendricks, Howard G. *Teaching to Change Lives*. Portland, OR: Multnomah Press, 1987.

Holland, Dewitt. *Preaching in American History*. Nashville: Abingdon Press, 1969.

Hoppin, James M. *Homiletics*. New York: Funk & Wagnalls, 1883.

Horne, Charles S. *The Romance of Preaching*. New York: Fleming H. Revell Company, 1914.

Hoyt, Arthur S. *The Work of Preaching*. New York: The Macmillan Company, 1936.

Jones, Ilion T. *Principles and Practice of Preaching*. New York: Abingdon Press, 1956.

Jones, Owen. *Some of the Great Preachers of Wales*. London: Tentmaker Publications, third printing, 1997.

Jordan, G. Ray. *You Can Preach!: Building and Delivering the Sermon*. New York: Fleming H. Revell Company, 1951.

Jowett, J. H. *The Preacher: His Life and Work*. New York and London: Harper & Brothers, 1912.

Kaiser, Jr., Walter C. *Toward an Exegetical Theology: Biblical Exegesis for Preaching and Teaching*. Grand Rapids: Baker Book House, 1981.

Kaiser, Jr., Walter C. and Silva, Moises. *An Introduction to Biblical Hermeneutics*. Grand Rapids: Zondervan Publishing House, 1994.

Kerr, Hugh Thomson. *Preaching in the Early Church*. New York: Fleming H. Revell Company, 1942.

Kidder, Daniel P. *A Treatise on Homiletics, Designed to Illustrate the True Theory and Practice of Preaching the Gospel*. London: Dickinson & Higham, 1873.

Killinger, John. *Fundamentals of Preaching*. Minneapolis: Fortress Press, second ed., 1996.

Kistler, Don, General Editor. *Feed My Sheep*. Morgan, Pennsylvania, Soli Deo Gloria Publications, 2002.

Knott, H. E. *How to Prepare a Sermon*. Cincinnati: The Standard Publishing Foundation, n.d.

Koller, Charles W. *Expository Preaching without Notes*. Grand Rapids, Baker, 1962.

Kroll, Woodrow. *Prescription for Preaching*. Grand Rapids: Baker, 1980.

Larsen, David L. *The Anatomy of Preaching*. Baker: Grand Rapids, 1989.

Larsen, David L. *Telling The Old Old Story*. Wheaton, Illinois: Crossway Books, 1995.

Leavell, Roland Q. *Prophetic Preaching: then and now*. Grand Rapids: Baker, 1963.

Lenski, R. C. H. *The Sermon: Its Homiletical Construction*. Grand Rapids: Baker, reprint, 1968.

Lewis, Ralph L. *Persausive Preaching Today*. Ann Arbor: LithoCrafters, Inc., 1979.

Lewis, Ralph L. with Lewis, Gregg. *Inductive Preaching*. Westchester, IL: Crossway Books, 1983.

Liefeld, Walter. *New Testament Exposition* (Grand Rapids: Zondervan Publishing House, 1984.

Lloyd-Jones, D. Martyn. *Preaching and Preachers*. Grand Rapids: Zondervan Publishing House, 1972.

Logan, Jr., Samuel T., editor. *The Preacher and Preaching*. Phillipsburg, New Jersey: Presbyterian and Reformed, 1986.

Loscalzo, Craig A. *Preaching Sermons that Connect*. Downers Grove, Illinois: Intervarsity Press, 1992.

Luccock, Halford E. *In the Minister's Workshop*. New York: Abingdon-Cokesbury Press, 1944.

MacArthur, Jr., John. *Rediscovering Expository Preaching*. Dallas, Word, 1992.

Massey, James Earl. *Designing the Sermon: Order and Movement in Preaching*, edited by William D. Thompson. Nashville: Abingdon Press, 1980.

Mayhue, Richard. *How to Interpret the Bible for Yourself*. Winona Lake, Indiana: BMH, 1986.

McComb, Samuel. *Preaching in Theory and Practice*. New York: Oxford University Press, 1926.

McDill, Wayne. *The 12 Essential Skills for Great Preaching*. Nashville: Broadman & Holman, 1994.

Bibliography

Mickelsen, A. Berkeley. *Interpreting the Bible*. Grand Rapids: Eerdmans Publishing Company, 1963.

Minnick, Wayne C. *The Art of Persuasion*. Boston: Houghton Mifflin Company, 1957.

Miller, Calvin. *Marketplace Preaching*. Grand Rapids: Baker, 1995.

Miller, Calvin. *Spirit, Word, and Story*. Grand Rapids: Baker, 1996.

Miller, Donald G. *The Way to Biblical Preaching*. New York: Abingdon Press, 1957.

Montgomery, R. Ames. *Preparing Preachers to Preach*. Grand Rapids: Zondervan, 1939.

Montoya, Alex. *Preaching With Passion*. Grand Rapids: Kregel, 2000.

Morgan, G. Campbell. *Preaching*. Grand Rapids: Baker, 1974.

Morgan, G. Campbell. *The Westminster Pulpit, Volume VII*. Grand Rapids: Baker, reprint, n.d.

Newton, Joseph Fort. *The New Preaching*. Nashville: Cokesbury Press, 1930.

Nichols, J. Randall. *Building the Word*. San Francisco: Harper & Row Publishers, 1980.

Noyes, Morgan Phelps. *Preaching the Word of God*. New York: Charles Scribner's Sons, 1943.

Olford, Stephen F. and Olford, David L. *Anointed Expository Preaching*. Nashville: Broadman & Holman Publishers, 1998.

Oliver, Robert T. *Persuasive Speaking*. New York: Longmans, Green and Co., 1950.

Oman, John. *Concerning the Ministry*. New York: Harper & Bothers, 1937.

Pattison, T. Harwood. *The Making of the Sermon*. Valley Forge: Judson Press, 1941.

Perry, Lloyd M. *Biblical Sermon Guide*. Grand Rapids: Baker, 1970.

Phelps, Austin. *The Theory of Preaching: Lectures on Homiletics*. New York: Charles Scribner's Sons, 1882.

Pierson, Arthur T. *The Divine Art of Preaching*. London: Passmore And Alabaster, 1892.

Potter, Thomas J. *Sacred Eloquence: or the Theory and Practice of Preaching*. New York: Fr. Pustet, & Co., fifth edition, 1903.

Pyle, Hugh F. *What Every Preacher Should Know!* Murfreesboro, Tennessee: Sword of the Lord Publishers, 1981.
Ramm, Bernard. *Protestant Biblical Interpretation.* Grand Rapids: Baker Book House, 1970.
Robinson, Haddon W. *Biblical Preaching: The Development and Delivery of Expository Messages.* Grand Rapids: Baker, 1980.
Rue, M. *Homiletics: A Manuel of the Theory and Practice of Preaching.* Chicago: Wartburg Publishing House, 1922.
Rummage, Stephen Nelson. *Planning Your Preaching.* Grand Rapids: Kregel, 2002.
de Sales, Saint Francis. *On the Preacher and Preaching*, translated by John K. Ryan (np: Henry Regnery Company, 1964.
Sanford, Jack D. *Make Your Preaching Relevant.* Nashville: Broadman Press, 1963.
Sangster, William E. *The Approach to Preaching.* Grand Rapids: Baker, reprinted, 1974.
Scherer, Paul E. *For We Have This Treasure.* Grand Rapids: Baker, 1944; paperback edition, 1976.
Shedd, William G. T. *Homiletics and Pastoral Theology.* New York: Scribner, Armstrong & Co., eighth ed., 1876.
Short, Roy H. *Evangelistic Preaching.* Nashville: Tidings, 1946.
Simpson, Matthew. *Lectures on Preaching.* New York: Nelson and Phillips, 1879.
Sizoo, Joseph R. *Preaching Unashamed.* New York: Abingdon-Cokesbury Press, 1949.
Skinner, Craig. *The Teaching Ministry of the Pulpit.* Grand Rapids: Baker, second printing, 1981.
Spence, H. D. M. and Exell, Joseph S., editors. *The Pulpit Commentary*, Vol. 21. Grand Rapids: Wm. B. Eerdmans Publishing Company, 1950.
Spring, Gardiner. *The Power of the Pulpit.* Carlisle, Pennsylvania: The Banner of Truth Trust, third ed.,1986.
Spurgeon, C. H. *An All-round Ministry.* Carlisle, Pennsylvania: The Banner of Truth Trust, reprinted 1986.
Spurgeon, C. H. *Lectures to My Students.* Grand Rapids: Zondervan, new edition, 1954.
Stalker, James. *The Preacher and His Models.* London: Hodder and Stoughton, 1891.
Stapleton, John Mason. *Preaching in Demonstration of the Spirit and Power.* Philadelphia: Fortress Press, 1988.

Bibliography

Stewart, James S. *Heralds of God.* Grand Rapids: Baker, reprinted, 1972.

Stott, John R. W. *Between Two Worlds.* Grand Rapids: Eerdmans Publishing Company, 1982.

Stott, John R. W. *The Preacher's Portrait.* Grand Rapids: Wm. B. Eerdmans Publishing Company, 1961.

Sweazey, George E. *Preaching the Good News.* (Englewood Cliffs, N. J.: Prentice-Hall, 1976.

Taylor, William M. *The Ministry of the Word.* Grand Rapids: Baker, reprinted, 1975.

Terry, Milton S. *Biblical Hermeneutics.* Grand Rapids: Zondervan Publishing House, ninth printing of flexible edition, 1981.

Thompson, James W. *Preaching Like Paul.* Louisville, Kentucky: Westminster John Knox Press, 2001.

Tizard, Leslie J. *Preaching: The Art of Communication.* New York: Oxford University Press, 1959.

Tuck, Robert. *The Preacher's Homiletic Commentary*, Vol. 30. New York: Funk & Wagnalls, nd.

Van Cleave, Nathaniel M. *Handbook of Preaching.* San Dimas, CA: L.I.F.E. Bible College, 1983.

Vines, Jerry. *A Guide to Effective Sermon Delivery.* Chicago, Moody Press, 1986.

Vines, Jerry and Shaddix, Jim. *Power in the Pulpit.* Chicago: Moody Press, 1999.

Vinet, Alexander. *Homiletics; or the Theory of Preaching*, translated and edited by Skinner, Thomas H. New York: Ivison & Phinney, 1854.

Wardlaw, Don M., editor. *Preaching Biblically.* Philadelphia: The Westminster Press, 1983.

Whitesell, Faris D. *Power in Expository Preaching.* n.p., Fleming H. Revell Company, 1963.

Whitesell, Faris D. and Perry, Lloyd M. *Variety in Your Preaching.* Old Tappen, N.J.: Fleming H. Revell Company, 1954.

Wiersbe, Warren W. *The Dynamics of Preaching.* Grand Rapids: Baker, 1999.

Wiersbe, Warren W. *Preaching and Teaching with Imagination.* Wheaton, Illinois: Victor Books, 1994.

Wiersbe, Warren W. *Treasury of the World's Great Sermons.* Grand Rapids: Kregel Publications, reprinted, 1982.

Wiersbe, Warren W. and Perry, Lloyd M. *The Wycliffe Handbook of Preaching and Preachers.* Chicago: Moody Press, 1984.

Wiersbe, Warren & Wiersbe, David. *The Elements of Preaching*. Wheaton, Illinois: Tyndale House Publishers Inc., 1986.

Willingham, Ronald L. *How to Speak so People Will Listen*. Waco, TX: Word Books, 1968.

Wilson, Gordon. *Set for the Defense*. (n.p.: Western Bible & Book Exchange, 1968.

Wood, John. *The Preacher's Workshop*. London: The Tyndale Press, 1965.

Zuck, Roy B. *Basic Bible Interpretation*. n.p.: Victor Books, 1991.

Subject Index

Abram/Abraham 282–90
abruptness, alleviation of 43–5
accuracy
 accurate understanding and purposeful preaching 236–9
 contextualization and 272–5
 terminological precision 234–5
Adams, Jay 67, 84–5, 117
 on preaching God's Word 190, 191–2
Alexander, J. W. 25
 quotation 329
anointing of the Holy Spirit (unction) 150–68, 212, 214
apathy 127
application 119–24, 125
 believer's compliance to God's Word 240–2
 developed connection 147–50
 purpose statements and 241–2
 specific intent 235–6
 volitional unity of purpose 230–2
 see also relevance
Armstrong, James 135
assurance 292–6, 299–304
attention gaining
 attuning the minds of the hearers 44, 75–92
 as a cumulative effect 22
 interest and 88–92, 103–4, 125–7 *see also* interest
 introductory material for 76–8, 82–8, 95–101
 maximizing attention 125–7
 necessity and difficulty of 78–82
 nonvoluntary attention 103–4
audience *see* congregations
Augustine of Hippo 322
authority 173–8
 authoritative declaration 173–9, 212–14
 biblical authority and purposeful preaching 221–30
 biblical preaching and 191–2
 preaching on God's authority 158–9
 preaching under God's control 157–8
 of the pulpit 212–13

Baab, Otto 167
Baird, John 62
Barclay, William 110
Baxter, Batsell Barrett (quotation) 104
Baxter, Richard 89, 118
Beecher, Henry Ward 111–12
Behrends, A. J. F. 246–7
Bible
 context *see* contextualization
 exposition *see* expository preaching
Black, James 135
Blackwood, Andrew 193–4
body language 207
 see also eye contact
Borden, Richard C. 48
boredom 117–18
Bourdaloue, Louis 215
Breed, David 57
brevity
 in sermon introductions 53–4, 55–60
 in sermons 54
Bridges, Charles 28–9
Broadus, John A. 38, 58, 123–4, 212
Brooks, Phillips 215, 250
Brown, Charles Reynolds 58–9
Brown, H. C. Jr., Clinard, H. G. and Northcutt, J. J. 245–6

Calkins, Raymond 215, 216–17
calling to preach 154–5, 156–7
Carnegie, Dale 168
 quotations 121, 123
Chapell, Bryan 141
Chapman, James B. (quotation) 195
Cicero 208–9
communication
 attention gaining *see* attention gaining
 body language 207
 certainty in 128
 communicative momentum/certitude 46–8
 emotion and 26, 63, 145–6
 eye contact 60–4
 information and 63

introductions as communication bridges 42–3
motivational 109
securing and holding the interest *see* interest
terminological precision 234–5
use of notes *see* sermon notes
compassion 105–6, 165
conclusions to sermons 86, 194, 208, 246, 263
congregations
   assessments of preachers 31, 51, 108
   attuning the minds of 44, 75–92
   compassion for 105–6, 165
   emotional effect of persuasion on the hearers 261–2
   favorable reception of preachers 45–6, 199–200
   gaining the attention of *see* attention gaining
   hearer's perception of sermonic integrity 338–9
   need of a sermon introduction 39–45, 80–1
   securing the interest of *see* interest
connection 268, 269–70
   examples in introductions to sermons by MacArthur 290, 291, 297, 305, 312
   reviews in the learning process 278–80
contextualization
   accuracy and 272–5
   assessed examples in sermon introductions by MacArthur 281–314
   benefits of 272–81
   completion and 278–80
   components of 268–72 *see also* connection; orientation; summarization
   as an introductory need 49–50, 267–72
   isolationism and 274
   learning theory and 276
   perspective and 280
   relatedness and 277–8
   retention and reviews 280
   thoroughness and 275–7
   volition and 280–1
conviction 160–1
courage 226
Cox, James W. 239, 240, 241
Craddock, Fred 319
culture
   and attention gaining 79–80
   preaching and 7–9, 56
curiosity 148–9

Dabney, Robert L. 43, 227–9
Dale, R. W. 196–8, 243
Davies, George Jennings (quotation) 317
Davis, Henry Grady
   plural noun (sermon) propositions 323–4
   quotation 317
Davis, Ken 244
   quotation 63
Davis, Ozora S. (quotation) 251
DeWelt, Don 104–5
distraction 127

earnestness
   earnest preachers and persuasive preaching 208–14
   purposeful preaching and 214–17
   see also sincerity
Edwards, Jonathan 64–5, 162–3
Eliff, Tom: sermon introduction 96–7
Elijah 153
eloquence 164, 170
emotions/feelings
   communication and 26, 63, 145–6
   earnestness and *see* earnestness
   emotional effect of persuasion on the hearers 261–2
   emotional manipulation 112, 171
   and the Holy Spirit 158
   passion *see* passion in preaching
   persuasion and 171, 204–6
enthusiasm 143, 156
   see also passion in preaching
Erasmus, Desiderius 222
evangelism 246–7
explanation 202–7
expository preaching 236–9
   accurate understanding 236–9, 272–5
   believer's compliance to God's Word 240–2
   biblical authority and purposeful preaching 221–30
   cognitive and volitional unity of purpose 230–2
   context setting *see* contextualization
   decline and renewal of 111–16
   instruction in righteousness 109–10
   interest and 104–16, 123
   need of a sermon introduction 49–50
   persuasion in 169–73 *see also* persuasion
   purpose and forceful delivery 194–6
   sermonic purpose and 189–94
   unction and 152–4
extemporaneous preaching 64–71
eye contact 60–4

faith-based promises 171, 306–12
   see also justification by faith
faithfulness of God 305–12
fear-based threats 171
feelings *see* emotions/feelings
Fenelon, Francois 69, 157, 164, 274
   quotation 161
Ferguson, Sinclair 247–8
focus
   attention and 87–8 *see also* attention gaining
   heightened 40
Forsyth, P. T. 212
Francis de Sales 209–10

Garvie, Alfred 26, 195
Gibbs, Alfred (quotation) 40
glory of God, as purpose of preaching 166–7, 239–40
goals

Subject Index

aims and 242–3
  dominant 241
  man-made and God-given 96–7
  persuasion, needs, values and 258–60
  purpose statements *see* purpose statements
  for sermon introductions 83
  see also objectives
grace, salvation and 292–6, 299–304, 305–12
Grant, Reg, and Reed, John 253–4
Gregory, Joel: sermon introduction 95–6
Gregory, John Milton 278–9, 281
Griffin, Em 128
  quotation 234–5
Guild, Claude A. (quotation) 30

Hagar 287
Hall, John 67–8, 184
Hamilton, Donald L. 321
hearers of sermons *see* congregations
Hendricks, Howard 109, 120, 145, 150, 182
  on authoritative declaration 213
hermeneutics
  biblical principles of exposition *see* expository preaching
  contextualization *see* contextualization
  procedure from the known to the unknown 276
Hitler, Adolf 215
Holy Spirit
  anointing/unction 150–68, 212, 214
  and the earnest preacher 211–12, 214
Horne, Charles S. 215
Hoyt, Arthur 39
human needs *see* needs

Ignatius Loyola 209–10
inductive preaching 173–5
integrity 135, 171, 227, 259, 323
  hearer's perception of sermonic integrity 338–9
  intellectual 144
  passion and 227
  in persuasion 157
  see also sincerity
intentional preaching *see* purposeful preaching
interest
  application and 119–24, 125, 149–50
  attention and 88–92, 103–4, 125–7 *see also* attention gaining
  and authoritative declaration 173–8
  through content means 135–43, 178–9
  through conveyance means 143–50, 179
  curiosity 148–9
  expository preaching and 104–16, 123
  hindrances to securing 117–18, 127–8
  persuasion and 150, 168–73
  results of securing 123–7
  in sermon introductions 48–9, 116–27, 133–79
  unction and 150–68
internalization 69, 152, 163

impact of the truth in the preacher's life 145–7, 163, 224
preaching first to yourself 224
introductions to sermons
  alleviation of abruptness 43–5
  application 119–24, 125
  assessed introductions to sermons by MacArthur 281–312
  as attention gainers *see* attention gaining
  as communication bridges 42–3
  contextual setting *see* contextualization
  convictions of the preacher for 21–35
  effectiveness 51–2
  efforts in preparation 31–5, 70–1, 134–5, 321–3
  as final step in sermon preparation 70
  heightening focus 40
  as integral part of sermon structure 236
  as interest securers *see* interest
  length 52–60, 345–6
  natural elevation 41–2
  overcoming inertia 40–1
  people's need for 39–45
  personal impact of the truth in the preacher's life 145–7
  persuasion and 208
  preacher's need for 45–9
  preaching elements in 124–7
  and preaching organization 317–20 *see also* sermon propositions
  problem-solution approach 139–41
  purpose statements *see* purpose statements
  questions and answers in 142–3
  securing interest through 48–9, 116–27, 133–79
sermon proposition *see* sermon propositions
Isaac 288–9
Ishmael 287–9
isolationism 274

Jeremiah, David 159–60
Jesus Christ
  gospel proclamation and 166, 246–8
  life-changing preaching by 192–3
John the Baptist 161
Johnson, Phil 114
Jones, Ilion T. 59–60
Jowett, J. H. 182–3, 214, 320–1
justification by faith 293–6, 297, 299–304

Kaiser, Walter and Silva, Moises 273
Kerr, Hugh Thomson 47, 223
keywords 326
  see also plural noun (sermon) propositions
Kistler, Don 225
knowledge 143–7
  completion and 278–80
  developed connection 147–50
  learning process *see* learning process
  retention 280
  see also understanding

379

Koller, Charles 62
Kroll, Woodrow 39

Lacordaire 170
learning process
   application 149
   momentum 139
   place of understanding 276
   relation of concepts 277–8
   reviews in 278–80 *see also* connection; summarization
Leavell, Roland Q. 134
   quotation 154
length of sermon introductions 52–60, 345–6
Lenski, R. C. H. 186
Lewis, Ralph L. 170, 171
   quotation 255
Liefeld, Walter 196
Lloyd-Jones, Martin 68, 106, 158
   on contextualization 270, 271–2
   on decline and renewal of expository preaching 111–13
   on preaching on God's authority (quotation) 159
   on purposeful preaching (quotation) 165
   on unction 150–1, 153
Luccock, Halford 321
Luther, Martin 222

MacArthur, John 113–14, 117, 159–60, 225, 240, 312–14
   assessed introduction to sermon on Romans 4:18-25 282–91
   assessed introduction to sermon on Romans 5:1-2 291–8
   assessed introduction to sermon on Romans 5:2-5 298–305
   assessed introduction to sermon on Romans 5:5-11 305–12
   on sermon introductions 267
Maclaren, Alexander 135
McDill, Wayne 137–8, 141
McDougall, Don 321–2, 341–2
Mickelsen, A. Berkeley (quotation) 277
Miller, Calvin (quotation) 327–8
Miller, Donald 237, 243
mind
   drawing the mind 91
   focusing of attention 87–8
   learning process *see* learning process
   tuning 44, 75–92
Mohler, Albert 221–2, 229–30
monotony 118
Montoya, Alex 61
Morgan, G. Campbell 81, 185, 318–19
Morgan, J. Pierpont 169
motivation
   motivating hearers into action 109 *see also* persuasion; preaching principles: changing lives
   preaching from God's motives 163–5

'must hear' preaching 21–35
   convictions of the preacher 21–35
   elements of a sermon introduction 34–5

natural elevation 41–2
needs 45, 46, 118–19, 258–60
   and the problem-solution approach to preaching 140–1
Newton, Joseph Fort (quotations) 115, 173–4
notes *see* sermon notes

objectives 185, 245–9, 251
   'behavioral objectives' 242
   statements of *see* purpose statements
   see also goals
Olford, Stephen 63, 184
   sermon introduction 99–100
Oman, John 200
orientation 268, 269–70, 312–13
   examples in introductions to sermons by MacArthur 290, 291, 297, 304, 305, 312
Owen, John 59

Packer, J. I. 173
passion in preaching 24–5, 28–9, 164–5
   body language and 207
   compassion and 105–6, 165
   earnestness and *see* earnestness
   eye contact and 62–3
   integrity and 227
   persuasion and 207, 208–10 *see also* persuasion
   unction and 162–3
   see also enthusiasm
pastoral responsibility 196–9, 250–1
Paul, Apostle 7–8, 78, 156–7, 227, 237
   as model for preaching purposes 249–50, 253
perseverance 292–6, 297, 299–304
perspective 280
persuasion 30, 150, 164, 168–73
   direct and indirect 207–8
   earnestness and 208–14
   emotional effect of persuasion on the hearers 261–2
   needs and 258–60
   the purpose statement as a persuasive proposal 201
   purposeful preaching and 199–201
   role of explanation 202–7
   values and 258–60, 261
Phelps, Austin 269, 270
Pierson, A. T. 184–5, 189, 243–4
plural noun (sermon) propositions 323–8
   crafting 330–6
   examples and assessments 328–36
   repetition 339–40
   words to avoid 336–8
Potter, Thomas 70, 202, 204–6
power in preaching 159–60
   see also unction
preachers

Subject Index

as ambassadors for Christ 172
assessments by congregations 31, 51, 108
biblical apostles and prophets 223, 249–50
burning with fire for the truth 24–5 *see also* passion in preaching
calling 154–5, 156–7
communication skills *see* communication
compassion 105–6, 165
convictions regarding introductions to sermons 21–35
deviant 122
earnestness *see* earnestness
enthusiasm 143, 156 *see also* passion in preaching
essayists and 112
as expositors 105–16 *see also* expository preaching
favorable reception 45–6, 199–200
impact of the truth in the preacher's life 145–7, 163, 224 *see also* internalization
knowledge and scriptural understanding 143–7
need of a sermon introduction 45–9
passion *see* passion in preaching
pastoral responsibility and purposeful preaching 196–9, 250–1
pulpiteers and 111–12
sincerity *see* sincerity
as surgeons 230
unction and the servant preacher 154–8
preaching principles
alleviation of abruptness 43–5
application *see* application
authority *see* authority
brevity 54 *see also* brevity
changing lives 190–4, 202–8, 233–4, 241–2, 254–5, 259–60 *see also* persuasion
communication *see* communication
conviction 160–1
courage 226
divine authority 158–9
divine control 157–8
divine glory 166–7, 239–40
divine motives 163–5
divine power 159–60
divine purposes 165–6
elements in sermon introductions 124–7 *see also* introductions to sermons
enthusiasm 143, 156 *see also* passion in preaching
expository preaching *see* expository preaching
extemporaneous preaching 64–71
gaining attention *see* attention gaining
'germinal and terminal laws' 243–4
impact of the truth in the preacher's life 145–7, 163, 224 *see also* internalization
inductive preaching 173–5
internalization *see* internalization
introducing the sermon *see* introductions to sermons
motivation *see* motivation

'must hear' preaching *see* 'must hear' preaching
organization and preaching 317–20 *see also* sermon propositions
persuasion 30, 150, 164, 168–73 *see also* persuasion
for the power of the Spirit (unction) 150–68
of preachers in the New Testament 223, 249–50
preaching Christ 246–8
preaching first to yourself 223–4
preaching with fire and passion *see* passion in preaching
problem-solution approach 138–41
purposeful preaching *see* purposeful preaching
relevance *see* relevance
securing and holding the interest *see* interest
sermon objects and subjects 242–4
sermon propositions *see* sermon propositions
standing up to resistance 229–30
use of notes *see* sermon notes
problem-solution approach to preaching 138–41
prophets 144, 154–5
  NT apostles and 223
propositional statements *see* sermon propositions
purpose statements 184–7, 191, 192, 194–6, 198, 231–6
  achievement 263
  application 241–2
  overt declaration 244
  as persuasive proposals 201
  role of unifying and clarifying content and intent 251
  specific 252–60
purposeful preaching
  accurate understanding and 236–9
  biblical authority and 221–30 *see also* authority
  changing lives 190–4, 202–8, 233–4, 241–2, 254–5, 259–60 *see also* persuasion
  cognitive and volitional unity of purpose 230–2
  earnestness and 214–17
  general purposes 245–6, 249–52
  goals and objectives *see* goals; objectives; purpose statements
  for God's glory 239–40
  need for 183–9
  pastoral responsibility and 196–9, 250–1
  persuasion and 199–201 *see also* persuasion
  the predominance of unintentional preaching 181–3
  purposeful expository preaching and forceful delivery 194–6
  sermonic purpose and expository preaching 189–94
  specific intent 235–6
  specific purposes 245, 246–9, 252–5
  statements of purpose *see* purpose statements
  terminological precision 234–5
  three-fold criteria for 232–4

questions
  introductory use of 142–3
  Socratic method 169
Quintillian 44, 83, 209

relatedness 277–8
relevance 104, 119, 137–8
  see also application
repetition 339–40
retention 280
reviews *see* summarization
Robertson, A. T. 110
Robinson, Haddon 17, 51, 58, 108
  on application 119
  attention gaining 84, 85, 100–1
  sermon introduction 100–1

salvation, security in 292–6, 297, 305–12
Sanford, Jack 177, 198–9
  quotation 254
Sarah 286–7
Scherer, Paul 134, 166
scriptural exposition *see* expository preaching
scriptural understanding 143–7
  see also understanding
sermon introductions *see* introductions to sermons
sermon notes 61–4
  extemporaneous preaching and 64–70
  sketchy pulpit outlines 69–70
Sermon on the Mount 177, 192–3, 334–5
sermon propositions
  clarity 320–1, 324–5, 338–40
  construction 321–3
  plural noun propositions 323–8, 339–40
  quality 340–2
  sermon structure and 320
sermon structure
  conclusions 86, 194, 208
  hearer's perception of sermonic integrity 338–9
  introductions *see* introductions to sermons
  purpose statements and 185–6
  sermon propositions and 320 *see also* sermon propositions
  sermonic unity 230–2
Shedd, William G. T. 55, 186–7, 322–3, 326–7
Short, Roy 166–7
Simeon, Charles 251
sincerity 63, 153
  see also earnestness; integrity
Sizoo, Joseph R. 110
Skinner, Craig 245, 249–50, 325–6
Socratic questioning 169
Spring, Gardiner 77–8
Spurgeon, C. H. 16–17, 23, 24–5, 155, 235, 254
  on gaining attention 80, 82–3, 84, 85
  on purposeful preaching 183, 187–8
Stalker, James 210
  quotation 226
Stephen, Sir Leslie 117
Stewart, James S. 32, 136

Stott, John 13, 80, 242
summarization 268, 269–70, 274–5
  examples in introductions to sermons by MacArthur 290, 291, 297, 304, 305, 312
  reviews in the learning process 278–80
Swindoll, Charles: sermon introduction 97–9

Taylor, William 27
  quotation 57
terminological precision 234–5
Terry, Milton S. 275–6
thoroughness 275–7
Timothy 8
Tizard, Leslie J. (quotation) 235
truth
  encouraging the discovery of 147–50
  knowledge of 143–7
  life and 137
  purposeful preaching of God's truth 184 *see also* purposeful preaching
  questions and 142–3

unction (anointing of the Spirit) 150–68, 212, 214
understanding
  accurate understanding and contextualization 272–5
  accurate understanding and purposeful preaching 236–9
  and application 149–50, 202–3 *see also* application
  through discovery 148
  explanation and 202–7
  through expository preaching 122, 192, 231
  God's gift of 203–4
  in the learning process 276
  passion and 163
  persuasion and 205 *see also* persuasion
  prophetic 144
  through sermon preparation 163
  textual knowledge and 143–7
  see also knowledge; learning process

values 258–60, 261
Van Cleave, Nathaniel 270
Vines, Jerry 60, 69
Vinet, Alexander 33–4, 43–4, 70, 75
volitional unity of purpose 230–2

Webster, Daniel 236
Whitesell, Faris D. 137, 325
Wiersbe, Warren W. 250, 252, 340–1, 346
  on gaining attention 83, 85–6
  quotation 63
Wilson, (Thomas) Woodrow 232–3
Wood, John 185
worship 259

Yim, Howard 16

Zwingli, Ulrich 278

Scripture Index

Genesis
13:2 286
17:9-14 238
17:18 287

1 Samuel
1 333–334

Psalms
7:11 302, 310
36:5 307

Proverbs
1:5 180
1:20 316
1:30-33 316
2:8 316
3:1-4 220
3:7-8 180
3:11-12 74
3:13-18 316
3:33-35 220
4:7-9 316
4:13 180
4:20-23 180
5:21 220
7:1-4 180
8:32-36 74
9:7-9 36
9:10 180
10:8 74
10:17 74
10:21 102
10:31-32 102
11:1 220
11:2 266
11:25 220
12:1 74
12:5 102, 132
12:8 20
12:15 74
12:17 266
12:19 266
12:25 20
12:26 266
13:2 266
13:14 132
13:17 266
13:18 74
14:5 266
14:6 180
14:25 266
15:1 102, 132
15:2 266
15:4 20
15:5 74
15:7 102
15:14 180
15:23 20
15:28 102, 132
16:2 220
16:7-8 220
16:11 220
16:13 20
16:21 132
16:23-24 102
18:4 20
18:21 102
19:8 20
19:20 74
20:15 102
22:4 132
22:10 36
22:11 20
23:9 36
25:11 132
25:12 36
25:13 266
25:15 102
26:4-5 36
27:17 132
28:23 36
29:9 36
30:5-6 20

Isaiah
32:17 302
61:1 212

Matthew
5:10-12 334–335
5:21-26 332
7:24 193
7:26 193

Luke
4:18-19 211

Acts
15 238
20:18-27 156–157

Romans
1:16 8
1:18–3:20 282, 291
3:21–5:21 282–283, 291
3:21-31 283, 291
4:1-8 289, 291
4:9-17 290, 291
4:18-25 282–291
5:1 301–302
5:1-2 292–298, 310–311
5:1-11 297
5:2-5 298–305
5:3 311
5:5-11 305–312
15:4 237

1 Corinthians
1:9 307
1:21 9
1:21-23 8
2:4 158
11:2-16 238
12:14-25 78

Galatians
4:21 288
5:2 303
5:4 303, 305

Ephesians
1:13-18 300–301
2:3 302

Philippians
1:6 309

1 Thessalonians
5:23-24 308

2 Thessalonians
3:3 308–309

2 Timothy
2:13 307
3:16-17 237
4:1 240
4:2 8
4:3 7

Hebrews
10:23 307

1 Peter
1:5 298, 304
4:19 308

Christian Focus Publications
publishes books for all ages

Our mission statement –

STAYING FAITHFUL
In dependence upon God we seek to help make His infallible Word, the Bible, relevant. Our aim is to ensure that the Lord Jesus Christ is presented as the only hope to obtain forgiveness of sin, live a useful life and look forward to heaven with Him.

REACHING OUT
Christ's last command requires us to reach out to our world with His gospel. We seek to help fulfil that by publishing books that point people towards Jesus and help them develop a Christ-like maturity. We aim to equip all levels of readers for life, work, ministry and mission.

Books in our adult range are published in three imprints.

Christian Focus contains popular works including biographies, commentaries, basic doctrine and Christian living. Our children's books are also published in this imprint.

Mentor focuses on books written at a level suitable for Bible College and seminary students, pastors, and other serious readers. The imprint includes commentaries, doctrinal studies, examination of current issues and church history.

Christian Heritage contains classic writings from the past.

Christian Focus Publications, Ltd
Geanies House, Fearn,
Ross-shire, IV20 1TW, Scotland, United Kingdom
info@christianfocus.com

Our titles are available from
www.christianfocus.com